Praise for *The Four*

"*Four Virtues of a Leader* is a true gift from one of the world's leading executive coaches. It should be at the top of the reading list for all business leaders who are seeking to fulfill their leadership potential."

KEVIN KRUSE, author of *Employee Engagement 2.0*;
Executive Director, Society of Pharmaceutical and Biotech Trainers

"Eric Kaufmann has done what no other business/self-help author has yet done—he has combined all of the lessons from hundreds of sources into one comprehensive and practical book. He understands the reader because he is just like the reader. He acknowledges his own faults throughout his own journey, which truly allows the reader to connect with and understand the learning experience. I recommend this book to anyone looking to grow as a leader for others and for themselves."

SCOTT SCHINDLER, Vice President, The Irving Group

"Eric Kaufmann's *Four Virtues of a Leader* is a truly visionary work. Read it, apply the principles, and you will be a hero in your organization!"

MARSHALL GOLDSMITH, "The World's Most Influential
Leadership Thinker," *Thinkers 50* global survey; bestselling
author of *Mojo* and *What Got You Here Won't Get You There*

"*Four Virtues of a Leader* by Eric Kaufmann should be required reading for every conscious leader, coach, or manager—and should be incorporated into their daily lives!"

PETER DAVIS, cofounder and CEO, IDEA Health & Fitness Association

"*Four Virtues of a Leader* asks tough questions. But they are questions that *every* leader must ask in order to experience lasting personal and market breakthroughs. I wish I carried this book with me when I began advising CEOs and Chief Marketing Officers twenty years ago!"

LISA NIRELL, founder of EnergizeGrowth®; award-winning *FastCompany*
contributor; author of *EnergizeGrowth® NOW* and *The Mindful Marketer*

"Effective leadership comes from the inside out, and those who courageously start within need both practical and inspiring support for the journey. Eric Kaufmann provides that and more in his compelling new book, *Four Virtues of a Leader*."

DAVID BERRY, Former Vice President, Leadership and Learning,
TaylorMade/Adidas Golf Company

"Finally, a truly fresh look at leadership. Drawing on decades of experience in both the corporate world and his Zen practice, Kaufmann provides wisdom and guidance to those who are serious about self-awareness and the courageous path of true leadership."

HAL DUNNING, President, Barney & Barney, LLC

"A heroic effort of heart, mind, and truth, Eric Kaufmann's *Four Virtues of a Leader* provides a beacon towards which all those on the forefront of leadership can confidently venture, and the means to get there."

SARAH MCARTHUR, author/editor of *Coaching for Leadership*

"Leadership is a journey that involves continuous learning. *Four Virtues of a Leader* provides insights in how to navigate this journey with purpose, regardless of level. Eric Kaufmann's thought-provoking questions and tangible examples will help you evolve the quality of your leadership and how you approach your work."

TOM WERNER, President and CEO, SunPower Corporation

"*Four Virtues of a Leader* is like having one of the world's best executive coaches as your personal mentor. It's filled with the author's own growth experiences, stories from his clients, and exercises that will certainly lead to better leadership results."

SHAYNA GOTHARD, PhD, forensic psychologist

"Eric courageously outlines leadership as a conscious and intentional path available to all through the commitment to awareness and practices outlined in this exceptional book. This book is accessible, personal, and a must-read for anyone on that path—and it provides a bridge on which to cross over from theory to practice. This is a wonderful synthesis of Eric's personal journey and practical wisdom founded in his own extensive and hard-won experience."

SUSAN PENN, Vice President of Human Resources, Evofem, Inc.

"As someone who is on a long journey into leadership, I found accessible wisdom, simple actions, and profound effects. Kaufmann's writing is very accessible, written as complex as it needs to be, and no more. Kaufmann's words touch me in a way that leads to taking simple actions that have profound effects. *Four Virtues of a Leader* is provoking in the finest way."

JASON MARTIN, Verizon Telematics

"Eric is a fantastic leadership coach. This book offers great ideas and tools for living a heroic life of leadership. Grit and Focus are my favorite takeaways. The wisdom in *Four Virtues of a Leader* will inspire many future leaders with practical ideas on how to be courageous and persevering."

JOHN FRAGER, Executive Managing Director,
CBRE Commercial Real Estate Services

"If you're a leader—or aspire to be one—the question is: How fruitful and fulfilling will your journey be? The insights and actions Kaufmann offers in *Four Virtues of a Leader* will make your work conscious, intentional, and successful. Not only is this a provocative book, it is exceptionally well-written. I highly recommend you make it well-read, too."

STEVE FARBER, author of *The Radical Leap Re-Energized*
and *Greater Than Yourself*; founder, The Extreme Leadership Institute

"Eric's book shows leaders how to transform themselves into masters of chaos and uncertainty. From this place of power, they become a force of clear and calm direction that aligns their people and accelerates results."

GARRY RIDGE, CEO, WD-40 Companies

"*Four Virtues of a Leader* is a perfect book for leaders looking to model a brave and connected leadership style. Eric challenges common thinking while giving you many practical ideas on how to stay focused, courageous, and persevering as you accelerate your organizational growth."

SARAH EBERHARDT-RIOS, MPA, Deputy Director of Program Support Services for the San Bernadino County Department of Behavioral Health

"This book will give you a perspective on leadership that can't be found anywhere else. I really appreciate the depth of knowledge and experience that Eric Kaufmann has and how he makes it so accessible in this book. As an owner of a small business with hopes of growth and expansion, I received some great insight into my blind spots, as well as things to avoid and to aspire to, in this book."

MIKEL BRUCE, CEO, Tiny Frog Technologies

The
FOUR
VIRTUES
of a
LEADER

The
FOUR
VIRTUES
of a
LEADER

NAVIGATING THE HERO'S JOURNEY
THROUGH RISK TO RESULTS

ERIC KAUFMANN

BOULDER, COLORADO

Sounds True, Inc.
Boulder, CO 80306

Published 2016

Jacket design by Rachael Murray
Book design by Beth Skelley

Illustrations © Nick Isabella

Printed in Canada

Library of Congress Cataloging-in-Publication Data
Names: Kaufmann, Eric, 1967–
Title: Four virtues of a leader : navigating the hero's journey through risk
   to results / Eric Kaufmann.
Description: Boulder, CO : Sounds True, Inc., 2016. |
   Includes bibliographical references.
Identifiers: LCCN 2015051122 (print) | LCCN 2016006813 (ebook) |
   ISBN 9781622037278 | ISBN 9781622037285
Subjects: LCSH: Leadership. | Risk-taking (Psychology)
Classification: LCC HD57.7 .K3795 2016 (print) | LCC HD57.7 (ebook) |
   DDC 658.4/092—dc23
LC record available at http://lccn.loc.gov/2015051122

eBook ISBN: 978-1-62203-728-5

10 9 8 7 6 5 4 3 2 1

To Shayna, Tara, and Maya
The triple gem that makes my path noble

CONTENTS

ACKNOWLEDGMENTS

I can't do justice to the scores of people I want to acknowledge. I owe a great debt to my family and loved ones. I feel tremendous gratitude for my mentors, teachers, guides, allies, friends, and helpers. Even my foes contributed to my learning and development. The insights and guidance I share in this book reflect my life and learning; they illustrate real-world application of leadership. While this book has been brewing for a couple of decades, it needed to mature, as did I, before it could see the light of day.

My father and mother, Eli and Norma, are my earliest and most enduring role models. They exemplify—both individually and as a couple—what it means to be leaders on a hero's journey. Their courage and commitment, their generosity and kindness, are remarkable to behold and inspiring to emulate. Their example and conduct have shaped me, and I'm proud to be their physical and spiritual descendant.

While the greatest teacher is life as it is, I have learned directly from several remarkable teachers. Their styles are as different as their personalities, and each has polished a different facet of my mind and heart. I was lucky to cross paths with Ingrid Coffin while I was a freshman in college, as she introduced me to a life of discovery and practice that shapes who I am and gives language and context to this book. Morris McCauley, the intrepid explorer of consciousness, brought magic and mystery to my life. Had I not met him and learned from him, my life would have been far less multidimensional and adventurous. Catherine Wambach provided the wisdom, patience, and space for some of my most profound transformations. Her generosity of spirit and time is a gift that I endeavor to pass along through my work and family. Ezra Bayda and Elizabeth Hamilton continuously offer invaluable wisdom in their teaching; their presence, practice, and lived compassion seep below the defenses of my mind and invoke awakening and evolution.

My friend Mikel Bruce has matched my curiosity and intensity for decades. It has been a joy and a privilege to share adventures with him, to be supported by his friendship, and to admire his heroic journey. Sharon O'Brien offered a beacon of kindness in a most precarious wilderness of my quest. Her ability to be present and accepting was a gift and a service.

I owe a great debt of appreciation to Sarah McArthur for her editing. Without her guidance and leadership, I would not have completed this writing project. When she first suggested that I abandon a dozen years of my material and start over, I thought she was crazy. Turned out she was the sane one between us.

My clients have been an inspiration. I am privileged to do my work of guiding, advising, coaching, and speaking. As clichéd as it sounds, I have learned more from all my clients than I have brought to any single engagement. While endeavoring to accelerate their growth, results, decisions, and behaviors, they have also shaped me. My CEO roundtable group, in particular, fortifies my passionate conviction about leadership as a hero's journey.

Lastly, I bow before my wife and daughters. There are no other people on earth I know as well who see me as fully as they do. We have our differences and disagreements, but the love and appreciation we share washes those clean every day. Tara, our firstborn, manifests compassion and has swelled my heart not just by our relationship but by her presence. Tara is deep and funny, competitive and caring; being herself, she makes a difference.

Maya, our beautiful youngest daughter, inspires me to strive to be a great dad and, consequently, an evolved man. Maya is a balance of fire and water, of intensity and depth, of expression and feeling. My heart is bigger because she's in my world.

Shayna means beautiful. My wife is a beautiful woman inside and out, and I love and respect her. Shayna is a powerful leader who touches people's lives and improves them; she's also a force of nature driven by service and guided by compassion. I feel inspired and encouraged by her courage, love, and commitment to her spiritual evolution. Thanks for being with me.

INTRODUCTION

I have no intention of adding to the convoluted mythology of leaders as special creatures. Many of the common notions of being heroic, as it relates to the work of leading, end up limiting the ability of leaders to be effective. When I ask leaders to name a hero, Superman often comes up. Well, Superman is the antithesis of our discussion in this book. Superman has superhuman powers. He is a perfect being and knows no fear. By contrast, every leader I've met possesses no superhuman powers, is flawed and complex, and is caught in anxiety and fear at new turns (even the exciting ones). Over the past two decades, I have coached and consulted hundreds of leaders in for-profit, nonprofit, and government realms. I've worked with privately held and publicly traded company leaders, community and social leaders, and spiritual and religious leaders. None of them was exempt from flaws and anxiety. It is precisely because of our flawed and anxious nature that we can be heroic. A hero is someone who seeks a great prize (something difficult and rewarding), leaves the comfort zone, makes sacrifices, and, ultimately, gives back to the community. If you regularly strive for enormous reward, often find yourself in discomfort or danger, and aim to serve the greater good, then you are poised for the hero's journey.

We expect leaders to achieve results, through and with other people. To lead is to drive toward outcomes that would not happen if the group were left to its own; leaders create outcomes that don't happen organically. And because they are tasked with achieving results, we hold leaders accountable. They are the final stop for praise or blame regarding the results of their team. When you are on your hero's journey, you willingly place yourself at risk and in discomfort in order to advance your vision, tend to your followers, and achieve results.

Leaders get to employ a variety of tools and approaches to ensure that they achieve results. Their work falls into three broad actions: *inspire* a culture of aligned and collaborative teams, *institute* effective systems and structures that support execution and decision making, and *articulate* a strategy that brings the vision and mission to life. Decisions influence everything leaders do. Decisions contain a rational element, but they also result from a leader's presence, attitude, and character. In this book I describe four virtues leaders must embody in order to inhabit a heroic character: focus, courage, grit, and faith.

Understanding the Hero's Journey

This book, like the hero's journey, is for seekers. Your job is not just to do but to think; I've written this book to be thought-provoking. The journey you're embarking on with me is one of leadership philosophy and psychology, not just prescriptive formulas. I've long been inspired by Joseph Campbell, the scholar and explorer of consciousness who brought the hero's journey into popular awareness. He characterized the journey by three elements: (1) leaving the familiar in order to seek a valuable prize, (2) encountering challenges and risks that demand personal sacrifices, and (3) sharing the hard-earned prize with fellow men and women.

I wrote *Four Virtues of a Leader* for people who have a passion for their own journey of growth, passage, and change. This journey requires and begins at the separation from the comfortable, known world. It is an initiation into a new level of awareness, skill, and responsibility that culminates when you bring your hard-earned prize back home. Along the journey, you change and return a hero—a different person, a different leader. While the hero's journey is defined by ambition, risk, sacrifice, and service, it requires the completion of the successive stages of separation, initiation, and return for the leader to become a hero. To turn back at any stage is to reject the need to grow, to mature, and to evolve.

Every manager and executive I talk with eventually asks the question, "What does it take to evolve into a great leader?" The answer is twofold: actions (things great leaders *do*) and attitudes (ways great leaders *are*). Actions manifest in competencies—skills and abilities—that include strategic thinking, team building, financial savvy, political acumen, operational excellence, recruiting and hiring, and coaching, among others.

Bring to mind the leaders you have followed passionately. It was more than their intelligent, educated, or skilled actions that compelled you to follow them. You gave your energy and effort to who they were—their beingness, their presence. You committed yourself to their vision and purpose because you believed in them; that's how great leaders inspire and engage us. Being adept at the required competencies is a baseline for entry into leadership. Climbing to the top of the ladder of commitment and engagement, however, results from a leader's personal energy and tone. Great leaders engage and inspire others to willingly commit themselves to their vision and purpose.

It's in this vein that we arrive at the distinctions of leadership as a hero's journey, a journey that unfolds on three levels: (1) results, (2) wisdom, and (3) spirituality. At the first level it is a journey of results. Your job as a leader, fundamentally, is to help usher a group of people from the state of the familiar and known through the unknown and unfamiliar to accomplish new outcomes and results.

At the next level, leadership is a journey of discovery. At this level, leaders commit themselves to experience and exploration, gain knowledge from lessons and trials, and, ultimately, discover new possibilities and innovate. This discovery leads to wisdom, which is the culmination of experience, learning, and experimentation.

The third level of leadership as a hero's journey is a spiritual one, the unfolding and expression of your authentic self. This means articulating and manifesting your unique gifts and contributions. This aspect of the journey is awakened by the prodding and shaping of leadership responsibilities; the spiritual level coaxes you to evolve into an authentic human being. In this state, you spend less energy defending yourself; rather than habitually focusing on survival, you become increasingly available and connected, engaged in expression and immersed in serving others' journeys.

I feel energized and inspired by the possibility of authentic expression and spiritual evolution through the practice of leading. Being authentic isn't a fixed condition; you don't wake up one morning and decide that you're authentic. Rather, it's a state of living in which anxiety, self-negation, and hiding behind protective strategies become less powerful than self-expression, curiosity, and genuine care for others.

A Journey through This Book

I've arranged this book in four parts, each addressing one of the four virtues of heroic leaders. Although each is complete unto itself, the heroic mind-set emerges at the intersection of these four interdependent virtues.

Focus sets direction and clarity for the journey.

Courage enables full engagement that is otherwise blocked by anxiety and fear.

Grit drives action forward in the face of fatigue and disheartenment.

Faith ensures agility and responsiveness in the place of rigidity and entrapment.

Part I, "Focus," answers the question, "What am I creating?" We are always creating something, either intentionally or unintentionally. Your responsibility as a leader is to be intentional and purposeful about what you, your team, and your organization are focused on creating. Your thoughts and beliefs and, by extension, the beliefs and thoughts of your team and organization, are reflected in your creation and behavior; what you focus on draws you and your organization toward results. Your power to intend, to deliberately reach for desired outcomes, pulls you away from the known and familiar on a journey into the unfamiliar and unknown—a journey toward discovery, innovation, creation, and results. In this part, I examine the relationship between self-awareness and achievement, and I explain how thoughts are actually things (and that we become, in time, what we think about most).

In part II, I dive headlong into courage in order to help you learn to answer the question, "What am I avoiding?" One of your initial responsibilities as a leader is to set out to create something new and challenging. You do this, in part, by intending, stretching out toward a goal, and forming a gap between what you have and what you want. You fill that gap with two critical elements for achievement: potential and uncertainty. With uncertainty come anxiety and fear—we feel excitement in the presence of uncertainty, as uncertainty carries the potential for innovation and creation. We are also bound to know fear. In this part, I share why fear acts as the gatekeeper of power, and I also explain how to retake your power from the clutches of fear.

Part III asks, "What am I sustaining?" Answering this question helps you develop *grit*. Grit, more than any other factor, reliably predicts achievement. I doubt that you're an overnight success; hardly anyone is. Your dedication and perseverance are the predictors of achievement, and focus takes passion and perseverance to sustain the choices and behaviors that turn potential into reality. Grit is how you overcome the addiction to comfort, an addiction that will pull you and your team right back into old patterns. In this part, I discuss how to persevere when your inspiration and motivation wane.

Part IV is about faith. Here we tackle the final challenge of awakening the heroic spirit, revealed by asking the question, "What am I yielding?" The label *hero* cannot be self-imposed; it is bestowed upon those who have made great contributions at some personal cost. When you sacrifice, you give up something of value to gain something greater. You sacrifice in order to serve, or to avoid calamity or evil. Effective leaders sacrifice daily; they give up time with family, personal time, recognition, and freedom from responsibility and scrutiny. But the most demanding leadership sacrifice is giving up comfort. In this part, we explore how to sacrifice without feeling weak, and how to apply mindfulness meditation to embolden the heroic spirit of leadership.

An Invitation to the Journey

I didn't write this book to please, but to challenge and inspire. If you are a leader, then there are enough sycophants swirling around you. You don't need more stroking; rather, you need to sharpen your thinking and broaden your heart. I intended for the following chapters to be thought-provoking, accessible, and illustrated with anecdotes and metaphors. Reading this book will equip you to skillfully dive into the unknown, inspire your people to commit to you and your mission, and grow results. As Emerson wrote, "An institution is the lengthened shadow of one man." I offer you this book so you can take responsibility for the shadow you cast and its influence on organizational outcomes.

PART I

FOCUS
What Am I Creating?

I came across a powerfully illustrative quote from the prolific philosopher Anonymous (often mistakenly attributed to Buddha): "The thought manifests as the word; the word manifests as the deed; the deed develops into habit; and habit hardens into character. So watch the thought and its ways with care, and let it spring from love born out of concern for all beings."

You are not a mere leaf floating on the wind, passively pushed along by circumstances. You actively shape your environment. As a leader, your job is more than arranging and directing resources; your job is to envision and create. Peter Drucker, the father of modern management discipline, said, "The best way to predict the future is to create it." Our unique human abilities to envision and to create are the heart of part I.

Focus allows you to answer the question, "What am I creating?" Focus and vision shape your leadership journey, as well as the journey of those who follow you. You are always creating, whether you're conscious of it or not, and by the end of this part you will become aware of it. You will recognize how your thoughts and beliefs play out in your role, relationships, team, and results, and you will be able to leverage this force of intention, attention, and expectation. Furthermore, you will understand that a thought is a thing, that you are what you think, and that you become what you think about most.

We begin our journey by investigating leadership from the inside out. Our first part is intended to explain the quality and nature of thoughts, beliefs, assumptions, and expectations and discover how they shape our results and relationships.

1

WHAT AM I CREATING?

You are always creating. You are always responsible for your results, relationships, and life. Whichever aspect of your life you examine—your job, team, body, or mental state—you realize that you are responsible for its creation. You form your experience of reality with the choices you make, and your beliefs and assumptions drive your choices. This doesn't happen in a vacuum: genetics have a hand in who you are. Environment and circumstances shape your reality, too. And then there's chance—the luck of the draw. But even in the context of these multiple factors, like it or not, you remain responsible for what you create.

I didn't always know that I was responsible for my own reality. I wasn't aware, for example, that I was responsible for shaping my relationships. When I was twenty-six years old, I broke up with my girlfriend. This was a pattern. My girlfriends were fun and affectionate, but I found a fatal flaw in every one of them. Frustrated and clueless about how to upgrade my relationships, I turned to my mentor, Morris.

I still recall the conversation we had over dinner. We were talking about my love life, and I felt eager for Morris to reveal the secrets of selecting the perfect girlfriend. As Morris asked pointed questions about my relationships, I felt my hopes build as I was sufficiently frustrated with my romantic history that I was open to approaching the process differently.

Suddenly, the conversation turned. Morris stopped asking questions about my girlfriends and started inquiring about my thoughts, beliefs, and expectations about relationships and about women. I can still recall the strain of disappointment that gripped my gut as I realized that Morris wasn't about to reveal any magical steps to acquiring a perfect girlfriend, but rather was impressing on me, once again, that my life is my responsibility. Morris insisted, as he did so many times, that beliefs precede behavior, and he worked diligently to expand my self-awareness.

Slowly and undeniably I realized that my relationship problems resulted from my beliefs, expectations, fantasies, and wishes about women. I was the common denominator in my frustrating experiences; I created, cocreated, and re-created the dynamics with my girlfriends. My responsibility was a bitter pill to swallow, especially as I'd hoped that Morris would reveal to me the secret of attracting the right woman. But he wanted me to reflect, grow in awareness, take responsibility, and recognize the beliefs that fueled and shaped my behaviors.

Finally, he asked me the question that unlocked my frozen pattern of unsatisfying relationships. It was a question that I proceeded to turn over and over in my mind for a decade, and that—when I finally answered in the affirmative—brought me together with my wife. Morris asked, "Are you the kind of man that would attract the kind of woman that you would want to be with?" Wait—don't rush on. Please read that question again.

The answer was no. I wasn't that kind of man. I was closed-hearted, self-centered, and needy. The kind of woman I wanted to be with didn't want to be with the man I was then. My girlfriends reflected me, just as your relationships mirror you; my self-centeredness attracted similar partners. My world is my reflection; just as your world is your reflection. You have to accept this paradigm as an act of maturity, responsibility, and power. If you don't, you disempower yourself and reduce your ability to effect change.

To lead you must take personal responsibility for what you create. To take responsibility you must develop self-awareness. Without awareness, how will you track and recognize your contribution to what you are creating? Leadership is a creative act. It is also a collaborative, relational, and risky endeavor—one accomplished with and through others. As a leader, your ability to navigate risk, collaborate with others, and establish trust and relationships fundamentally emanate from your beliefs and assumptions, from your focus. And the depth of your self-awareness is proportional to your strength of personal and professional responsibility.

The Unwitting Creator

Just as my romantic life reflected my self-concept, beliefs, and expectations, your self-concept as a leader directs and shapes the quality and results of your team. Your self-concept (sometimes called self-perspective) is a compilation of beliefs about yourself that you have drawn from your life experiences and circumstances. These include your educational achievement and academic performance, sexuality and gender-role experiences, religious and racial identity, successes and failures, social connections, and family roles and relationships. Most generally, your self-concept represents an answer to "Who am I?"

Tom's leadership experience illustrates how beliefs impact one's environment. At forty-six, Tom was the president of a company that he led on a five-year growth spurt, but that was four years ago. The past four years had yielded flat results—no growth. Tom's credentials were impressive; he was a CPA with an MBA, had extensive marketing experience, and was extroverted and charming. The staff and team liked him personally, but the shareholders were scratching their heads, puzzled by Tom's recently poor results. The company was well established, well regarded in the market, and employed smart and creative talent. Research and development, production, distribution, and customer service were quite effective. They had a compelling mission and vision, and a gripping purpose statement that engaged their customers. So why, then, was this well-honed operation stalled in terms of revenue growth? The obstacle to growth, it turned out, was Tom. Specifically, the obstacle to growth was Tom's focus; he was focused on safety and control rather than taking risks and growing.

Tom insisted that he touch every aspect of the business. He required that he be informed about each detail and development in all areas of the company, and his personal focus drew him toward a detailed involvement in decision making at all levels. His need to contribute to most decisions caused a logistical and mental bottleneck of activity, which disempowered his people, slowed innovation, and overwhelmed him. His overwhelm fanned his natural anxiety about failure and drove him to control the process even more. This vicious cycle—focus on control and being controlled by the focus—robbed the organization of its vitality and agility. The flat financial returns represented the only results that the organization could produce within the limits of Tom's focus.

Tom's self-concept prioritized safety, which manifested as controlling and micromanaging. Fortunately, Tom's self-concept was malleable. When I was in my twenties, Morris explained to me that consciousness precedes action, and that I could change my experience and outcomes by changing my thoughts. I can still hear Morris saying, "A thought is a thing. You are what you think. You become what you think about most." My late mentor was passionate about respecting and acknowledging the power of a focused mind. Focus is more than the ability to concentrate on the task at hand—problem solving, planning, or coaching. Focus is a key trait of a leader on the hero's journey, a trait that blossoms into an ability to steer a team toward a desirable shared vision. More than just paying attention, it leverages self-awareness in order to answer the question, "What am I creating?"

A Thought Is a Thing

Picture, imagine, or feel that you are standing by a lemon tree. The scent of lemons wafts around you, and you notice the rich yellow fruit hanging from a branch. Now picture, imagine, or feel yourself reaching for a lemon and plucking it from the tree. Notice the weight of it in your hand. Notice the texture and temperature. Notice the color and shape. Even as you read these words, allow your imagination to conjure up a lemon in your hand.

Next, imagine that you have a knife in your other hand, and, safely, cut the lemon in half. Using your vivid and creative imagination, bring one half of the lemon to your mouth and take a bite. Go ahead, bite into the lemon and picture, imagine, or feel the lemon juice splashing and flowing into your mouth.

I find that most people, when visualizing the lemon juice in their mouth, experience more saliva. They might even taste the familiar sour tinge of lemon juice. This happens because your brain retrieves tangible memories in response to the exercise; in this case, it retrieves the images, smells, and textures that a lemon brings to mind. By directing the mind to think about eating a lemon, you generate real-time physical reactions. Imagining that you're eating the lemon triggers the distinctive reaction, and your body responds with a conditioned reflex. Salivating from an imaginary lemon demonstrates that thinking alone can affect the body—*that a thought is a thing*.

While we can't weigh a thought or hold it in a jar, it has presence and impact. In *The Selfish Gene*, British evolutionary biologist Richard Dawkins expanded on this idea as he described the concept of memes. The term explained the spread of ideas and cultural phenomena, and examples include melodies, catchphrases, fashion, and the technology of building arches. Dawkins explains that a meme is "an idea, behavior, or style that spreads from person to person within a culture." A meme resembles a gene in that it can replicate, mutate, and respond to environmental influences and pressures. This meme—a thought that is a thing—acts as a unit for carrying cultural ideas, symbols, and practices from one mind to another through writing, speech, gestures, and rituals.

This is important to us as leaders because we spend a great deal of energy shaping and transmitting memes—turning our ideas into symbols and practices that take on a life of their own. But, alas, much as you might wish, you can't tell people what to think; it is challenging even to manage what we ourselves think. As a leader, you can tell people what to think *about*—you can shape the focus of their thinking and, consequently, the reactions of their thinking process. I can't tell you to salivate, but I can direct your attention to recalling a sour lemon and expect that you will salivate. Similarly, as a leader, I can't tell you to think creatively, but I can shape your environment to focus on innovation and creativity and on novel ways to problem solve. By directing my team to think about the ideas, processes, and practices of creativity, I influence their focus and attention.

The most direct way that leaders influence what their people think is by modeling—exhibiting the behaviors and traits that others are to imitate. A Chinese proverb says, "Tell me and I'll forget; show me and I may remember; involve me and I'll understand." Your leadership effectiveness draws more from your behavior and actions than from your words. Your focus, your cumulative efforts at what to nurture in your thinking, becomes the foundation of the thoughts you amplify around you.

Similar to leading, parenting is transmitted more in modeling behavior than in words. Try as I might, I can't tell my daughters what to think. Certainly, I'm actively educating them—sharing ideas, exposing them to experiences, discussing their thoughts and feelings, and setting limits and boundaries. Yet in spite of my best efforts, they have their opinions and beliefs and are far from being my clones. While my children learn a great deal from me, most of what sticks is the result of what they see me do, not what they hear me share. How I treat my wife influences what they think about relationships far more than what I say about connection and love. How I tend to the household teaches them more about stewardship than what I preach about responsibility. The way I attend, listen, and engage with them teaches them more about the quality of our relationship than anything I might say about love and respect. If I'm disrespectful toward my wife, neglectful of our home, and distracted by my mobile phone while in conversation, I reinforce these behaviors regardless of the values and ideals I might preach.

A thought is a thing, and even if it can't be measured and boxed, it can become evident in its manifestation. Just as in parenting, your thoughts as a leader are contagious and replicable through others—your thoughts shape and influence people, situations, and results. You shape yourself by your thoughts, and you affect others with them, too. A thought is, in fact, a thing, and you are what you think. This is not a philosophical statement about existence; it is a statement about the power of focus—what am I creating?

You Are What You Think

The Dhammapada (a collection of Buddhist verses from the third century BCE) explains that we are the result of all we have thought. We are founded on our thoughts; we are made up of our thoughts. If a person speaks or acts with evil thoughts, pain follows, like the wheel follows the foot of the ox that draws the cart. By contrast, if a person speaks or acts with a pure thought, happiness follows, like a shadow that never leaves.

You are what you think. If you think that you can only manage a small team, and believe that you can't lead a large organization, you're probably right. If you think safety is the ultimate leadership goal, you are likely to have safe and predictable experiences. In *Psycho-Cybernetics*, Maxwell Maltz elaborated on this phenomenon, which he discussed as the powerful idea of "self-image," the view we each have of ourselves. This view—which is an aggregate of thoughts—shapes and predicts our capabilities, as well as our limitations. Maltz compared our self-image to a recording in the brain that relives experiences as real as the original experience. Your self-image is how you see yourself, both positively and negatively. It is based on memory, crafted from beliefs, and is formed from relationships with significant others and interpretations of events. The beliefs you hold right now were formed without effort and with no willpower. In contrast to your pattern of circumstantial beliefs, the objective of psycho-cybernetics is self-realization—the firsthand appreciation of your own uniqueness as a human being, a sense of deep and wide awareness of all people and all things, and an approach of constructively influencing others through your own personality. Your self-image has a directional influence on your leadership and your hero's journey; this self-image can be reshaped by forming a clear mental image of your desired self, and practicing consistently to reach that goal.

I was a lousy student as a youngster. From elementary through high school, my grades were below average. I found schoolwork boring, and I was more focused on easily getting by than on demonstrating excellence. My teachers were perplexed: I had all the necessary ingredients for high grades—intelligence, self-direction, and the potential for a strong work ethic as the son of hardworking entrepreneurs. But I envisioned myself—my self-image—as lazy and efficient (putting in the minimal effort, that is). I expected little of myself academically, and followed through on that expectation. Fortunately, my self-concept changed. It transformed into one of ambition, drive, and goal achievement in large part because of the influence of my mentors and guides and the influence and expectation of my leaders.

Expectations are powerful thought patterns. In 1964, Robert Rosenthal, a Harvard professor, conducted a seminal study on their power. His setting was an elementary school in south San Francisco, and his experimental goal was to determine if students' results could be shaped by their teachers' expectations. The researchers instructed the teachers that certain students were destined to become successful based on a new test of learning potential (actually a standardized IQ test dressed up with a new title). After every child in the elementary school was given the test, Rosenthal randomly selected 20 percent of the student body (whose test scores were no better or worse than their peers) and told their teachers that these students' test scores indicated that they were poised for a leap of intellectual growth and ripe for academic excellence.

Rosenthal followed the children's performance for the next two years and discovered that teacher expectations demonstrably affected these kids: teachers had been led to expect greater gains in IQ from children in this group, and these kids subsequently gained more IQ.

What Rosenthal found was that our expectations shape our experience; that we become what we think about most. As the teachers in the study thought about the high potential of their high achievers, they changed how they engaged with these students. Rosenthal explained that the results were not caused by mental telepathy; the teachers simply treated the "special" group of students in different ways. They received more smiles, nods, and affirming touches. They were given more time to answer questions and more specific feedback on their answers.

Leaders, too, influence their followers in the same way. And it is the same principle that shapes our internal experience as we define ourselves with our thoughts and beliefs. We become what we think we are or what others expect us to be.

You Become What You Think about Most

Your outcomes today result from the thoughts you dwelled on yesterday, and your present thoughts build your tomorrow—in other words, your results, and for that matter your life, are the creation of your thoughts, beliefs, and expectations. The life of your team and your organization is the creation of your collective reactive or deliberate thoughts: reactive thoughts are triggered by the environment

> *Your outcomes today result from the thoughts you dwelled on yesterday, and your present thoughts build your tomorrow.*

and your history; deliberate thoughts are the ones you hold with your intention and your vision of a desirable future. Our minds, though intangible, form the experience of our tangible reality. When you focus your mind by holding deliberate and intentional thoughts, you set in motion the cumulative power of mental attention, and you accelerate your ability to create and produce. When your mind is unsteady and not fixed on a clear path, it wavers from its vision and purpose, and never quite reaches the fulfillment of achievement.

There is a reason every book on leadership discusses vision. Vision is the act of focus. Intentionally holding a steady mental gaze toward your chosen horizon is an act of leadership; it shapes choices and informs decisions.

At the core of shaping and sharing a vision is the steadiness of a focused approach. The mind, however, is restless, fidgety, and difficult to pin down; the wise leader who willingly steps into the hero's journey works to steady the mind and its stream of thoughts (much more on this in part IV). Not content to allow the mind to make random flights of fancy, a wise leader guides the mind, for a mind intentionally directed is a source of great power, creativity, and accomplishment.

Your group becomes what it thinks about most, too. As I mentioned before, you can't tell people what to think, but you can tell them what to think about. Articulating and reinforcing a desirable outcome—a vision—harnesses team members' attention and influences their thinking. As a leader, your task is to set everyone's eyes toward the same horizon, so that their feet can all follow the path to the same result. By holding the future as a constant variable in present decision making, you provide your team and organization with a focus, and, by design, it will become drawn toward that focus.

2

FOCUSED INTENTION

I recall an evening relaxing in my hotel room after facilitating the second of a three-day strategic planning retreat. It was a cold night in Toronto in early January; I was practicing a light yoga routine to unwind from the day's tension, and the TV was on. As the local news spilled into the room, an authoritative reporter captured my attention. She spoke about a research program performed by the provincial police investigating backcountry collisions. In particular, they wanted to uncover the reason why drivers who lost control on icy roads were likely to crash headlong into telephone poles.

What the research discovered about cause and effect in these accidents on icy roads also holds true for conditions in the boardroom: we gravitate toward the object of our focus. Anyone who plays golf, soccer, tennis, or any other activity that requires goal orientation knows this to be true. Golfers learn that their swing, posture, and the final placement of the ball are all determined by where they place their attention. The Canadian researchers realized that some drivers, when their cars momentarily seem out of control (if, for example, the tires slip on a patch of ice), become scared and anxious. Their minds furiously and intensely scan the environment for danger. The looming danger of a telephone pole draws their attention, and, unfortunately, the intensity of that focus draws them directly toward the object of fixation: they steer their cars directly toward the pole.

The training that race-car drivers undergo takes this phenomenon to heart. One of the first lessons these drivers learn is to focus on the road, not on the wall surrounding the track. If you focus on the wall while rounding a curve at two hundred miles per hour, you will drive right into it. If you focus on the road, you will follow the road.

Leading an organization is like that. There are a thousand things that can go wrong. If you focus on them, you will drive yourself nuts and crash your company. Focus on where you want to go rather than on what you hope to avoid.

Race-car drivers are trained to acknowledge and honor this mental function. Many leaders, unfortunately, are not, and they don't realize the influence that focus has on physical action and behavior. Our minds are wired toward goal attainment. This has nothing to do with ambition. Our minds naturally orient toward the desired outcome and compute the necessary behaviors and intermediate outcomes needed to reach it.

When you articulate a goal or desired outcome, you begin to marshal your natural processes of attainment. When you do not express a specific goal, you still mobilize your natural processes of attainment, but they merely reinforce and re-create historical patterns of thought and action. Consider something as fundamental as eating. We have to eat to survive. How and what we eat will change, though, depending on our goal or desired outcome; your intentions will influence your behavior. If you set out to gain muscle mass, you will eat differently than if your goal is to lose fat. If you decide to cleanse your system of gluten, you will eat differently than if you are preparing for a triathlon. If you don't have any intention or goal that relates to food, then your diet will reflect your past training and habits.

When a leader asks, "What am I creating?" he or she deliberately activates the first virtue of leadership as a hero's journey—focus. This is critically important. Focus is more than psychological; it has a neurological foundation, too. When we focus intently on an object or direction, we activate the sympathetic mode of our autonomic nervous system. The word *sympathetic*—*sym* and *pathos*—means "with feeling." The sympathetic mode entails an upsurge of energy that, if expressed, involves movement toward the object of focus. Sympathetic physiology increases energy and readies the body for action, so it is also about the need to do, express, and act. In this mode, our muscles and movements align our physical action with our mental focus. A driver whose focus on the telephone pole activates the autonomic nervous system simply follows through on moving toward her point of intense focus; whether the object of focus is front and center because we want to avoid it at all costs or because we want to reach it at all costs is irrelevant to that part of the brain. By concentrating intensely on the telephone pole, our physical motions begin to move us toward it, steering the car (even against our rational judgment) toward an inevitable collision.

We function throughout our typical day believing that we are rational decision makers, that we understand the mechanisms by which we decide, plan, and relate. We may be surprised, therefore, to discover that our body navigates our car toward the telephone pole, even against our conscious wish. For all we know, the car, apparently out of control, randomly hit the pole. We refer to this as an accident—an unintentional event—but it was not entirely out of our control. Although it might seem inexplicable, this phenomenon is predictable and consistent; we naturally move toward our focus. The key issue is not whether we shape our decisions and actions by our focus, but what we choose to focus on.

Unregistered Negativity

Having the capacity for singular focus is a powerful skill. While it takes much effort to cultivate a benevolent use of this skill, it's easy to default to letting the skill work against us. My golfing friends often lament about the challenge of trying to "avoid" the rough or bunker. I've heard their exasperated and frustrated discussions over what they call a "magnetic force" that seems to draw the golf ball directly into the bunker. Much like the car careening into the telephone pole, our bodies adjust as we follow through on the swing with our eyes directed toward the rough. Our mind is goal directed and cannot perform inaction; our minds can only process actionable commands. By telling yourself "don't go in the rough" while setting up your golf swing, you establish an inaction, and the mind simply edits the sentence in order to fit its task of accomplishing a goal. In this case, the mind removes the negative orientation of the thought: "don't" falls away, and all that's left is "go in the rough."

Our minds are designed to move toward something; we are wired to create, form, and accomplish. Through trial and error I learned not to yell, "Don't run!" to my children. I noticed that they only heard the "Run!" part of the command. I have learned to intentionally yell "Walk!" and now they have a specific request and direction to follow. Similarly, I noticed that when I pleaded with my team at work not to make any mistakes, they paid attention, but mistakes didn't stop. When I asked them, instead, to strive toward 100 percent accuracy, they were far more consistent in getting the work done without mistakes. Again: I can't tell them what to think, but I can direct them toward what I want them to think about, and therefore shape their behavior.

> *Our minds are designed to move toward something; we are wired to create, form, and accomplish.*

Alignment

Asking "What am I creating?" on a personal level organizes your personal choices and actions; asking "What am I creating?" on a leadership level organizes your team's choices—it creates alignment. Partnerships, teams, and organizations exist to harness the collective power of the group. *We* can accomplish more than *I*, and our collective efforts are most impressive when they surge forward in unison. Alignment amplifies individual contributions. It produces a multiplier effect in which the whole exceeds the sum of the parts. Teamwork, however, can also prove challenging and frustrating as we subjugate our needs and impulses and emphasize consideration of others and emotional intelligence. Teamwork can also rob us of our spontaneous expression and blur our coveted individuality. On the upside, teamwork can provide a platform from which we can accomplish meaningful and breathtaking achievements.

We choose to engage with a team in order to tap the amplified force that teams produce. When each member internally asks, "What am I creating?" the larger team generates power and everyone focuses on the same horizon, answering the question in similar terms. When team members collectively focus—set their attention and intention—on the same objective, they harness the power of alignment.

Tug-of-war is a practical example of the power of alignment. As a kid growing up in Israel, my friends and I played this game a lot: tug-of-war cost nothing and took little to set up. It was also intensely competitive. With a heeled shoe we'd scratch a line in the dirt, then split our group in two. Each group took hold of opposing ends of a strong rope, and on command we'd begin to pull and heave. I remember the strain and effort that my team and I expended as we pulled and tugged on the rope with all our strength in an effort to draw the other team toward us and over the midway line. If you've played this game, then you know that the biggest and heaviest team member gets the "anchor" position planted at the end of the rope. I was always taller, stronger, and heavier than my age-group peers, so I spent my tug-of-war "career" as the anchor. From this vantage point I had a clear view of my team as well as the opposing team. What I learned watching both teams is that the size, weight, and strength of the team were not the most important predictors of who would win the game.

Alignment was the winning factor. Teams whose members pulled in the same direction at the same angle were rewarded with cumulative force. When our backs, feet, and waists lined up and pointed in the same direction, we became unified, and the combined force of our aligned team exponentially magnified our individual contributions. I remember many sunny days anchored at the end of the line staring down the rope and hoping that the opposing team would look disjointed, that their guys would be out of sync, pulling the rope with all their might in multiple directions. When even one person on the rope pulled at a different angle, the entire team lost the power of cumulative force, and, rather than win, they struggled.

Your organization constantly pulls against the competition in an ongoing contest for market share, resources, and talent. You also experience nonstop tug-of-war with consumers and patrons. Each organizational function is a hand on the collective rope. Aligning your functions is not a mere philosophical abstraction; it is a dictate of mechanics and physics. Team members pull the rope at the operational level; if R&D pulls the rope north and production pulls the rope west, the organization falters.

Leaders engage in a continual tug-of-war with not just one but multiple ropes pulled by several teams in various directions. As so many factors push and pull leaders' attention and energy, it is focus—"What am I creating?"—that shapes the most effective decisions. Clarity of choice and decisions arises when you can definitively answer "What am I creating?" as a person, as a leader, and as a team. This focus is your vision and your commitment to the future, and it illuminates a path of decisions, relationships, and behaviors that pave your unique path to success.

3

PERSONAL METAPHOR

Walking up Eighth Avenue in New York on a blustery September day, I recall the feel of the wind flapping my jacket and whipping my hair. But as soon as I turned onto Forty-First Street, the force of the wind tripled and I was turned into a human sail—pressed backward by its power. Invisible yet powerful wind—moving air—is a shaping force in our world: it carves rocks, forms waves, and moves clouds and rain. Similarly, our self-concept acts as an invisible yet powerful force that plays a pivotal role in shaping our behaviors, relationships, and results.

When my director asked me to prepare for our annual review, the power of this invisible self-concept became clear. I was the marketing manager, and I was expected to prepare a self-evaluation for our review meeting. I took the process seriously, as it was an opportunity to reflect and learn and to promote my intentions for increased responsibility and pay. In order to gain insight and to anticipate the feedback I would receive, I imagined myself first in my boss's seat, and then in my team's seats. Considering myself through their eyes, I thought that they would probably describe me as somewhat detached—that I was passionate about the work but not fully connected to the team. I knew that I was onto something accurate, but I wasn't sure how to change.

I decided that if I could articulate my self-concept as a leader, the self-awareness would provide options for change. I began by making a list of adjectives that described me—driven, self-directed, ambitious, caring, exploring, risk-taking, and so on. The list alone, however, didn't illuminate a path to change as I wanted to capture my mental model, the self-concept from which I made decisions. So I stared at my list and allowed the words to form a pattern, which turned into an image, which finally formed a metaphor that reflected me. A metaphor is a comparative figure of speech in which a phrase that ordinarily describes one thing is applied to describe something else. If I describe Vivian as having a bubbly personality, I don't mean that bubbles are actually pouring out of her, but that she's a cheerful person. A broken heart, for example, doesn't indicate that a person's physical heart is cracked, but that they feel hurt and sad.

The metaphor that I eventually came up with to describe me at that time was an Explorer: I enjoyed discovering new ideas and territories and thrived on risk and exploration. I also pursued new ventures, product ideas, concepts, and market applications passionately. However, there was also a disadvantage to identifying with this metaphor: my focus on exploring and discovering, in time, directed my attention away from our "camp" and toward the periphery of the familiar. As a leader, I discovered that my Explorer self-image put me out of touch with my team and its day-to-day projects and efforts.

Fortunately, self-concepts are malleable. I knew that I could change my behavior if I changed the focus of my personal metaphor. I wanted to connect and engage more with my team, but I still needed the fuel and energy of adventure and discovery. I wanted to keep the best of what motivated me, while also updating and upgrading my effectiveness. I searched for a new metaphor that would provide both motivation and growth, and found it in the metaphor of a Spelunker—a cave explorer. Specifically, I was a Spelunker who descended into caves by rope; my team controlled the rope, and as they lowered and raised me I could explore and find treasures, but I depended on, and was always connected to, my team. As I embraced my new metaphor and focused on it daily, I began using this metaphor to evaluate my choices; I found myself naturally changing certain behaviors. In meetings, for example, I would silently ask myself if I was being an Explorer or a Spelunker as I assigned tasks to my team. If I noticed myself pressing my attention toward an adventurous new project, I'd think about spelunking and consider how to involve my team to safely lower and raise me by my imaginary rope.

The invisible can be made visible. You can actually visualize and express your self-concept. Additionally, you can manage and update your personal metaphor as needed. For more than a decade, I've guided leaders to identify their self-concept and harness the power of this mental feature rather than just be blown and pushed by it. I call this simple process the Personal Metaphor Exercise. What follows is an exercise combined with real-world examples of how it works.

Personal Metaphor Exercise

Your personal metaphor is a word picture that describes you as a leader. More than a static list of adjectives—passionate, thoughtful, analytical, and so on—the metaphor paints a mental portrait. Museums, galleries, and our homes are filled with pictures and paintings; each image invokes thoughts, feelings, and memories. For example, the photo hanging in our living room of a four-hundred-year-old oak tree reminds me of our wedding in Louisiana—the image makes me smile in the delight of the memory. A metaphor describes something that does not literally apply in order to show a resemblance. Shakespeare applied theater to life: "All the world's a stage, and all the men and women merely players. They have their exits and their entrances."

By defining your metaphor, you refine and strengthen your focus. You answer the question "What am I creating?" with your self-concept, a metaphor that captures and communicates your assumptions and expectations as leader. One VP of engineering, upon reflection, told me, "I'm a Wolf, and I'm surrounded by sheep." I asked if he meant sheepdog. "No!" he barked back unequivocally, "I'm a Wolf, and I have all these sheep around looking at me with big, frightened eyes. But I'm not a bad Wolf. I'm a good Wolf." I'm certain that his sheep don't know the difference; they just know that they feel defensive and anxious in his presence.

Another leader reported, after some thought, "I'm the Little Dutch Boy standing by a dike and holding back the ocean. I've got my fingers plugging the holes in the wall, but the whole thing is about to explode, and I'm barely holding back disaster." Another leader said, "I'm a Train. I'm at the station, and I'm leaving quickly and on time. You'd better get on board and we're going. I have no time to wait for latecomers or anyone hesitant." An executive in his early fifties caught my attention when he called himself a Priest. Another executive described her role as a Mother, caring for all her children on the team. One of the more creative metaphors came from a marketing executive who, after staring at the ceiling for a minute, referred to himself as a Thoughtful Clydesdale.

A metaphor articulates your self-concept, your current vision of yourself in the role of leader. The unspoken mental picture or metaphor that you have of yourself informs your decisions and choices; it is your internalized vision of who you are at this time. This story you tell about yourself to yourself shapes and influences your activities and choices, just as a vision for your team members shapes and influences their decisions and actions.

Our mind is a data filter: we pick and choose streams of information from our environment that fit into our story, into the narrative of our lives and roles. It's called "selective attention." We notice more of what we are attuned to; we select data consistent with our expectations, attitudes, and interests. Just recall the last time you bought a new car. Can you remember the surprise of noticing how many cars just like yours suddenly filled the streets around you? The real reason you saw so many cars just like yours is that your mind became acutely attuned and attendant to your particular make and model.

What is your personal metaphor? Take a moment to describe your leadership metaphor as it is today. Not as it should or could be, but in this moment. Inspect your thoughts and opinions, tap your imagination, and express a metaphor that accurately expresses you as a leader. There isn't a right or wrong answer; there is only your honest reflection and imagination.

Is your personal metaphor, your vision for yourself, good or bad? Well, it depends. It depends on whether your self-concept advances or impedes your success. Is your self-concept current, or is it an outdated vision? Was it crafted by default or by design? Does it fit in with your articulated goals and values or is it out of alignment with them? The question isn't whether your vision of yourself is good or bad, but whether it serves who you are now and where you want to go.

What kinds of behaviors would you expect to witness from the executive who sees himself as a Wolf? Just ask his sheep. How is the relationship between them? Ask them about the fear they experience in his presence. While his people feel passionate about the company's product, they fear their leader and become guarded around him. This Wolf of a vice president has complained about the lack of creativity on his team even as he's fired and hired talented people in his quest to surround himself with creativity. The problem, as you can imagine, is not a lack of creative team members; the problem is that there is an inverse relationship between fear and creativity: as one goes up the other goes down. The creative people who join his team get stripped of their creativity as he methodically (although not consciously) intimidates them.

The Wolf metaphor worked for this VP when he was a young and ambitious salesman. He was intense, driven, tenacious, and smart. As he rose through the ranks of leadership, these same qualities were recognized and rewarded, but their limitations began to show. The Wolf began to strike fear in those around him. As people began to steer clear of him, he became more intense in his pursuit of them, which exacerbated his reputation as a vicious predator.

The Little Dutch Boy executive with his fingers in the dike is caring and concerned. Along the way he realized that his talents and skills allowed him to solve complex problems and hold teams together when they appeared to fall apart. But he became deeply frustrated as his career stalled; he had become so integral to the safety of his business unit that he was passed over for promotion—not because he was unqualified but because of the consensus that he was irreplaceable. His self-concept as the sole protector and savior of the division prevented him from developing and coaching his people; accordingly, he was not mentoring and grooming his replacement.

The Train leader stayed on track. She had tremendous power and perseverance and always focused on leaving the station on time and with efficiency. With her Train mind-set, she primarily paid attention to punctuality and secondarily attended to people and relationships; she left laggards and latecomers behind. While she was terrific at follow-through and execution, she struggled to adapt and connect to her people. It was extremely difficult for her to leave her tracks and forge a new path as the environment of her business changed. And the passengers she leaves behind? Well, that's her current problem. She laments that her direct reports aren't on the same page as her, and that the frequency and intensity of miscommunication is growing. With the Train metaphor guiding her choices and behaviors, her future seems bound for more of these troubles.

Everyone loves the Priest. He acts as the spiritual center of his company. People flock to him, confess, seek counsel, share concerns, and listen to his advice. Is there even a downside to this metaphor, you might wonder. While he is acutely aware of the power of his role and relationships, he is concerned and discouraged about his company's financial control and expense management. When we examined his Priest metaphor more closely, we realized that his one-dimensional self-image didn't allow for discipline, only love. He was enabling and permitting subpar performance in the name of caring for his people.

The Mother is mired in a limited application of her metaphor as overly protective. Her team trusts her; they know she would protect and defend them with vigor and intensity. But her people feel coddled and micromanaged. She feels anxious for their well-being, so she hovers nearby, examining their choices and actions in order to keep them safe. Her staff members, like many children, appreciate Mother's care but resent her smothering presence.

All of these metaphors possess value and power, but they are woefully out-of-date. These metaphors originate in the decisions and lessons of my clients' personal histories that no longer fit their current realities or where they envisioned themselves going.

You assemble your self-concept from the ingredients of your journey's experiences; it contains your strengths and talents, fears and hopes, and conclusions and assumptions. It is normal and natural to have a self-concept for your role. In our discussion of leadership as a hero's journey, however, you must examine whether your metaphor is current or out-of-date. Are you being steered by a focus that serves your future or one that simply reinforces your history?

Recall the lesson from race-car drivers. When you commit your full attention to an object or direction, your choices and actions follow suit. The metaphor you have for yourself commits your direction. This is physically and mentally true. Your movement is directed toward the object of your attention. That direction is inevitable. A vision for your organization serves that purpose—to focus the movement of effort and action. It's nearly impossible not to have a vision, but you do have a choice whether to harness your imagination or let it run unchecked or reflect a self-concept that is out-of-date. If I were to ask you, "What is your vision for your department, your company, or your product?" you would likely answer with a well-rehearsed picture. Why is it, then, that when I ask for your vision of who you are as a person and a leader, it is difficult to respond with an intentional vision?

> *Unintentional actions are driven by impulse, habit, and history, not by choice. Leaders on the hero's journey strive to act from choice, not from scripted habit.*

Each of us has a metaphor—a mental image—for our role. We have a collection of metaphors that match our roles—leader, spouse, community member, and so on. Whether you are a Wolf, a Train, or a Little Dutch Boy is irrelevant. What is important on the journey of leadership is that the self-concept be up-to-date and reflect what you intend to achieve. The question "What am I creating?" is significantly affected by this metaphor. In the absence of a thought-out and deliberately articulated self-image, your behavior is unintentional. Unintentional actions are driven by impulse, habit, and history, not by choice. Leaders on the hero's journey strive to act from choice, not from scripted habit.

Now is a time for you to be intentional. You reflected on your current metaphor, read about other leaders' metaphors, and understand the power of a deliberate vision for yourself as a leader. What, then, do you chose to be? Project your imagination forward, past the challenges of implementation and personal change, and allow a metaphor to arise that contains the essence of who you are becoming as a leader. Think past the adjectives and let your imagination bring forth a metaphor;

call forth a mental image that expresses the kind of leader you want to be and the kind of leader your people need you to become. Willfully ignore your self-limiting thoughts and accept my permission for you to expand your self-concept.

So, what do you choose to be? How do you want to go about it? What's the value? What vision of yourself do you want to hold and project to others?

4

THE CO-CREATIVE LOOP

We answer the question "What am I creating?" with our outcome-directed minds. We have no choice but to comply with the inquiry; our choice lies in what we focus on as the answer. Your vision, your personal metaphor, is a response to the question "What am I creating?" Environment, opportunity, luck, and circumstances are forces and elements that shape and influence us, but we are not merely passive conduits of our environment; we exert an influence on our environment, too. I'll illustrate this influence with the Co-Creative Loop.

Imagine a clock face with numbers. Let's add a few labels to key numbers in order to understand the cycle of thinking and being. At high noon imagine the word *Beliefs*, at three o'clock picture the word

The Co-Creative Loop

BELIEFS

RESULTS

EXPECTATIONS

BEHAVIORS

Expectations, at six o'clock place the label *Behaviors*, and at nine o'clock is the word *Results*. The clockwise movement from twelve to three, three to six, six to nine, and back to twelve represents a closed loop of co-creation, from expectations to outcomes.

Beliefs start the loop; they are amalgamated thought clusters of your conditioning, values, desires, fears, biases, memories, and so on. Deeply seated beliefs seem natural and normal, as they have formed through direct and indirect exposure to family, culture, religion, and experiences. You ingrained your typically preverbal beliefs before you could express yourself or select your opinions. They drive your expectations and form belief-colored lenses that tint everything you see.

Expectations act as lens filters through which we perceive, judge, and evaluate the world around us. If, for example, I've come to believe that I can't do math, I'll feel nervous whenever my job requires some mathematical input. I'll expect that math and numbers-related activities are too harrowing, and I'll make efforts to minimize or avoid them. As my "numbers angst" persists and my math skills remain low, I will fret over my incompetence and struggle with a strong urge to avoid any numbers situations.

As a manager, though, I have budgeting responsibilities. Allocating income and expenses and managing finances are key functions of my professional role. If I perpetuate my expectation that I'm incompetent at math, I will make choices (the next part of the Co-Creative Loop) that will compensate for this belief and expectation. There are various behavioral paths I might follow:

- I might circumvent financial reports altogether.

- I might find someone to serve as my proxy and depend on his skill or judgment.

- I might play down numbers and insist that people skills are the "real" measure of leadership.

- I might fabricate reports to my bosses.

• I might reject a promotion, arguing that I serve the organization better in my current position.

Beliefs and expectations guide my choices, which, in turn, create my behaviors. Thoughts precede every action. If I feel, speak, and behave from an outdated and unexamined belief about my "numbers incompetence," then those around me will believe me and relate to me accordingly.

Behaviors are the third part of the Co-Creative Loop, the needle that pulls the thread of attention to sew together the fabric of resources. The higher you rise in your leadership responsibility, the more removed you are from direct means of production, and the more dependent you are on achieving your outcomes through and with others. Your beliefs about yourself, about people, and about the world shape your observations, expectations, and decisions, which, in turn, determine the direction and quality of your behaviors.

Behaviors are dynamic—a back-and-forth exchange of energy and attention. Leadership is a relational competency that depends on skillful behaviors. This shouldn't be confused with being liked or loved by everyone; it means that your actions generate the most power when they engender trust and alignment. The Gallup organization has polled millions of professionals on the topic of employee engagement—the level of emotional commitment at work. Their findings have shown that the overarching factor determining engagement (which also predicts retention) is the quality of relationship with the supervisor. People join companies, but they leave their managers.

Having looked at beliefs, expectations, and behaviors, we finally arrive at results—the last step in the Co-Creative Loop. These are the results we manifest in our worlds. Our outcomes, the life events we experience, reflect the beliefs that started the cycle, and in turn confirm them.

Tom, the president we met in chapter 1, oversaw a flat company performance for four years. A contributing factor to the firm's results was Tom's belief about relationships and dependence. His behavior with his team was shaped by micromanaging, which had its roots in his belief that he worked in a dangerous environment that he needed to control closely in order to succeed.

Inside this cycle of co-creation we create and re-create our experiences from moment to moment, from event to event, and from person to person.

Upgrading your leadership experience requires you to learn, practice, and implement new beliefs and thoughts. But this is only a beginning; philosophy and intellectual theorizing are not enough to generate an upgrade in competence. To achieve greater leadership satisfaction requires effort and work. It requires that we align our behaviors and relationships with new beliefs in order to produce new outcomes in our lives.

Co-Creation

You constantly affect your environment and contribute to the outcomes you experience, but you are not the sole hand that shapes reality. The creative act of leadership resembles the production of a play. A play germinates in the mind of the author. Trusted advisers help nurture and mature the ideas, and editors provide fine-tuning because their objectivity improves the author's message and process. But an undirected script is not a play; it's an idea. The author must transfer her prized possession to a director, who uses the script as a foundation for her interpretation of the writer's concepts. And there's more as the actors, without whom the play is a mere collection of words on a page, take on the work. They are the conduits for the story, as they infuse the characters with life and bring their energy into the interpretation of the lines. Finally, the audience interacts with the actors and influences how the actors deliver the play night after night, as they interact with the mood and energy in the theater. By performance time the writer's original vision and material is not her pure brainchild anymore—it has been codeveloped.

As the author's vision transforms during the production process, so does the leader's vision change and mature. As peers, staff, and investors work to interpret and personalize the vision, it changes. When the manifest product of the vision arrives in the hands of customers, they, in turn, change it. The final outcome, the manifestation of the leader's original vision, is both recognizable as and different from the initiating idea.

The intention of the leader is an urge to create. Leaders cannot afford to passively observe events and situations, they actively participate in creation—they cocreate. God, I'm told, has the power to create something from nothing, but I haven't met a person who can match that divine power. As a leader you create through your people. When you remember that

> *Because we lack the power to create something from nothing, we have to rely on working with others to redirect and recombine resources.*

your job is to cocreate, you can avoid the ego trap of grandiosity and remain connected to your people.

When I was in my twenties, I believed that I could do anything, and I could (and still can), but I can't do it all simultaneously. What I didn't know was how my beliefs affected my actions and outcomes, and how impactful relationships and collaboration were on my ability to produce outcomes. I was convinced that I alone could make things happen. I was quite certain that people would follow me because they were compelled or convinced by my willpower and persuasiveness. I fully expected that I was the author and the actors were dynamic dolls that I moved and manipulated to express my story. I was driven, intentional, and visionary. I was also an emotional moron.

Because we lack the power to create something from nothing, we have to rely on working with others to redirect and recombine resources. Relying on team members and allies to get things done isn't a sign of weakness, but hard-won maturity. My leadership succeeds when those I lead elect to emotionally and practically commit themselves to our common shared vision. Commitment sets the foundation for co-creation, for collaboration, for the comingling of effort and energy that accelerates results and outcomes.

Commitment is one of the outcomes of being focused. Repeatedly answering "What am I creating?" serves to align you with your highest and best use of time, energy, and effort. The wise companion to this question is "What are we creating?" This ignites commitment to purposeful thinking and to leadership as a hero's journey. More than just setting targets, objectives, and milestones, knowing your thoughts and beliefs and how they shape your experience (and the experience of your team) sets you on the heroic path of service and responsibility.

5

FOCUS GOBBLERS

Pausing during the day to ask yourself, "What am I creating?" is a powerful exercise in focus and productivity. Holding a focus and being intentional is the first step in transforming ideas from concept to reality. Kathy, our business manager in the firm, regularly asks us, "Is this the highest and best use of our time?" In order to answer this question, we must know what to focus on, what we're committed to creating, doing, and being.

My coaching clients are seasoned leaders, CEOs, and executives who focus on skillful ways to solve the problem of the moment. When we meet, rather than diving right into their stream of thoughts and attention, I typically begin by asking them to describe their visions for themselves and their organizations. I ask them, "What are you creating?" Their answer to this question is more than a personal alignment: it is a fundamental inquiry into organizational alignment. Leaders determine their followers' priorities, not only by what they say but also by what they do.

Your actions signal organizational priorities, and what you focus on becomes the finish line toward which your people race.

As an executive and leader, your actions signal organizational priorities, and what you focus on becomes the finish line toward which your people race. You have to expend real effort and energy to remain on target and keep yourself and your people focused on your deliberate creative targets.

Why, then, is focus such a fragile flower? It's fragile because we must repeatedly overcome three hurdles in order to remain focused—biology, psychology, and geography. Biology is our body, which has competing needs and limited energy. Psychology is our mind, ever occupied and distracted as a multifaceted processing machine. And geography is our environment, which is stimulating, volatile, and distracting.

Oh, If Only I Could Focus!

Our biology works against our effort to focus for practical and well-honed reasons. You're right if you've ever felt that prolonged and intense focusing seems unnatural. Our body and brain are ingenious systems finely attuned to survival, and therefore highly dependent on effective energy conservation. We have a built-in feedback process that strives for consistency and steadiness in our body, a process called homeostasis. In order to maintain homeostasis, our body balances through movement, food, sleep, and chemical management of stress hormones. Focusing—intentionally and consistently directing the mind—is a willful mental activity that devours energy and creates tension.

We can more successfully accomplish the mind's tendency toward homeostasis by short bursts of activity and reaction rather than long, sustained work. You know how your mind tends to flit and skip around? There's nothing wrong with you; that's an exercise of homeostasis trying to prevent burning up all your energy on thinking. While survival is enhanced by long-term thinking and preparation, it is driven by effective and efficient reactions to stimuli and environment. Our environment is both stimulating and potentially threatening; our ancestors didn't survive because they were envisioning and planning all the time. We are the genetic offspring of ancestors who survived because they kept alert, scanned their environment, and attended to sounds and movements, also known as stimuli. Our attention is designed to jump around and scan, not hold steady and plan.

You are, no doubt, bombarded with information from emails, articles, conferences, telephone calls, meetings, and social and traditional media, enough to trump most people's focus. However, allowing these stimuli to control you will result in neither heroic leadership nor productivity. *Getting Things Done: The Art of Stress-Free Productivity* by David Allen and *The Effective Executive: The*

Definitive Guide to Getting the Right Things Done by Peter Drucker are time-tested resources for efficiency and effectiveness. I highly recommend them. They will help you refine your productivity processes, thus freeing up valuable energy you can use for focusing. This is a critical first step because leadership as a hero's journey is born from clarity of both mind and body, both action and thinking. Mastering the techniques of focus and organization is one part of the equation; the other part is mastering the mind and heart.

Three Subtle Obstacles to Focus

Our ability to focus—to answer "What am I creating?"—is constantly undermined by stimuli, circumstances, events, people, information, and thousands of messages that bombard us daily. It might seem like a Herculean task to tame the screaming hydra of distraction all around us, but there is another source, equally powerful, that robs focus, that pulls attention away from the question "What am I creating?" This distraction emanates from our minds and hearts. Your leadership journey is an expedition that calls you to address the world within even as you engage with the world around you.

Mastering focus requires overcoming three subtle, internal obstacles that inhibit our ability to stay the course toward our commitments. These mental obstacles—distraction, confusion, and desperation—sneak into our thinking and make off with our attention.

I saw a bumper sticker that made me laugh and reflect: "Honk if you love Jesus. Text while driving if you want to meet him." Distraction can be lethal while driving, and it can be fatal to your ability to lead. Distraction smudges focus and erases your vision bit by bit. Rather than answering "What am I creating?" the distracted mind dwells on "What's this? What's that? What am I even doing?"

Our mind is a finely tuned instrument calibrated to notice, interpret, and predict what's happening, what it means, and what will happen. Our ancestors survived because they could discern between situations, objects, and people to avoid and those to embrace. These attributes are still critical to our survival, as we are geared to notice danger and opportunity. According to evolutionary scientists, the ancestors who didn't notice danger did not pass along their genes; they died because they didn't react to threats and opportunities, and we are the descendants of those who scanned and attended to their environment. Evolution favors focus and attentiveness over unawareness, and this behavior is rooted in the most ancient "lizard" part of our brains, estimated to have developed 285 million years ago. This reptilian controller sits atop the brain stem and drives us to perform primeval actions. When I feel threatened, the processing core of my brain calculates one of three simple responses—fight, escape, or stay still.

Focusing on long-range vision, on the other hand, comes from the newest part of the human brain: the neocortex—the seat of reasoning, language, planning, and problem solving. It answers the critical question "What am I creating?" and we need it in order to successfully navigate the inevitable deluge of the modern world's distractions. While your brain is susceptible to ancient patterns of distraction and wandering attention, your ability to cultivate focus and prolonged attention is critical for being a leader.

Confusion is a lack of clarity, an absence of the *fusion* or blending together of ideas or information. I consistently encounter two kinds of confusion in leaders: *learning confusion* and *defended confusion*.

New streams of knowledge and data, when introduced into an existing pool of information, stir up the pool and produce eddies and swirls, mixing things up. This whipped-up pool of existing and new knowledge produces a temporary froth of information, which results in confusion. This learning confusion typically resolves as time and repetition help integrate the new knowledge.

When I updated my computer with the newest version of Windows, I experienced learning confusion. Buttons, layouts, and functions changed, and actions I recently performed without thinking required more time, discovery, and attention. Grasping the particulars of the new software confused me. It wasn't inherently difficult, but I was already trained to interact with the previous version, so the new data and features did not align with my thinking and expectations. The path out of learning confusion requires an energetic climb up the learning curve, and because the climb can be intimidating or strenuous, some leaders would rather remain in their familiar state than learn something new. Though learning confusion is the easier of the two confusions to contain, it consumes attention and can bait attention away from "What am I (or *we*) creating?"

Defended confusion, on the other hand, is a form of psychic protection. It is a way for the mind to steer us in circles in order to avoid potential danger or damage from uncertainty or failure. Defended confusion is not fed by data or information, but by anxiety and an inherent commitment to self-preservation. For example, once a month for the past ten years, I have facilitated a dozen CEOs of established and growing businesses to help deepen their wisdom, sharpen their decisions, and accelerate their results. At one of our meetings, Parker, a six-year member, shared that he felt frustrated about his firm's growth rate. At fifty-three, Parker had the astuteness of three decades of work in his field. He was a senior vice president in the leading firm prior to starting his own business. So when he expressed that he felt confused about how to grow his firm, the rest of us around the table were incredulous.

Parker's confusion was a defensive mental attitude that kept him relatively safe and out of the way of danger and risk. This defensive behavior is neither conscious nor intentional, but self-protective and mechanical. Confusion is the opposite of focus, and it blots out both the horizon and the path toward that horizon. While Parker didn't like feeling confused, it served his unspoken desire to avoid danger or disappointment, and protected him from risk and letdown. By claiming confusion about how to grow his business, he conveniently kept to his comfort zone of familiar routines and expertise. Confusion was the safe and easy solution for him to avoid his fear of failure.

Should you find the mists of confusion swirling in your thoughts, examine whether they emanate from a barrage of information or from an upwelling of anxiety. On the heroic journey of leadership, we address learning confusion with repetition and practice. We resolve defended confusion with courage, which we'll discuss in great length in part II.

The Greek myth of Pandora and her box is a story rich with teachings. Pandora (meaning "all gifts") was made from clay and infused with life by Hephaestus, the blacksmith of the Greek gods. She was sent to earth to satisfy Zeus's revenge against Prometheus (from the Greek meaning "forethought") for sharing fire with humans; Hephaestus created Pandora to wreak havoc on humanity. Prometheus gave Pandora to his brother, Epimetheus (from the Greek meaning "afterthought"), as his wife. The myth reminds us that a leader with forethought would not accept a loaded gift from a suspect source, but a leader who doesn't think ahead would become involved in a troublesome situation.

Pandora came to earth bearing a locked box from Zeus, which he warned must never be opened. He did, however, give Epimetheus the key to wear around his neck. Zeus fully expected Pandora's curiosity to overcome her compliance, and one evening Pandora stole the key from her sleeping husband and opened the box. To her dismay, the lid burst open and out flew every kind of disease, hate, envy, and despair. She let loose on the world all the dreadful things that people hadn't experienced before. Gripped with guilt and shame, she struggled to press the lid down, but the flow of calamities was so great she succeeded in trapping just one item in the box. When Epimetheus awoke, Pandora told him what had happened, and as he opened the lid of the box in disbelief, he saw just one thing left—hope. Now it, too, flew out into the world.

Focus, or "What am I creating?" is rooted in hope, and while your leadership experience is fraught with challenge and difficulty, it is also synonymous with hope. Hope is a strong expectation—an optimistic feeling that what you want is possible and that events will turn out for the best. As the last "gift from the gods," hope counterbalances the vicissitudes of the journey. Hope emboldens your actions and nurtures your commitments, ambitions, achievements, confidence, and endurance. A leader without hope can't lead.

Viktor Frankl, author of *Man's Search for Meaning*, renowned psychotherapist and survivor of the Nazi concentration camps, places hope as the precursor to survival. He wrote, "The prisoner who had lost faith in the future—his future—was doomed. With his loss of belief in the future, he also lost his spiritual hold; he let himself decline and became subject to mental and physical decay."

A desperate leader lacks hope and will find his focus eroding. Just as focus is commitment to a distant vision, desperation urgently presses attention to the hopelessness of the immediate. Desperation is a loss of hope and focus. When the odds seem stacked squarely against us, the seed of the solution is contained within hope.

6

HUMAN UNIQUENESS

Leadership is the art of setting everyone's eyes toward a common horizon as you foster alignment by harnessing collective energy and effort toward the same horizon—the same desired outcome. As a leader, you set the horizon by activating your unique human gift of looking into the future. Great leaders throughout time have shaped history and societies by leveraging a desirable vision to influence and create. There are leaders who have brought out the best in humanity—Nelson Mandela, Gandhi, Golda Meir, Abraham Lincoln, John F. Kennedy—and there are leaders who have invoked the darkest aspects of people—Adolf Hitler, Attila the Hun, Ayatollah Khomeini, Pol Pot, and Idi Amin.

Just what is it that allows leaders to influence and shape behavior? What is unique about human beings that can be leveraged by leaders? If leaders bring out the best in humanity, we should have some idea of what that means. What makes us uniquely human is critically important for you to know and understand. Consider this short list of features unique to humans and instrumental for initiating and navigating the hero's journey: remorse, emotional resonance, rationality, and future orientation.

Remorse is uniquely human. I felt remorse after firing a team member, even though it was the necessary thing to do, and I didn't second-guess the decision. While I knew firing her was appropriate, I also knew how painful it was for her, and I had (and, to this day, still have) real sorrow for the anguish she experienced. Remorse differs from guilt. Remorse is a tenderness of the heart that relates to empathy, the ability to recognize and share the pain of another. Empathy is a leadership trait that invokes loyalty and respect. As a leader, you make difficult decisions that impact people's lives, and hiding your remorse hardens your heart and gnaws at your trustworthiness.

Remorse is a personal heartfelt experience; we express it to others as an apology. Aaron Lazare, writing in *Psychology Today*, says, "The main reason that people do not apologize is because they are afraid the apology will be seen as a sign of weakness and/or guilt. In reality, an apology indicates great strength as it is an openhanded act that restores and rehabilitates the self-concept of the offended party." Leadership is a relational competency. Remorse and heartfelt apologies are restorative acts that repair and strengthen relationships. Strong relationships yield employee commitment and engagement.

Emotional resonance is another defining human trait. Neuroscientists, using functional magnetic resonance imaging (fMRI) technology, have gained remarkable detail and clarity in producing maps that show which parts of the brain are activated and involved in particular mental processes. One of the newly found features of our brains is a distinctive class of neurons called mirror neurons, which provide us resonance with another person's experience. When you cringe at the sight of a stranger crashing his bicycle, you are engaging your mirror neurons. The anxiety you feel in your gut when your colleague flails during her presentation is due to mirror neurons. Mirror neurons allow us to internalize and personalize another person's experience. We can learn by observation; we do not learn solely from direct experience. Mirror neurons and emotional resonance are, therefore, at the heart of behavior modeling. By repeatedly concentrating on "What am I creating?" you will modify your behavior to match your focus. Consequently, your team and followers will mirror you.

Another human feature is *rationality*. The Greek philosopher Aristotle believed that being rational was the primary distinction between humans and animals. We are affected by anger, jealousy, lust, and fear, but we are also able to refrain from our instinctive drivers and engage the world in a deliberate and purposeful manner. Emotional energy radiates from within us like light from the sun. However, like too much sun, emotional energy can burn us. Wearing a hat, long sleeves, and sunscreen is a wise precaution against strong sun exposure.

Similarly, our rational thinking provides a screen from the intense radiation of emotions and base instincts.

Rationality and objective problem solving are among the key features of leadership. In the face of change and uncertainty, it takes a collected and objective mind to remain on track. In the chapters to come, we explore how to cultivate grit and courage. Both draw on focus and both require a measure of rationality.

Future orientation is the last of the human distinctions I'll discuss. Future orientation allows us to hold the future as a variable in real-time decision making. We can project into the future and consider that future in the present. Our remarkable mind has the ability to travel back and forth in time; we can equally revel in memories and goals. All animals have memory. This capacity enables my dog to remember where the door is located and the time for our evening walks. Some animals demonstrate future-facing behaviors (think of squirrels and ants stashing food for the winter), but these seem to be instinctive. It doesn't appear that animals project their minds into an imagined future. Making up possibilities about what's going to happen down the road is a uniquely human experience, and we call that imagination.

Our minds easily conjure up—intentionally or unintentionally—scenarios for the future that may or may not become reality. Our capacity to imagine lies at the very core of the leadership skill of vision. Albert Einstein said, "Imagination is more important than knowledge. For knowledge is limited, whereas imagination embraces the entire world, stimulating progress, giving birth to evolution."

Vision refers to our ability to project the mind into the future, to imagine a possible outcome, and to imbue it with enough concrete evidence that we can articulate and share it. Crafting a strategic plan, articulating goals, formulating a budget, describing new product families, and crafting financial models for new business ventures all exercise the power of imagination and yield the gift of creativity.

Discussions about creativity typically involve artists, poets, or others who channel their visions into tangible form. I believe that all human endeavors are creative, not just recognizable art. This narrow view of mashing up creativity with art prevents people from grasping the fact that entrepreneurs and leaders are also artists who use business and commerce as the medium to create their visions.

An articulated vision is an act of creativity. Articulating a vision for an organization is an exercise in practical imagination. You can and must develop the talents of imagination and vision if you want to successfully lead. This is part of the skill of focus: blending vision and intention. Intention is the ability to stretch toward, and vision is that toward which we stretch. In some respects, vision and intention are synonymous as they answer the question "What am I creating?" When you set a vision for the organization, you provide a common point for everyone in the organization to stretch toward.

In the absence of a vision—a coherent point in the future—toward which we apply our skills, efforts, and attention, each person will exercise his or her natural capacity to reach out but will end up traveling in different directions. We see this play out as team members leverage their natural capacities for intention and end up diluting the collective power of the organization by pulling in different directions. Many failures of organizational execution are not failures of goodwill, but failures of coordination and alignment. They reflect the inability to integrate the multiple contributions of individuals. They represent failures to exercise the fact that the whole is greater than the sum of its parts.

In the absence of a vision— a coherent point in the future— toward which we apply our skills, efforts, and attention, each person will exercise his or her natural capacity to reach out but will end up traveling in different directions.

As a leader on the hero's journey, you learn that intention trumps precedence. Holding this principle in mind emboldens you to trust that the future can be different by design. In setting our intention, we can draw on the past, on a storehouse of wisdom gleaned from experience. If we fail to harvest the wisdom from our past experiences, we doom ourselves to make the same mistakes over and over; we also doom ourselves to experience futures that are mere variations on the past we've traversed.

As a leader who embraces the hero's journey, focus (your intention and vision) is more powerful than that which has come before. Literally, leadership is about going to places no one has been, and it requires you to be more future focused than past focused. You can't deny the past, but your attention must be on what's to come rather than what has been.

Imagination

As Einstein proposed, the power of imagination expands our world and ushers in growth. As a leader, you are charged with growth, not mere maintenance; growth happens when we pass the border of our comfort zone. Imagination acts as the vehicle in which our mental scouts first cross that border. We can project our imagination as far and wide as we'd like without any danger or damage. An imaginative flight of the mind can be an unfettered thought experiment, freely exploring possibility and creativity. After consideration and calculation, the scope becomes clearer, narrower, and more articulate, and at that point we can share it with others. Now this refined and articulated flight of imagination has a new name: vision.

Where do we apply our intention? If it is natural for humans to stretch toward a desirable horizon, how do we determine which horizon is desirable? Easier said than created—the answer is vision. My colleagues and I consistently discuss vision as a distinguishing feature of leadership. Lack of vision is one of the fatal flaws of leaders; it is a sure way to terminate an otherwise promising leadership career. Yet I have had countless conversations with executives who struggle to understand their visions and how to communicate it to their teams. Your ability to set a clear and compelling vision for the organization is a key element for facilitating collaboration, efficiency, and synergy.

On the heroic journey, there is another aspect to vision—the vision you hold for yourself. The power of personal vision stems from its tendency to align, synergize, and integrate your personal strengths, talents, and motivations. The challenge we all face is that we already have a vision of ourselves as leader, a vision that pervades our thinking, actions, and decisions; our imagination and vision are always active. By asking the question "What am I creating?" you initiate an active quest. The answer, though, is either intentional, something I'm creating on purpose, or habitual, something I'm creating by default. Consider these books for an immersion in crafting your vision: *Vision: A Personal Call to Create a New World* by Ken Carey; *The Personal Vision Workbook* by Tobin Burgess; *The Art of Possibility: Transforming Professional and Personal Life* by Rosamund and Benjamin Zander; and *The 7 Habits of Highly Effective People Personal Workbook* by Stephen R. Covey.

Vision is the act or power of anticipating that which may come to be. You have engaged in vision your whole life. Projecting into the future is a full-time occupation for the mind. Just think of how much energy and focus we place on planning and goal setting, on the one hand, and fretting and "awfulizing," on the other hand. This process typically goes unchecked, but we can harness it. Like other skills or talents, some leaders are more attuned to imagination and vision. As imagination is a human capacity, all leaders possess it and can harness its power; more important, all leaders must do so if they want to articulate a vision.

Leaders guide a community on an uncertain expedition toward a desirable shared vision. The expedition is uncertain because it requires leaving the zone of the known, the comfort zone. Why must we stretch the comfort zone? Because potential and growth lie outside it. Within the comfort zone, potential has been turned into reality—prospects are now clients, innovation is now integrated, inventions are now tools, goals are now accomplishments—what was once new is now standard.

Leaving the comfort zone is not a goal unto itself; it is a necessity for reaching toward a desirable vision. You awaken your hero's journey by taking steps in the direction of a vision, steps that take you away from the comfort zone. Teams and communities are drawn toward a desirable future vision, and so are individuals. You have a vision for yourself as a leader, whether you have crafted it on purpose or by reaction to circumstance. Let's turn our attention next to your inner vision, your mental aspiration toward which you are heading.

7

FIGHT OR FLIGHT?

Neuropsychological studies of the brain have confirmed what philosophers and teachers have observed for millennia—that the mind is oriented toward goals and outcomes. The mind constantly reaches toward something. It seeks to fulfill an intention. Remember our race-car driver who focuses either on the road or on the wall: she moves toward her intention, toward her focus. She might not want to drive into the wall, but when she holds it as her focal point, she invariably moves toward it.

In the absence of an articulated intention—a vision—leaders and their teams are reduced to operating in habitual patterns, which function largely in concordance with the "fight-or-flight" mechanism. Leading people and accomplishing results through others involves a lot of stress, stress that arises in the tension between current experience and a desired, different, future experience. You are, undoubtedly, familiar with what anxiety and stress do to people: both ignite the fight-or-flight reaction process.

When we get startled or triggered by a stimulus that we judge as threatening, our lizard brain (the most primitive part of our brain, specifically the amygdala) quickly evaluates whether we want to fight (engage the situation) or flee (avoid the situation). This lizard brain sets up a constant calculation of either moving toward or away from something. I was taught that fight-or-flight instincts move us toward pleasure or away from pain, but having studied and observed human behavior in general, and leadership in particular, I disagree with this premise. I disagree that we either chase or escape, that we either fight or flee. My investigations reflect recent brain research that supports the premise that we are *always* moving toward something; what seems like fight or flight is actually a consistent drive toward a goal.

It is easy to conceive how the fight mechanism is moving toward something: we move into the struggle to engage with the stimulus. It's harder to see how the flight mechanism also reveals a movement toward something, but consider that the flight response is an intentional move toward safety. When we decide to fight, we have done so because we calculate the odds of winning as high. When we decide to flee, we've done so because we believe the odds of winning are low. In either case, we make a decision to move toward something—either toward domination or toward safety. Even when we decide to avoid a stimulus, we move toward something—toward a perception of comfort.

> *If you don't determine your focus, then your focus will be determined for you by your team and the environment.*

Imagine or recall attending a team meeting with your manager and peers. A recent organizational change has increased your team's workload and added new members. As a result, collaboration is ineffective, deadlines are missed, and your internal customers are grumbling about your team's performance. This day's agenda includes a consultant who will facilitate a conversation about increased collaboration, and you are a key focus in this discussion. No doubt you have mixed feelings, wanting to forcefully explain and promote your decisions (fight) *and* wanting to avoid the meeting altogether (flee). In either case you desire to achieve something—either assertion or safety. Both are outcomes on which you can focus.

We are intentional (outcome-directed) creatures by design, and leadership effectiveness depends on harnessing intention—a purposeful aim—to direct efforts, decisions, and relationships. If you don't determine your focus, then your focus will be determined for you by your team and the environment. We are not the sole shapers of our outcomes; none of us are entirely autonomous in our goal setting and achievement. We live within a context and concurrently create and respond within its boundaries.

You are responsible for achieving results and accomplishing strategic objectives and goals; you are expected to orchestrate people's efforts toward attainment. As a leader you are an agent of change who coordinates an organizational expedition toward a desirable shared outcome. Effective leaders are intentional—they are deliberate and purposeful in their focus. And we are, by our nature, intentional. Intention originates from the Latin word *intendere*—a stretching out. Your thoughts, actions, and commitments are all rooted in the natural inclination to stretch out.

I remember once, as a department head, when I engaged in intentional fleeing. During that time, I set our department goals lower than what our GM wanted; I knew I was going to be pressured to raise our targets. You might think that setting the low goal was a lack of vision or boldness, or evidence of poor leadership, but that was not how I thought about it at the time. Setting low goals was a flight response for me, a way to stretch toward safety and to ensure at least some measure of success. While it's conceivable that I was trying to avoid failure, the deeper truth was that I was stretching toward my own sense of accomplishment and success.

Setting my sights low was an act of self-preservation, as well as a subtle act of sabotage that affected my team and peers. In focusing on my own safety, I compromised the goals of my organization. I was a leader with mixed intentions—I wanted to orchestrate success for my organization and maximize my own ego safety. Mixed intentions, especially combining a conscious vision for growth with an unconscious vision for safety, can undermine leadership effectiveness. My own impulse for safety was a neglect of responsibility.

I needed help to see my mixed intentions, help that my mentor provided in a series of conversations. Our blind spots are, by definition, invisible to us. Seeing and labeling the desire for safety wasn't enough to transcend it, but it was enough to corral it. My early career decision to lower my goals was not an act of deliberate cowardice; it was an expression of my mixed intentions. While some of my intentions remained hidden, operating below the radar of awareness, they silently influenced my decision making. I was unable to behave differently as long as I was unaware of how these hidden factors influenced my decision process. With my mentor's help, I found the self-knowledge and self-awareness that form the initial steps to purposeful change. By understanding my motives, I could consider the essential elements of my decision making and commitment, and I finally grasped how my self-concept affected my focus, vision, and creative output.

8

WHAT DO I STAND FOR?

As a leader, you have to stand for something. Stand for your focus. Stand for intentional purpose. Stand for the essence of vision and strategy that you and your team reach toward.

It takes far more energy to create than it does to destroy. When I was thirty I built a small house, almost entirely by myself: a 625-square-foot cabin in the high mountains surrounding Albuquerque nestled in the woods. This little house was built to be green: it had a composting toilet, five-hundred-gallon catch tank, and an 8/12 pitch roof for maximizing snowmelt and rain capture. I even created a French drain system to direct the gray water into the drip circles of nearby trees. The cabin was isolated but in the vicinity of friends who supported me in my year of silence and isolation.

I retreated to this forested corner in order to live out my dream of practicing meditation with undistracted focus and attention. I wanted to experience a level of spiritual practice that eluded me with my regular life of work and community. I committed to building my cabin with a spirit that embodied my experiment; I was determined to build with the smallest environmental footprint possible and, whenever possible, recycle and reuse as many materials as I could. Fortunately, a friend of mine owned property down the hill in Edgewood that had on it three run-down structures. We struck a deal that if I helped him demolish these older buildings, I could take any salvageable materials. Surprisingly, tearing down structures that someone else spent great effort and energy to build was easy. Using my strength and wielding a ten-pound sledgehammer, I quickly and effectively broke down the walls.

I admit that slamming a giant hammer into the wood and stone thrilled my inner ten-year-old boy. Using brute force to strike the structures until they collapsed and fell apart didn't take any intelligence or design. I just had to hit hard and get out of the way to avoid falling objects.

Building the house, on the other hand, took energy, consistency, and a tremendous amount of dedication. It required vision, planning, and near flawless execution. As a leader, your focus is not to tear down but to build—you must stand for something, reach for something, *build* something. But first you must determine the purpose of your creation or structure. A clear purpose allows all your people to turn their eyes in the same direction and build together. How are you going to get people to focus in the same direction?

Part of the hero's journey is discovering your vision of success. I've coached hundreds of successful leaders, and their success formulas have been as diverse as the people themselves. Of course, some leadership practices and principles apply well to all leaders, and yet your way, your vision, your design for the team and organization that you are building is unique. It's up to you to figure out what you stand for, what you believe, and what you champion. What is your intention? What are you reaching toward? What is your goal? What is your purpose, both for your team and for yourself as a leader?

Answering the question "What am I creating?" requires an intentional answer. It's not enough to stand against something. It's not an act of leadership to just tear things down, to negate. Although creating a common enemy can galvanize people and move them closer together, it doesn't move them forward. The late Steve Jobs, founder and (twice) CEO of Apple Computers, knew how to both stand against and stand for something: he cast Microsoft as the antagonist in his vision. "Let's not be like them," he proclaimed, while also rallying his employees, investors, and customers to "put a dent in the universe." His people had something to stand against, but they also had something to stand for.

What am I creating? What do I stand for? You answer these questions at both the macro (vision) and micro (conduct) levels. You might, for example, stand for a culture of adaptability. The next question is, how do you promote that value as a behavior everyone reaches for together?

Promoting Values

The two primary ways to promote values are to publish them and practice them. *Publishing* means clearly articulating and documenting your intention. It means that you take the time and make the effort to clarify your thoughts and intuition and communicate them clearly and consistently: you articulate what you stand for and what you want your people to stand for. But articulating a value isn't enough. As you publish your expectations, you also have to practice the behaviors that demonstrate that value. Let's consider adaptability, for example. In publishing adaptability, you might announce and emphasize that adaptability is important in your company. In practicing adaptability, you might actively solicit new ideas from employees and customers.

Your practices will either reinforce or undermine what you publish. Imagine a heated meeting in which a team passionately pursues a creative solution to a thorny problem. Imagine that Brian shares an idea that is both unusual and contradictory to yours, and you respond sarcastically, shutting him down before he can fully mature his thought. Your team will believe your practice more than they will believe what you've published. You may say (publish) that you stand for adaptability and its implications of staying open to novel and innovative problem solving, but you just demonstrated (practiced) that you stand for habitual repetition, power dynamics, and status quo management.

Your actions will either reinforce or contradict what you publish, and your team will take as much direction from what you do as from what you don't do, or what you do or don't tolerate. You communicate leadership expectations by role modeling, by living and breathing your values, expectations, and point of view. As a leader, you reinforce what you tolerate. Consider a different meeting during which Brian shares his novel idea, but this time you sit in silence as Tom jumps in and sarcastically interrupts Brian. If you allow this behavior and tolerate Tom's actions, you have implicitly approved his behavior and communicated to the team that adaptability is not a value you support.

Responsibility

The old adage "the buck stops here" definitely holds true when it comes to leading. Regardless of whether you are in middle or senior management, you have a scope of authority and decision making, and your effectiveness is proportionate to your responsibility. I resonate with Denis Waitley's comments: "A sign of wisdom and maturity is when you come to terms with the realization that your decisions cause your rewards and consequences. You are responsible for your life, and your ultimate success depends on the choices you make." Your decisions are what you stand for, and what you stand for is your responsibility. You are accountable.

What does it mean, then, to be responsible in leadership? A leader in a responsible position has ownership of the process and outcome of decisions and actions. A responsible leader wields control and authority, and makes critical decisions without supervision. When principles of conduct are clear and articulated, they give rise to

In the short term, you may experience some relief by not taking responsibility and blaming problems on others or on circumstances, but there is a price to pay. Your cost is loss of respect, authority, and the ability to accomplish your goals and move toward your vision.

responsibility, judgment, and effective decision making. These principles arise from the spring of your vision, focus, and answer to the question "What am I creating?"

George Bernard Shaw observed, "Liberty means responsibility. That is why most men dread it." When you choose (and it *is* a choice) not to take responsibility for your decisions, you squander your leadership power and authority. In the short term, you may experience some relief by not taking responsibility and blaming problems on others or on circumstances, but there is a price to pay. Your cost is loss of respect, authority, and the ability to accomplish your goals and move toward your vision.

There is another costly by-product of not taking responsibility—loss of self-respect and self-esteem. When you practice responsibility, you cultivate self-respect, and when you eschew responsibility, blame others, and fall into a victim mentality, you nurture a mind-set that limits relationships, ambitions, and achievements. Owning your responsibility and refraining from blaming empower your sense of achievement while signaling authority to your people. You also reduce your reliance on external validation and praise from others to feel good about yourself. I have yet to meet a leader who doesn't desire validation, which is an inherently human need, but there is a spectrum of validation drive. On one end, "validation dependence" shapes your decisions in favor of receiving praise; on the other end, "validation appreciation" allows you to enjoy praise from others while maintaining your independence of thought and judgment.

If you won't embrace your responsibility, you will play out a victim mind-set, one driven by circumstances, not by focus or intent. The victim convinces himself that he's at the whim of chaotic events, the outcome of which leaves him casting about reactively without any apparent rhyme or reason. He's on the receiving end, not the creating end. The responsible leader has a mind-set of ownership of her experiences. She is responsible for who she is, what she has, and what she does. She can't create and control everything, but she has the capacity to choose how she participates with the people, situations, and conditions that arise.

The lesson here is that what you choose to do in the moment has an impact on where your conversation, relationship, and team will go. You calculate your choices by measuring whether each of these elements brings you closer to or further away from your focus.

Leadership means responsibility. So how do you take responsibility? It's an important choice that you have to make. In this part, I outlined reasons to keep your mind attuned to the value of responsibility and focus, but a word of caution is necessary. Staying focused and doing the right thing is hard to sustain, and even harder to perform meticulously, so don't aim for perfection. Commit yourself to continuous and deliberate practice and do the best you can moment to moment.

By adopting the practices of focus and shouldering the weight of responsibility, you develop the capacity to stick to your path, and cultivate the habit of owning your experience. But don't mistake your urge to improve for a reason to beat yourself up. Self-awareness is the key to your development, even when you become aware of beliefs or habits that you don't like or need. It takes courage to grow in awareness. It takes perseverance to change your self-concept. Courage and perseverance are the next two virtues we discuss on your hero's journey of leadership.

PART II

COURAGE
What Am I Avoiding?

Your focus, your vision of something possible, sets you on a deliberate departure from the familiar comfort zone, and with that comes uncertainty and the companions of uncertainty: fear and anxiety. Face it: you can't eliminate fear. You can't be fearless; fear is biological. It is activated in the face of real or perceived threats. You can, however, find your courage in the presence of fear, and while it is unreasonable that you remain fearless, you can become skillful in how you manage your fear and anxiety. Since leadership is a hero's journey into opportunity, uncertainty, risk, and sacrifice, it is a journey into fear territory.

When you're done reading part II, you'll be better equipped to be courageous. You'll understand what we're all fundamentally afraid of, why courage is critical to achievement, and how you can bolster your leadership courage. Mark Twain wrote, "Courage is resistance to fear, mastery of fear—not absence of fear." Let's examine how to apply this practically.

9

WHAT AM I AVOIDING?

At some point in my twenties, I realized that the biggest barrier in life was my collection of well-rehearsed fears. I had heard this so many times from so many people it eventually crystallized. My relationships, work success, creativity, spiritual connection, and even my goals were all governed by my ability to conquer my fears. The instructional choir in my head, made up of the voices of Zig Ziglar, Anthony Robbins, Brian Tracy, and Tom Hopkins (among others), convinced me beyond doubt that when I finally conquered my fears I would have an unlimited life with the ability to realize my full potential.

I could feel my fears and anxieties weighing me down like a waterlogged woolen cloak. What were some of my fears? I feared that if I committed myself to a significant project or relationship and I wasn't able to make it happen, it would demonstrate that I was, in fact, incompetent; it would prove that I was a failure. I feared looking bad to other people, to women in particular, and to my friends and competitors. I attempted to appear cool and uncaring, while anxious about whether my hair looked okay or my choice of clothes was acceptable or hip enough for my crowd. I worried that I might sound like an idiot while giving a presentation. I fretted about whether my friends liked me, and whether strangers found me likable. I was a poster child for the adage, shared by one of my psychologist friends, that people are motivated by two desires: to look good and to avoid looking bad.

Convinced that conquering my fears was the path to a fully realized life, I took it upon myself to conquer them. I went deep-sea diving in the Gulf of Mexico with hammerhead sharks. I went skydiving twice because I was promised that this would cure the fear of heights that had haunted me since childhood (which, by the way, didn't cure it!). I walked barefoot across a bed of nails only to step into a thirty-foot-wide pit of fire and burning coals, from which I emerged without a scratch or a burn. I fasted for two weeks to prove my superiority over my physical body. I logged more bungee jumps from bridges and cranes than I can even remember. I spent hours in sensory deprivation tanks—locked in pitch-black, floating in warm water, cocooned in absolute silence, facing my demons. I confronted my parents, disclosing my frustrations about their parenting and my childhood disappointments. This is a short list of some of my more dramatic "fear-conquering" behaviors. By all accounts I should have earned a golden merit badge for fearlessness.

Fearlessness is not the gospel to study and follow, rather we are called to cultivate courage and bravery—a willingness to press forward in the presence of fear.

But, alas, while my confidence swelled from many repetitive efforts to face and confront my fears, I am still not fearless. More important, I no longer wish to be fearless. While I encourage you to press the boundaries of your comfort zone, I would discourage any sane human being from setting out on the absurd expedition to become fearless. Being fearless is an immature, delusional, and misguided objective. As I asserted before, fear is biological. It is a survival imperative so deeply woven into our neural system that it practically defines what it means to be alive.

While I agree that our fears hold us back, I reject that we have to banish our fears as a condition of success. Fearlessness is not the objective of a fully realized life; the objective is courage. To be courageous requires that we fully recognize, feel, and acknowledge our fears while making a choice to do the very thing that our fear would like to avoid. To be courageous is to walk toward what you'd rather run away from; to be courageous is to embrace the hero's journey. That instructional choir in my head had been off-key in its message. Fearlessness is not the gospel to study and follow, rather we are called to cultivate courage and bravery—a willingness to press forward in the presence of fear. As Aristotle said, "Courage is the first of human qualities because it is the quality which guarantees the others."

You are far more likely to wrestle with the angst of failure than the danger of falling off a cliff. The courage and bravery you have to activate are most critical in tackling fears of the mind and heart rather than fears of physical danger. One of the privileges of my coaching role is the depth and intimacy of my conversations with executives. In order to accelerate their results and sharpen their decision making, we almost always find our way to uncovering the fears and anxieties that block their thinking, feeling, and relating. I've never heard an executive mention fear of heights or fear of drowning as a legitimate leadership concern. Practically all the fears mentioned are mental and emotional in nature; they are ego- and relationship-based fears. See if you recognize yourself in these examples:

- "I'm afraid that I'll fail and therefore let people down."

- "I'm afraid that I'll be perceived as incompetent."

- "My worth is defined by what I do for others. If I don't provide, I'm afraid people won't value me and my connections will go away."

- "I'm afraid that I will lose credibility. This literally hurts my heart and makes me feel terribly vulnerable."

- "I'm afraid that if I fail to have significance and make a difference around here, people will lose respect for me."

- "I'm afraid of losing the respect and trust of my team and peers. If I lose this respect, I'll lose my authority and with it my ability to be effective and successful."

- "I worry that I'll lose self-respect, that I'll blow my responsibility to others, lose credibility as a leader, and be rejected."

- "I have a fear of failure, so I avoid making certain difficult decisions, or put off the decision until the very last possible minute."

- "I'm afraid of not being in control. If I lose control, I'll be irrelevant."

Kathy, a recently promoted CEO of an 850-employee organization, knew firsthand the inner voice of fear. She spent countless sleepless nights riddled with anxiety, fretting over how her decisions would affect the lives of thousands of employees, shareholders, and customers. She was intimately in touch with the nervousness of having to fire tenured executives who no longer fit the organization. She recognized that she had a perspective of the organization that no one else could fully share, and that her decisions had an unequal impact on the organization, even as her certainty was questioned. By her own account, she knew she was growing in courage when she shared with me, "I'm no longer scared to death. I'm just scared now."

In spite of several years of organizational growth, Kathy felt nervous and anxious about the financials, worrying that the top and bottom lines were out of alignment. While her firm had been recognized in the Inc. 5000 list as one of the fastest-growing companies in the United States for three years in a row, her financials were not as strong as she hoped. Although Kathy knew this at an intuitive level, she felt too afraid to face the reality of the organization's financially precarious situation. She was a responsible leader—caring deeply for her people, for their market, and for the vision of the company—but her fear obscured her ability to make effective leadership decisions.

Kathy was not facing a fear of heights or injury, but a fear of failure—or, rather, she was avoiding facing her fear of failure. After some wrangling and cajoling, she assembled and activated a forensic financial team that reviewed her financials from top to bottom. The objective reports were, in fact, as bad as she had intuited. She felt as if she had taken the company to the brink, and she was not certain of her ability to bring it back to solid ground. In describing her situation, Kathy said that the company felt like a car that had spun out of control, slid to the edge of a cliff, and was now perched on the verge with the front wheels hanging over the abyss. As the driver, her weight could tip the car into oblivion, or swing it back to get the rear tires traction with the ground. She no longer slept properly, lost her appetite, experienced persistent headaches and stomach pains, and constantly dealt with fatigue. Kathy was gripped tightly in the debilitating embrace of deep anxiety and fear of failure.

Through our work, Kathy became willing to face the reality of the situation. The leadership journey turns heroic when it meets three criteria: (1) going after a great prize, (2) facing risk and sacrifice, and (3) serving the community. When Kathy's sense of duty to her people—her commitment to serve her community—squared up to the depth and intensity of her fear of failure, she was able to place her feet back on the hero's journey.

Kathy understood that fearlessness is not an option, since fear is a biological reality, and she began to embrace her courage when she started moving toward the facts that her fear instructed her to run away from. Courage is an option, and it's a defining trait of leaders. It involves the willingness to put your own well-being at risk in order to serve your people.

10

COSTS OF FEAR

Fear and anxiety are not bad. Saying that fear is bad is like saying that the sun is bad because prolonged exposure can produce melanoma. Fear occurs naturally in the brain and, more important, in the body. On the heroic journey of leadership, fearlessness doesn't exist; fear does, but so does courage—the willingness to bravely face that which we'd rather avoid or eliminate. Learning how to manage and contain naturally occurring fears and developing skills for relating to our fears are critical skills for leaders. Left unchecked, fear and anxiety exact a heavy toll not only on you but on your team, organization, and even the market.

Instinctively, we react to fear by contracting (getting small), complaining (finding faults), and controlling. Erin, for example, was a newly appointed director of a large marketing department. Congress had announced new regulatory legislation that would directly affect her company's ability to remain competitive, and her department needed to initiate strategic changes.

> *Fear and anxiety are not bad. Saying that fear is bad is like saying that the sun is bad because prolonged exposure can produce melanoma.*

While Erin's boss felt confident in her ability to meet the challenge, she started losing sleep as a result of fretting and anxiety. The changes were going to directly affect the 130 members of her team, how they distributed work, and how they delivered value to their clients. Fueled by her unexamined fears of loss of control, of being discovered as a fraud, and of failing in her job, Erin experienced terrible anxiety. Worse, she was subtly communicating her anxiety to her employees, whose response was to shrink to safety by disengaging from her and the organization.

Employee engagement—the emotional connection to work—is one of the holy grails of modern organizations. Safe working conditions were the hallmark of the nineteenth century, as fair salaries were focal in the twentieth century, but it is employee engagement that energizes the workplace of the early twenty-first century. Fear is an engagement solvent; it dissolves and dissipates emotional connection. The costs of disengagement have been documented by numerous researchers including the Hay Group, the Gallup Organization, and the Corporate Executive Board. The 2012 report "Engagement at Work: Its Effect on Performance Continues in Tough Economic Times," the Gallup's meta-analysis of 1.4 million employees, demonstrated that lost productivity of disengaged employees in the United States amounted to $370 billion. Specifically, they found that disengaged employees did the following:

- Take more sick days and are tardy more often.

- Undermine their engaged colleagues with constant complaining.

- Cost employers $3,400 to $10,000 in salary owing to decreased productivity.

- Miss deadlines and turn in poor sales results.

- Experience an increase in customer complaints, creating disengaged customers.

- Contribute to inadequate company performance.

- Increase the number of high-potential employees desiring to leave.

There is an important reason to discuss your personal anxiety. Fear, you see, is reflected back by those you lead. Ralph Waldo Emerson's words, "The institution is the lengthened shadow of one man," keep us focused on the influence leaders have over their followers. Nobody expected Erin to not experience fear, but when she wallowed in her anxiety and wore a mask of angst, her team began to reflect her state. Vision and enthusiasm are contagious, and so are anxiety and worry. As a team registers their leader's fear, they begin to resonate with their boss's anxiety and slip into defensive behaviors. Defensiveness is an instinctive grasping for self-protection, and there are several defensive patterns common in anxious groups. Here are a few patterns that inhibit your team and organization:

- **Hoarding:** In the 1950s, at the height of the Cold War, some families in the United States built up large stocks of survival materials because of their anticipatory anxiety about the possibility of a nuclear war. Their retreat and hoarding weakened their community morale, terminated relationships, and significantly amplified fear in their friends and family. Similarly, when your team members feel the radiation of your anxiousness, some will adopt a bunker mentality and begin to hoard "survival resources," including information, process expertise, relationship capital, materials, and time. Such hoarding stalls the forward momentum of the team, department, and organization.

- **Sabotage:** While hoarding indirectly disrupts the flow of knowledge, relationship, and materials, sabotage acts more directly. A sabotaging employee may act out consciously or unconsciously. Either way, the intent of sabotage is to disrupt or halt the work process and, by extension, prevent change from taking root. The word *sabotage* derives from rebellious and disruptive actions of workers in fifteenth-century Holland. The Dutch workers wore wooden clogs—sabots—which they threw at the looms (the weaving machines) in order to stop the encroachment of automated production and their possible job losses. Anxiety is anticipatory—it arises in advance of any real event. An imagination that churns uncertainty into worst-case scenarios produces anxiety. Seeing fear in my boss resonates with my fears and ignites my worst-case-scenario thinking. In the absence of facts, we make stuff up; usually the stuff is more negative than reality. We formulate theories about some danger lurking in the future. Some folks will turn to sabotage as ways to prevent the future from coming any closer to reality. Sabotaging behaviors range from active to passive: equipment destruction, computer viruses, stealing, working slowly, or purposely treating customers rudely.

- **Team disintegration:** An organization derives its power from the ability to coordinate and align processes, efforts, and people. Why should you even have an organization? Because a group of aligned people—a team—has the ability to accomplish exponentially greater outcomes than the work output of individuals. Teaming and team building are a pervasive focus of any leader. Like in tug-of-war, teams become effective when the individuals align their effort and direction, and these are energized by your leadership. In the absence of team cohesion, there is merely a group—a bunch of people who happen to work in the same place at the same time. Groups are chaotic and don't amplify everyone's output through collaboration. In the 1960s, Bruce Tuckman identified four stages of team development: (1) forming (coming together), (2) storming (working out differences), (3) norming (arriving at mutuality), and (4) performing (functioning as one). Teams, whether small or large, short term or long term, travel through these stages. A leader whose team is in the performing stage can benefit from efficiency, engagement, and high productivity. However, when levels of fear arise within the team, people contract and pull away from one another. A high-performing team operates well because trust is present and each member feels at liberty to collaborate and cooperate with their team members. When fear and anxiety take root, trust turns to self-preservation and cooperation gives way to survival. Under these circumstances, the bonds of the team loosen and weaken.

- **Reduced creativity:** Creativity has been a hallmark of human experience for as long as humans have gathered and communicated. The competitiveness of an organization—its ability to produce value—requires creativity and innovation. *Creativity* is the capacity to imagine and formulate new possibilities. *Innovation* is the ability to transform creative ideas into practical solutions and applications. Creativity and innovation together are the trademark of organizational renewal. Iron and steel, when subjected to cold, shrink and contract; similarly, the mind and heart, subjected to fear, shrink and contract. Gripped by fear, the contracting mind withdraws from creative and innovative thinking, and a mind gripped by fear sticks with familiar and safe routines and engages in repetition rather than innovation. Group dynamics are etched deeply in our social minds. We look to our leaders to determine our collective "mood." Because the role of leadership is to look forward, scan the horizon, and orient toward the future, we choose leaders with the power to shape our sense of safety. An atmosphere of safety brings warmth that facilitates the meandering process of the creative output. But when I sense danger and fear in my leader, I contract, complain, and attempt to control what I can. Under these conditions, I become hyperfocused on my survival rather than on the well-being of the team or innovation for the organization.

- **Flawed decision making:** While vacationing at an all-inclusive resort in Jamaica, I entertained myself by conducting a little research. Throughout my ten-day stay, I asked two dozen other guests what was most relaxing about their vacation. Practically everyone's first answers focused on the unlimited food, sun, and alcohol. This was, after all, an adult play camp. Moreover, because all the activities, food, drink, and games were prepaid, we didn't have to think about money, calculate tips, or budget our holiday expenses. And since the property was dotted with entertainment and activities accessible day and night, planning and time management were unnecessary. Stripped of the need to decide how to spend time and where to spend money, people relaxed. My semiscientific investigation revealed that the relaxation resulted from three factors: warm weather, unlimited food and alcohol, and the absence of decision-making pressure. Work in general, and leadership in particular, is a constant process of making decisions. Deciding and making judgment calls requires calculations and scenario planning and takes constant mental focus and energy. There are two key components in my choice to promote a team member—their competence and judgment. Competence is their demonstrated skill; judgment is their applied intelligence to decision making. Mental fear and anxiety impede skillful judgment. Sustained apprehension clouds focus and drains energy. A leader who perpetuates a state of anxiety actively fosters an environment of poor decision making. Fear-fanned defensive thinking focuses on near-term issues, not on value-adding generation of growth.

11

FEAR AND ANXIETY

We often think of *fear* and *anxiety* as synonyms. In the course of conversations, we toggle back and forth between fear and anxiety, freely exchanging one for the other. There is, however, a distinction between the two terms: fear is biological; anxiety is psychological. Fear is rooted deeply in our brain structure; it leaps fully formed from our amygdala. Anxiety, on the other hand, emerges from the neocortex, the most recently developed layer of our brains. Fear is an instinctive survival reaction to danger and threat; anxiety arises from our imagination. Fear springs from the present state—an immediate sense of real or perceived menace. Anxiety is anticipatory, resulting from projecting our mind into the future and imagining threat.

Mental time travel gives birth to anxiety, while fear is fed by real-time perception. Anxiety is always anticipatory. Your apprehension about possible future misfortune or danger is felt as a tense uneasiness; it is born from an active imagination that runs rampant and conjures a painful future.

> *Fear springs from the present state—an immediate sense of real or perceived menace. Anxiety is anticipatory, resulting from projecting our mind into the future and imagining threat.*

While fear and anxiety differ greatly, we often treat them as interchangeable synonyms, so I will address them interchangeably in order to mirror common usage. We talk about fear of the unknown, rather than anxiety of the unknown, and we know anxiety of failure as the fear of failure. Even though they are not the same phenomenon, fear and anxiety have the same impact on leaders. Either way, leadership becomes a hero's journey in the presence of fear and anxiety, not in their absence.

What are some of the fears that affect your leadership? What are you really scared of and how does it touch your life as a leader?

Fear of the Unknown

Nowhere does anticipation—mental projection into the future—wreak more havoc on us than when we face the great unknown. Confronted with this chasm of perceived danger, the mind races to create visions of pain and loss, great or small. I've seen executive teams convince themselves of an unknown so awful that they defaulted to fighting for the status quo rather than for growth. I've struggled with my own doubt and indecision in the face of the unknown, opting at times to keep busy rather than commit to action in a new direction. For most of us, few things are as paralyzing as fear of the unknown.

Leading is rife with unknowns: regulations, competition, technology, tastes, emotions, market conditions, loyalties, and temptations. Our fears hold us hostage as we attempt to remain safe and unhurt financially, socially, and professionally. The unknown and its twin, uncertainty, are ever present. There are times when their presence is magnified and highlighted, like when we are accountable for results while pressing forward toward a new horizon.

What do we fear? For most of us, the answer is one or more of these: failure, humiliation, loss of control, loss of power, looking stupid, feeling incompetent, losing time, losing money, or getting hurt. What about any of these is really unknown? Essentially, we fear the undesirable and uncomfortable outcomes that we can't control; the unknown stretches out like a vast movie screen onto which we project our familiar and unknown fears. Follow this exercise to understand the futility of fear of the unknown: Imagine that you are among the first wave of European pioneers to sail across the sea to the New World in the early 1600s. As you stand on the ship's deck, you hear the creaking of the wood, the wind pressing the sails, and the cry of seagulls overhead. The stars and sun guide your voyage, measured with a compass and sextant. Wouldn't it be great to have some of the productivity and connectivity tools of the modern age?

Imagine yourself, a pioneer on the ship, with GPS. How proficient you would be and how efficiently you could organize and coordinate your shipmates! But, as GPS technology didn't exist yet, your mind contained no knowledge of the device—you didn't crave it, resent it, love it, or appreciate it. Because it was unknown, you had no relationship, belief, or feeling about GPS. The unknown, by virtue of the absence of knowledge and awareness, cannot evoke any reaction from us—neither excitement nor fear.

Although we use the term "fear of the unknown," it isn't mentally possible to entertain fear of the unknown. We experience fears of known conditions that we don't like and feel powerless to avoid. The vastness of the unknown provides a backdrop against which our minds parade a host of known and unwanted possibilities. I've tasted the bitterness of failure before; that's not unknown. I've had my heart broken by rejection; I wish that was unknown. I've lost money on investments that seemed great at the time, and I've lost time on projects that were well conceived but poorly timed. All these sources of pain and loss come rushing back to my mind when risk presents itself. Risk is ushered in by uncertainty—when a situation is not clearly or precisely determined or can't be accurately known or predicted. We react with anxiety to the parade of negative and harmful possibilities that we recall and imagine.

Strategic planning is an effort to lay order over uncertainty. By planning, we project our imaginations forward and conceive a path and pattern to manage risk and opportunity. Planning, though, depends on the unknown, on the vast reservoir of potential that lies around us. So many plans falter because leaders fall prey to their negative mental projections of the unknown; rather than venture into the realm of possibility, they are drawn back to the safety of the known. Yet we require access to these possibilities, to their potential, in order to craft new outcomes, true to the adage, "If you always do what you've always done, you'll always have what you've always had."

In partnering with leaders and executives as an adviser on their journey toward new results, I appreciate our conversations and the depth of honesty and courage we achieve because it allows us to peel back the obscuring layers of the "unknown" and decipher the unnamed fears lurking below. Once we name the fear, we can actually address and defuse it, and a reasonable plan can emerge.

Leadership requires willingly staring into the unknown and not freezing. It does not mean we eliminate fear; it means learning to name it, engage it, and ride its energy as a path to unlocking personal and organizational power. Ultimately, the unknown contains all untapped potential. This is the real power of the unknown: limitless growth.

While each of us has our own particular mix of anxieties and fear, we draw from a finite pool of elemental fears. Much like my printer's ability to produce 256 colors from permutations of red, green, and blue, our minds can produce dozens of versions of anxiousness based on permutations of the essential code of fear. Let's turn our attention to the four primary colors of fear and anxiety: pain, failure, rejection, and worthlessness.

12

FOUR UNIVERSAL FEARS

Mary put forth a question to our CEO roundtable: "How do I eliminate my anxiety over a looming financial shortfall?" After two years of continuous growth and the recent best quarter in company history, Mary witnessed an alarming and sudden loss in February owing to an aggressive hiring run combined with a major client who cut his account by half. Mary could well recall several times in her executive journey when she had faced tight financials. As the group delved deeper and asked more questions, a double-layered picture of her fear began to emerge: on the surface, Mary felt genuinely concerned about the financial viability of the business, but on a deeper level, she hated what she knew was about to arrive—tightness in her neck and back, an upset stomach, the elephant sitting on her chest, inevitable disruption of her sleep, and constant sluggish heaviness.

Our initial approach to the problem was logical and operational: We made sure that she had a backup plan in the event that the financial losses continued. We outlined where to cut costs, who to let go, how to bolster short-term business development, and sources of funding and bridge loans. We helped articulate a plan for the worst-case scenario. Mary felt better prepared, but not better.

It was imperative to formulate a wise and rational plan for addressing Mary's business concerns, but rationality alone wasn't enough to tame the stampede of fear-based thoughts that roamed through Mary's mind. We needed to delve into the more personal side of her fear and anxiety. In order to bolster her courage, Mary had to identify the fears dominating her thoughts. Mary could begin to tame her fears by naming them.

Through my education and training, analyzing thousands of hours of individual coaching and group facilitation, and years of personal development and meditation, I have observed four primary patterns of fear, patterns that contain our anxieties. Interestingly, these prototypical fears mirror the four motivations that push us forward to accomplish our goals in life.

The motivations that drive behavior are also referred to as *needs* or *hungers*, and they are universal. They affect all people regardless of culture, race, geography, or gender. Each of us has our unique blend of these hungers; we each formulate a mix of fears and anxieties that affect our decision making and daily conduct. They whisper in our inner ears with such a hushed tone that our conscious minds miss the message even as our unconscious minds attend and obey.

Our life is an insatiable quest for these four hungers: safety, control, connection, and expression. Our fears and anxieties are the hunger pangs of these unmet needs. As I described earlier, fear is biological and is hardwired into our survival mechanism, whereas anxiety is psychological and emerges from our ability to project into the future and anticipate. The hunger pangs—these psychological fears and anxieties—come from our motivational drivers: our drive for safety yields a fear of pain or discomfort, our drive for control brings to bear the fear of failure, our drive for connection lays the groundwork for fear of rejection, and an inherent drive for expression makes possible the fear of humiliation.

Our life is an insatiable quest for these four hungers: safety, control, connection, and expression. Our fears and anxieties are the hunger pangs of these unmet needs.

Fear contracts. When caught in fear, our perception shrinks, our creativity diminishes, our thoughts become more basic, and our bodies tense and tighten. Watching two boxers squaring up in the ring, we see them turn their bodies sideways relative to their opponent: by turning the body sideways, they become a smaller target. This is the primordial fear response—contract (become smaller in thoughts and action), control (fixate on some aspect that can be directly affected), and complain (find fault in the situation, people, or process).

You don't set out on the hero's journey to eliminate fear, but rather to find skillful ways to acknowledge and include it without becoming paralyzed. The idea that you should remain fearless is counterproductive at best, and promotes psychopathy at worst; rational human beings experience fear and anxiety in the face of uncertainty and risk. The contribution that you make to your team is proportional to your willingness to guide them in the face of uncertainty and within the inevitable fear and anxiety. You need courage to walk through fear. Invoked by uncertainty, courage finally comes into focus.

Pain: The Hunger for Safety

Safety is a primordial driver, a never-ending effort to avoid pain and loss. If you're reading this book, then your personal safety is likely not in jeopardy. Survival and safety concerns, however, are not usually about the availability of basic food and shelter, or a threat from wild beasts or natural phenomena. If you serve as a leader in an organization, the safety concerns and fears that you face are social and psychological, not physical. Certainly a loss of livelihood and the financial pressure that it invokes can trigger our survival instinct, but the vast majority of safety concerns in the modern economy have to do with comfort.

The modern version of fear of pain has morphed into a fear of discomfort. Mary, the CEO, quickly recognized that one of the drivers for her anxiety about financial pressure was fear of physical distress. She also felt concerned for her staff, for the well-being of the business, and even for vendors and clients. Yet it was her fear of discomfort that plagued her mind. Having experienced the situation before, Mary knew what to expect from her fears about the loss of safety and comfort: stress manifesting as muscle tightness and headaches, a churning in her stomach that affected her appetite, and poor sleep and fatigue. Pain and discomfort, while not resulting from being mauled by a saber-toothed tiger, are nonetheless physically depleting.

Failure: The Hunger for Control

The drive for control is intended to wield power and influence over our environment, and the fear born from this drive is the fear of failure. I vividly remember a conversation my daughter and I had one evening before bed about a new rule that the principal had established for the school lunch break. She was upset and indignant about what she considered an unfair rule, even though it was intended to reduce misbehavior among kids during lunch. What I clearly remember was that at the young age of eight, she was highlighting and complaining about children having no power.

This is the essence of our drive for control: it is our hunger for autonomy and an ability to affect our environment. It is about having power. Each of us has a drive to shape and impact our relationships, processes, and results. We want to make those things happen that we deem important, necessary, or desirable.

We differ in the amount and intensity of power that we crave; some of us tend toward aggressive and some toward passive. These are two ends of the continuum, and each of us resides somewhere along the spectrum. Infants attempt to assert control over their environment in infantile ways, while adults attempt to assert control over their environment in more mature ways. If we watch ourselves, we can note the unique ways we try to assert control. Infants cry and throw temper tantrums, since their power tools are unsophisticated, but as we mature, our power tools become more sophisticated and can include negotiation, manipulation, threats, bribery, the "cold shoulder," flattery, and gifts intended to establish a future quid pro quo.

When we lose power, when we fear that we can't control and make things happen, then we must face our fear of failure. Mary began to examine the anxiety that she felt, and all of us around the table resonated with the familiar tremor of the internal fear of failure that she identified. It's practically impossible to navigate the journey of leadership without consistently staring into the taunting face of failure, and here lies one of the great ironies of our hungers and drivers: they never end, and they regularly defy evidence. Regardless of how many successes we rack up, the fear of failure continues to reside in the dark crevices of our unconscious thinking.

Fear of failure plays with our perceptions. The fear is not entirely irrational, because it arises from real risk and uncertainty. Leaders who guide teams and organizations past their comfort zones and into their growth zones commonly experience fear of failure. They lead their teams beyond the zone of accomplishments and into the field of possibility, where potential can be harnessed and transformed into new outcomes and results. Failure—falling short of expectations or desired outcomes—is entirely possible. It is not the possibility of failure that awakens our fear and anxiety; that possibility is inherent in the leadership role. Rather, we become fearful and anxious due to our concerns about the possible implications of failure.

While each leader is unique, I've seen a common scenario that frightens and infuriates every executive I've ever met: being blindsided. Every executive I know—when caught by surprise with information that his team knew but did not share—becomes angry. Underneath this anger resides a layer of fear. The potential loss of control of the situation invokes possibilities of failure. Perhaps even more disturbing, it raises the specter of the leader's potential incompetence.

June was a VP of operations in her mid-fifties. She was one of my first coaching clients and wanted to become a more skilled strategic thinker. Twenty years earlier she was hired into her pharmaceutical division as a customer service rep answering incoming calls, and over the decades her hard work, savvy problem solving, and leadership contributions earned her increased power and responsibility. During our first meeting she shared with me her deep and private fear: "I was hired as a receptionist," she said. "I've been promoted, and they're about to offer me the COO role. Sooner or later they're going to find out that I'm a fraud, that I don't belong here, that I don't really know what I'm doing. Once they discover that I'm not cut out for this, I'll be sent back to answering the phones!" In spite of her successes, June feared that she was an imposter fundamentally incompetent to fulfill her role.

I admit that among my reactions to her disclosure was a self-focused concern. My heart sank as June talked. She was only my second paying executive coaching client, and I was gripped with my own fear of being found out as an imposter myself. We shared this common fear that, for many of us, lurks far below the surface of the drive for control, even deeper than the fear of failure. June and I shared a deep and abiding concern that we were not competent.

Rejection: The Hunger for Connection

Connection and relatedness, participation and belonging, are primordial shaping forces of the human experience. When this motivation, this drive for connection, becomes threatened it gives rise to fear of rejection. Researchers have long known that some infants, in the absence of human touch, become depressed, depleted of vitality, and even die. We are social creatures, and connection and membership lie at the core of what it means to live as a social creature. As a teenager, I declared that I didn't care what people thought about me, and I prided myself on my ability to remain alone and detached, convincing myself that relationships were too tedious for me. But these were times of emotional pain for me, and it was untrue that I didn't care. Rather, I adopted a defensive mental attitude to contend with my insecurity and fear.

Being connected is a basic human drive. As our ancestors formed societies and established rules of conduct intended as means of social control, threatening behaviors—those that endangered the well-being of the community—had to be limited or eliminated for the greater good. Punishing offenders involves some form of disconnecting: We commonly punish a child by sending her to her room, and similarly punish adults by sending them to prison. We may privately punish an acquaintance or friend by giving him the cold shoulder. In some religions a high form of punishment is excommunication: officially excluding someone from the sacred community.

For more than a decade, the Gallup organization has conducted polls using the Engagement Index, which measures the level of commitment and buy-in that employees have to their organizations. This commitment predicts performance, productivity, and profitability. Interestingly, results have shown that relationships primarily drive engagement. Engagement, a critical component for organizational success and a leading indicator of leadership effectiveness, is a function of emotional linking—of connection.

We use a variety of synonyms to express our hunger for connection: love, recognition, acknowledgment, friendship, bonding, appreciation, and belonging. Children who grow up without a healthy sense of connection develop attachment issues, and they struggle to find healthy relationships.

Fear of rejection affects us as we visit and revisit our unfulfilled drive for connection. This anxiety stays with us because we are perpetually aware of the uncertainties of life, we are intimately familiar with resource scarcity, and we have the experience of never feeling fully satisfied. When our anxiety turns to the scarcity of love, affection, or recognition—of connection—we dwell on the possibility of rejection. To lead means to flirt with rejection. Leaders on the hero's journey serve an organization, but they can never satisfy all the people in the organization: to lead means to propel a group through the unknown and the uncertain, and not everyone will agree on your chosen path. Thus, rejection is an ever-present possibility.

My wife spent two years as president of the PTA at our daughters' elementary school. She served with passion. She stayed up late night after night, pressing programs forward, overseeing fund-raising, coordinating school beautification projects, contributing to the newsletter, analyzing data to help the teachers, strategizing with the principal, and corresponding with dozens of other parents with wonderful ideas (and some bizarre ideas, too). The hardest part of the presidency for my wife, especially in the first year, was the rejection. In spite of her tremendous efforts and pouring her heart and soul into the school, she could not satisfy all the parents or all the teachers. Although the PTA board made all the significant decisions, my wife was the president, and she became a target for anyone upset with the PTA. Some tried to sway her actively through discussion or argument, and others tried to manipulate her passively. A popular means of passive manipulation was leveraging the power of connection, or rather, leveraging its inverse: disconnection. Some parents and teachers would actively avoid my wife, knowing that the cold shoulder works as a powerful manipulative force. Some team members use rejection as a blunt weapon intended to sway and influence people, including their leaders.

Our fear of rejection can throw a bucket of water on the fire of our passion. I don't know how to be immune to the fear of rejection. While I used to tell myself that I didn't care, it was a thinly veiled lie, an immature effort to mask the quivering of uncertainty and vulnerability that I felt. I occasionally find myself in conversations with people who claim not to care whether people like or accept them. In reality, they are unwilling or unable to acknowledge their fears about the vulnerability of their position.

Worthlessness: The Hunger for Expression

The fourth universal driver in our human experience is the drive for self-expression, which includes creativity and spirituality. This is the drive to satisfy our need to be unique and to be acknowledged in our uniqueness; when this drive is blocked, we experience fear of worthlessness and humiliation. My own fear of worthlessness became illuminated through a dialogue with my mentor about how to lead my business to growth. Over the course of several conversations, we covered a lot of ground—strategy and mission, team makeup, operational efficiency, financial management, ways of monetizing and productizing services, and organizational values and culture. As we walked together one October day, our conversation turned from strategy, operations, and team, to me. Specifically, my mentor asked bluntly what permission I needed in order to grow my business and take it to its next level. At first I was perplexed. I'm a responsible adult with a history of successes, and I take pride in being a motivated self-starter. His question seemed off-base and irrelevant, but he persisted in asking "What permission do you need?" I realized he didn't intend the question to elicit a rational and logical answer. It was designed to cause me to reflect and search within myself; it was an invitation to self-awareness, not a call for one specific data point.

We walked in silence for at least half a mile. I let the question sink into my body. I let it settle into my mind like a stone descending into a pond. I walked and let the question reverberate within me, not thinking about it in my typical problem-solving way, but rather letting it move about in my body and mind. The question had a gravitational force all of its own and slowly pulled into words a constellation of insights, ideas, and, eventually, an answer.

When the answer finally crystalized, it felt immediately accurate. I knew the permission that I was looking for was the same permission that I'd been seeking for decades. This quest had driven many of my decisions through a variety of relationships, situations, adventures, and experiments. It was a deep hunger, and it has worked as a strong driver. It might well be the only permission I've ever really sought, and the one permission that no one could ever afford me: I wanted permission to be myself.

The natural drive we all share for expression is an urge to bring out what is inherently within us—our uniqueness and our creativity. Mary, so busy growing her firm, was also engaged in the process of self-expression. She once remarked to me that she felt as though she were pulling energy from her spirit and soul in her effort to build her company. My artist friends—those who make their living through music, painting, and sculpting—typically perceive themselves as doing quite different work from business executives. They believe they engage in a process of creative expression, and that organizational leaders do not, but that's not accurate; an entrepreneur is an artist whose medium is the marketplace and whose brushes are her people. Creation and artistic expression also mark Mary's experience, as she creates value where, prior to her efforts, there was none.

We constantly journey on a quest to bring forth that which is uniquely us; we deeply want to feel valued for our intrinsic worth. We want others to see and know us, and we feel frightened at the prospect of humiliation. Our fear of humiliation connects to the deep concern that somehow we are not worthy, that we are, in fact, worthless. Marianne Williamson captured our hunger for expression when she wrote in *A Return to Love: Reflections on the Principles of a Course in Miracles*: "Our deepest fear is not that we are inadequate. Our deepest fear is that we are powerful beyond measure. It is our Light, not our Darkness, that most frightens us. We ask ourselves, who am I to be brilliant, gorgeous, talented, fabulous? Actually, who are you not to be?"

13

THE SIGNS OF FEAR

A moonless sky hung like a heavily spotted veil over the vast stretches of the desert. My family and I were enjoying springtime camping in the beautiful state park of Anza-Borrego, two hours east of San Diego. Admittedly, we prefer camping under the full moon; the absence of the moon makes the desert floor seem spooky. The girls were in the tent, my wife was putting away the last of our dinner, and I was preparing to douse the fire and set our camp for sleep. I headed over to our SUV, parked eighty feet away, to confirm that it was locked, and the dying flames of the fire reflected in an amber dance on the shiny gunmetal blue of the car's body. Although I was alert, I was unprepared for the sight on the other side of the car: there, in the palest light of stars, I barely made out the fattest, biggest snake I had ever seen. In an instant my heart leaped into my throat and my gut lurched down to my feet. I turned and raced back toward the tent to get a flashlight and a big stick.

Had I been camping by myself I might have ignored this dangerous creature, but I was there with my wife and my two daughters, and all three suffer from a deep fear of snakes. My own fear was dampened by my sense of duty. I couldn't share with them what I had seen or why I was coming back for the flashlight and the stick, as that would have ruined the rest of our camping trip together! Fearfully, but with determination, I crept back around the car and jumped around the corner, raised my stick, and clicked on the flashlight. Adrenaline flowing, heart pounding, teeth clenched, I was ready to take on the menace, and there, extremely still in the yellow pool of light, lay a neatly coiled yellow-and-green rope, my old climbing rope from college that I still use to tie down loads on top of the car. The lesson? My fear was real even though the danger was not.

Fear is the essential mood of our ego. Our ancestors successfully survived challenges by remaining vigilant. Anticipating harm, pain, and risk continue to serve us today just as it served them; we continue to anxiously scan our environment for potential mishaps. In our professional and social lives, though, few legitimate environmental threats exist, and the majority of our fear and anxiety is generated by threats to our relationships and our self-concept: threats to our ego. While fear and anxiety insinuate themselves into every aspect of our decision making and thinking, it is rarely obvious to us that they are present. We have spent a lifetime learning strategies to cope with them, and have developed socially acceptable and personally workable behaviors that mitigate our fear and anxiety.

> *We have spent a lifetime learning strategies to cope with them, and have developed socially acceptable and personally workable behaviors that mitigate our fear and anxiety.*

These strategies—coping behaviors—enable us to function under conditions that we would rather detach from or avoid altogether. Our creative minds manufacture numerous coping strategies that we use as shields. Withdrawing—detaching and disengaging—from the danger is the most passive coping behavior. However, I want to address five other fear-based strategies that are more active, and quite common among leaders and teams. These fear-masking behaviors are so prevalent that you are likely exhibiting them yet don't recognize them as originating in fear: blaming, micromanaging, avoidance, sarcasm, and anger.

Blaming

Peter Drucker wrote, "Effective leadership is not about making speeches or being liked; it is defined by results." Blaming is the antithesis of leadership because when you blame, you place responsibility for a fault or error on somebody else. Multiple factors—situational, environmental, personal, interpersonal, systemic, regulatory, and financial—might influence a situation to turn out differently and therefore not produce desired results. In fact, the odds of a plan manifesting exactly as intended are stacked against us. Even the most quantitative business aspect, finance, embraces this reality. We track our accounting with two columns: projected and actual. A responsible enterprise prepares a budget with which its leaders can make financial decisions, and while this budget is an earnest effort to predict and plan for financial income and expenses, we all expect some deviance. In order to account for the deviance, we create a column labeled *actual*. When the time comes to balance projected versus actual, we search diligently for the causes of the gap, but we have expected it, so it doesn't come as a surprise. Committing ourselves to understanding the reason for the discrepancy is an act of refinement and growth. It does not have to be a dance of blaming—a game of projecting responsibility onto others and avoiding self-responsibility.

It is precisely because of the probability that they will miss their projected target that leaders are on a heroic journey; they journey to bring value to their community while fighting the odds of failure. Those unwilling to enter the arena of unfavorable odds—those unwilling to take on failure—twist their leadership role into the bureaucratic defender of the status quo.

Victor faced these struggles as president of his family-owned business. Since his father passed away, Victor had been the primary leader in the business along with his uncle and cousin. Victor was a member of our CEO roundtable, and he debriefed us one afternoon with a diatribe of blaming and complaining. He described the challenges of leading his family business while sharing ownership with two other people: his uncle was "old school" and approached the business from a conservative perspective. The uncle was trying to withdraw as much cash as possible from the business while minimizing investment in its growth and renewal. His cousin, on the other hand, didn't even want to be there: he showed up to work, but only in body.

We all empathized with Victor's frustration. He was working diligently to create an engaged workforce, but the behaviors of his co-owners invited detachment from his people. Victor felt frustrated and powerless to single-handedly change the situation, so he blamed and complained. We easily turn to this behavior when we feel powerless to affect a situation; we complain when we get caught in the belief that what we do doesn't matter or that we can't make things better. When complaining doesn't satisfy the frustration and powerlessness, we escalate to blame.

Blaming is a self-defense mechanism. It seems practically instinctive to point the finger away from us in order to avoid accountability. I recall countless scenes of one of my daughters dropping or breaking something, and almost immediately pointing the finger to her sister and saying, "She made me do it. It's her fault." I don't have to travel that far in my own memory to find my instincts for blaming. Just recently, I turned the key in the ignition to my car early one morning ready to drive off to an appointment, but all I heard was the sickening *click-click-click* of a dead battery. Instinctively (and embarrassingly), I blamed my wife for doing something to *my* car. The thought was so automatic and so quick that I was a little surprised, especially since my wife doesn't even drive my car. The impulse to blame, the drive to push away responsibility for undesirable outcomes, is a safety mechanism fed by our fear of negative consequences.

The legal system plays several roles for our society and ideally acts as a system of checks and balances. The legal system is also awash with angry and bitter—hurt and frightened—individuals who, rather than taking responsibility, choose to sue and blame. In the United States, we've made personal responsibility a negotiable dimension of thought and action. It was a sobering education for me decades ago while studying law classes in college to discover that guilt did not exist as a black-and-white distinction within the legal system. There are, it turns out, degrees of guilt and responsibility. A person could be positively identified in a criminal act, but their degree of responsibility and accountability can be negotiated among attorneys and decided by a judge and jury.

Leaders are accountable for the results of their organization. At the heart of what makes leadership a hero's journey is the dynamic tension between accountability, on the one hand, and uncertainty, on the other. Leaders work to guide people toward an outcome that has yet to be accomplished, and approaching this new accomplishment is fraught with uncertainty. Once a path to an outcome is well-worn and well-mapped—once certainty and familiarity are abundant—your role as a leader is significantly decreased and the position is better suited to project management. The word *leader*, in fact, originates from the old Anglo-Saxon word *lithan*, which means "to travel, to go"—literally, leading means to journey away from the known and the familiar. Your leadership contribution excels when you press against the membrane of the comfort zone, when you stretch your organization beyond the well-rehearsed, repetitive patterns of past accomplishments. Accountability—the capacity to be responsible—is a necessary element to counterbalance the drive for growth that can turn unhealthy and even dangerous.

Blaming works as the antithesis of accountability. It is a person's outward manifestation of an internal shirking of responsibility; it is definitely not a leadership competency. When Victor expressed his frustration with his partners as blaming, he retreated from his position of authority and integrity as a leader. Blaming encourages sinking into the foggy embrace of fears. Victor's anxiety was fueled by his legitimate concerns that if the business declined, he would be perceived as incompetent. It was possible that his personal stock and reputation would be tarnished, and, as a result, that his colleagues and investors would abandon him.

Rather than studying his reflection in the mirror of accountability, Victor cast his gaze through the window of blame. It was easier to find fault and culpability in his partners than to admit his own shortfalls or powerlessness; blaming energized him with a righteous indignation that felt morally strengthening, reinforcing a narrative in which his partners were wrong and he was right. In actuality, however, they were all stuck. His friends confirmed the unfairness of the situation and piled on the blame. As long as he continued to blame, though, he was neither taking responsibility nor exhibiting leadership; he was running about like a pony ridden by a master horseman called fear.

Within the shelter of our roundtable, we safely challenged Victor's blaming. As the group's questions and comments peeled back his defended and frightened thinking, Victor recognized the weakness and ineffectiveness that his blaming produced. As he distinguished his feelings of powerlessness from his real power, he began to form a plan of approach. I could see his face relax and his body straighten as his thoughts moved from feeling trapped to taking action.

Micromanaging

There is a healthy and unhealthy expression of micromanaging. We express the healthy version with a new team member or a team member new to a task—they don't know the mechanics and the specifics, so paying close and meticulous attention to their actions and decisions is a form of teaching. As a leader you have a responsibility to ensure that new members of the team get up to speed on what's expected of them and learn as quickly as possible how to satisfactorily execute their role. On the other hand, we manifest the unhealthy version of micromanaging when we try to control competent team members by strictly directing their choices and behaviors. This version of micromanaging is fed by the wellspring called "control"—some people refer to it as *perfectionism*. While it seems like a search for excellence, perfectionism is a variation on the theme of controlling to avoid failure.

When I was promoted to manager of a marketing department, I felt keenly aware that my new position had outstripped my competence. I was promoted to the position based on my gumption, performance, and potential: I knew this, my boss knew this, and my deep fear was that my team knew it, too. I desperately wanted to do a good job, I wanted to prove that my boss had made the right decision, I wanted to earn my team's respect, and I wanted to silence the incessant questioning voices whispering inside my head. It didn't take long for my team to call me a perfectionist. I believed that I intended my comments to improve their work, and I spent lots of energy fixing flaws and aspiring toward perfect product outputs. I experienced pride of ownership in our product, but I also felt driven by incredible anxiety and a deepseated concern that someone would find me unfit for my new role. Micromanaging as a performance driver for "perfect" outcomes was my attempt to erase any possible evidence of my inexperience. I used the tool of micromanaging to bend my team to my will of perfectionism.

In his book *Drive*, Daniel Pink concluded from his research that motivation derives from three aspects of work: autonomy, mastery, and purpose. The desire for *autonomy* is the urge to direct our own lives, the desire for *mastery* is the urge to get better and better at something that matters, and the desire for *purpose* is the yearning to work in service to something larger than ourselves. If autonomy, mastery, and purpose fuel motivation and high performance, then micromanaging siphons away the fuel and energy of motivation. When a leader micromanages, he actively curtails autonomy; he directly controls and dictates both behavior and decisions. The micromanaging leader expects his people to follow close directions and instructions and to execute exactly as he has taught; mastery—getting better and better—is pushed off the table and is replaced with obedience. And purpose—a macro perception of work and life—is obscured by the microfocus of micromanaging.

Sometimes a member of your staff might complain that you're hovering too closely or watching too intently when you teach, but at other times your expertise and experience are necessary to closely direct a person or a team. Mary spent a year managing Chris in a laissez-faire style. He was a senior director and Mary assumed that he knew what to do. However, the grumblings and complaints from his team and managers did not taper off over the course of the year. In fact, after six months, the complaints about Chris turned to accusations about Mary: others blamed her for Chris's incompetence. During our coaching conversations, it became clear that Mary had to switch approaches and manage Chris in a direct and detailed way. Mary intentionally adopted a micromanaging style. In her case this was not driven by fear, but by a sense of responsibility to the team at large and to Chris's success.

The hallmark of fear-based micromanaging is the unconscious, impulsive urge to control every detail and decision. The fear of not being able to control people and circumstances and outcomes is, at its root, the fear of failure, incompetence, or unworthiness. As a leader, you are removed from the final means of production, but you are held accountable for results that you personally cannot bring about—results that must be accomplished through other people. The vulnerability of being evaluated not on your immediate skills and creativity but on your ability to create through and with other people is a fertile environment for the growth of fear and anxiety.

Avoiding

While micromanaging arises as an active expression of fear-based behavior, avoidance represents a passive expression of our fears. When I started my consulting firm, I faced great uncertainty, which produced both excitement and anxiety. I launched the consultancy in June, the following March I got married, by August we bought a house and our daughter was born in February. I worked like a madman to support and finance this new life. I was also scared, anxious, and grappling with doubt. I wasn't conscious of the ways I was acting avoidant. In a twist of ego self-defense, I tried to avoid my angst in two ways: designing marketing brochures and networking. When the cold hands of anxiety that squeezed my heart became too much to bear, I would turn on my computer to redesign my marketing brochures. Rather than make calls, network with new contacts, revisit my allies, or perfect my presentations, I would sit in the safety of my office and make "difficult decisions" about content, font style, and margins. My productive output and creative input were permission enough to rationalize my avoidance of doing anything meaningful to move forward.

My other form of avoidance also didn't seem like avoiding at the time, as I attended networking functions that appeared like business development. I was, however, attending safe functions where I was known and liked. I was turning a blind eye to the obvious fact that there were no new contacts and no real opportunity for new business. I was actively avoiding the awkwardness and discomfort of going to places where I was not known; I was avoiding the fear of rejection.

In the course of avoidance, we focus our attention on noncritical tasks and relationships as a way to distract ourselves from a difficult task or relationship; we avoid things that cause us anxiety and fear. I asked

Bill, the CFO of a food manufacturing firm, what he was avoiding at work—a person, project, situation, or client—that he knew needed to be addressed. He reflected for a short moment, then mentioned Kathleen, his most tenured employee who, unfortunately, had no role in the new iteration of the company. Bill shared that he had done everything he could to help Kathleen upgrade her abilities, but the company's new direction had rendered her skills ineffective. Bill hoped that he could quickly scale up the company in order to ensure that he could secure a place for Kathleen. Yet he knew this was not realistic.

When I asked him how he felt physically when he thought about letting Kathleen go, he described feeling sick to his stomach and drained of energy. Bill's self-concept was rooted in being a responsible employer and a passionate caretaker of his people, so having to fire his most tenured employee was, to him, a sign of leadership inadequacy. He struggled to face the failure implied in his decision to fire Kathleen. Bill wasn't putting off the decision; he was putting off implementing the decision. By staving off the conversation, he was trying to avoid the physical and emotional discomfort of uncertainty, anxiety, and humiliation that he was "not good enough" as a leader. However, the longer he avoided the conversation and required action, the sicker he felt: every time he passed Kathleen in the hallway, every time he sat in a meeting with her, his anxiety increased. Yet he continued avoiding the inevitable. I do this, too. We all do this at one time or another. It's a well-honed strategy to avoid the sickening feelings, doubts, and anxiety-fueled fatigue that arise when we have to do something difficult.

Avoidance is the adult version of the child pulling the covers over his head and staying in bed until an unpleasant situation miraculously vanishes. I'm not suggesting that we should immediately address and resolve every single issue; time and timing are critical considerations in resolving issues and pursuing opportunities. Our wisdom is a good guide for determining how quickly and when to apply effort and energy, and this differs from avoiding. Executives can become highly adept at righteous avoidance by pouring effort into some benevolent or creative endeavor and appearing too busy to address something difficult. These difficult issues, more often than not, are interpersonal decisions.

Chief among the tools of an executive is decision making. Leadership decisions can be complex because of multiple considerations, implications, and parties. Complexity, however, is different than difficulty. More often than not, we consider a decision difficult because someone will be negatively affected or unhappy about its consequences.

Practically every conversation I have with my executive clients includes an inquiry into their avoidance, whether passive (simply ignoring and pretending it's not there) or active (intentionally focusing attention on something more fulfilling). Leaders, I believe, are called to make sacrifices on their hero's journey, and the most common sacrifice is giving up comfort. Avoidance is an immature clutching at comfort. It is a failure of leadership to avoid the people, situations, or ideas that make us uncomfortable. Fear and anxiety always fuel this kind of avoidance. The hero's journey demands that you lean into the discomfort you would rather lean away from and choose to engage what your comfort-seeking mind would prefer to avoid.

Sarcasm

Sarcastic behavior occurs so regularly it hardly seems like a cover for fear and anxiety. Russ, a VP of operations, described two of his managers as perpetually sarcastic. Since Russ was sarcastic in his own right, he didn't consider how their sarcasm negatively impacted either the leadership team or the rest of the company, and he had no reason to consider that the persistent sarcasm they threw around was driven by fear. So when Sean, his newest manager, announced that he was quitting, Russ suddenly woke up to the negative impact of his tenured managers' sarcasm. Sean shared that he felt henpecked, belittled, and cut down by the constant sarcasm and the disempowerment that it inflicted.

Russ had gone to great lengths to recruit Sean and felt it was a coup for his department because of his industry and functional experience. Now Russ was forced to evaluate the impact that sarcastic behaviors were having on his team and their business performance; since Russ liberally used sarcasm, he struggled to see the costs of that behavior. When Sean tendered his resignation, his reasons were not limited to personal offense from being too thin-skinned: Sean felt deeply concerned that he was being robbed of his ability to be effective. Sean recognized that sarcasm was a sharp weapon wielded to assert power and force defensive behaviors from the target. Russ became determined to investigate the impact that sarcasm was having on his team, in particular, and on the rest of his organization, in general. Of necessity, he began to pay attention to the impact of his own sarcastic behavior.

Because I contend that sarcasm is a form of fear—inherently disempowering and intended as a form of manipulation—I've had multiple conversations with leaders about it. Sarcasm occurs so commonly that people rarely perceive it as a weakening factor, and several of my conversations have explored whether sarcasm is inherently negative or whether it has some redeeming qualities. I've come to see the application of sarcasm in the same light as the levels of spiciness in Thai food: on a scale of 1 to 10. At levels 1 to 3, sarcasm comes across as funny and harmless, but as the numbers go up it starts to burn and hurt.

If used benevolently and with care in a meeting, you can sometimes use a well-timed sarcastic joke to break the tension in the room, refresh the energy, and provide a form of release. Sarcasm derives from the Greek word *sarkazein* meaning "to tear the flesh"—it is typically wielded as a sharp weapon to cut an opponent down. Sarcastic comments that arise in a team meeting are usually signals of helplessness and powerlessness; they communicate a fear of loss of power and provide a crude way to regain that sense of power. Within leadership teams, an inverse relationship exists between sarcasm and trust. As sarcasm and mutual tearing apart increase, defensive behaviors rise, and trust plunges. In the absence of trust, a team is rendered ineffective at best and paralyzed at worst.

Russ committed to coach his two managers, and began by sharing with them examples of their own sarcastic behaviors. He explained the impact and negative consequences of their behaviors and initiated a dialogue about how to make a positive contribution to the team. One of the more compelling elements Russ provided was a commitment to reduce—or even eliminate—his own sarcasm at the same time his managers were working on reining in theirs. In a conversation we had a month after he made this commitment, Russ expressed frustration at how difficult this change was for him, but in adjusting his behavior Russ also developed a heightened sensitivity to the presence of sarcasm in general. Russ was able to change his sarcastic reflexes because he was willing to face his fears and anxieties as a leader and as a man. The height of his achievement in this change process was proportionate to the depth of his awareness.

Anger

Just as sarcasm is an expression of fear, so is anger. We perceive anger, however, as assertiveness and power. You can feel the weight of righteousness behind it, and regard it as a sign of dominance and authority. But it is rooted in fear.

As soon as we sat down for our coaching conversation, John, the president of an engineering consulting firm, began railing about how angry he felt at Rachel, his go-to staff person for quick-turnaround problem solving, because of the poor quality client document that she had created. Details were well represented, but style and formatting were sloppy relative to John's standards. He felt angry about Rachel's lack of follow-through, about producing a subpar document, and about—above all—disappointing the client.

John told Rachel what she did wrong and how angry it made him. When John got angry everybody knew it, as he was not one to hide his feelings; in fact, John was convinced that showing anger was important for his leadership. He believed that a certain measure of anger demonstrated his passion and reinforced his dedication to the mission. A little edge of anger, John told me, was an important motivational tool.

During our meeting, I challenged John to see that his anger was rooted in fear. He didn't buy this idea. His anger was justified, he told me. He wasn't careless with it but used it to help him make a strong point and drive home a lesson. He felt his employees were more productive when they made the effort to avoid his anger.

Anger occupies a special place among the strategies of avoiding our fear and anxiety. Because anger occurs in a flash of energy and intensity, people usually don't see it as an expression of fear. We have further complicated our cultural relationship with anger by making it fashionable to display unchecked anger—political debates, for example, have regularly been reduced to opposing diatribes of righteous indignation. Being angry has become cool. Television shows in general, and news commentators in particular, tout their anger as evidence of their passion, moral standing, and deep caring. The voices of caution that would remind us that anger is divisive and violent are angrily shoved to the sidelines.

The emotional and psychological structure that undergirds anger is composed of two layers. Directly beneath anger is, commonly, a layer of hurt, an injured ego. More deeply beneath that lies fear. Fear of rejection, fear of humiliation, and fear of failure make up the "triple crown" of fears. When John would not budge from his strongly held belief that anger was power, not cowardice, I pressed him to tell me what most upset him about Rachel's document. "She just didn't seem to care," was his indignant response. "So," I said, "you're angry with her because she was careless?" That hardly seemed reason to generate this much energy and heat. "What's the real damage and cost of Rachel's carelessness? What's really making you angry?"

As I continued to question John, I eventually teased out his underlying feelings: he revealed that if the report disappointed the client, they would take their business elsewhere, and John would feel like a failure. I had one last question, "What would failing as a leader communicate about you as a person?" John's face was now visibly different from just seconds ago when the energy and fire of anger was dancing in his eyes. His voice was softer, his eyelids no longer stretched wide-open, and his shoulders slumped a little. "If I fail, it signals to my bosses that I am not competent or worthy of my position in the company. Honestly, they might realize that I'm faking my way through this role."

This was the root of John's anger: his fear of unworthiness. Of course, maintaining high quality and standards and keeping clients happy and engaged are critical leadership functions. And anger, used selectively and purposefully, can serve as a powerful communication tool. But unchecked, anger is an effort to control the environment in order to mitigate our underlying fears.

Anger figures into every aspect of life, at work and away from it. When my younger daughter was eight, I would often get angry with her. We clashed and engaged in arguments from which neither of us emerged happy. This was an unwelcome pattern in our relationship. I became angry because she would not listen to my advice and counsel, and she refused to do what I asked or wanted her to do on certain occasions. I doubt there's a parent out there who doesn't understand my frustration at this headstrong child who believed she knew exactly how the world works. I would get frustrated, raise my voice, and threaten her to try to bend her to my will. This was not a proud process for me, nor was it effective in accomplishing my parental goals.

I earned some valuable insights about this behavior while meditating. In addition to my regular practice, I attend a couple of five-day silent retreats every year. These extended quiet periods are a chance to mentally and emotionally slough off the busyness and confusion that accumulate in the course of my life. As I set off to one of these retreats, I determined to use some of the intense reflection time to focus on my relationship with my daughter.

I decided to use the space of silence and reflection to investigate what it was that frightened me. Because I was so emotionally caught up in the situation, it was a difficult process, but some clarity rewarded my perseverance: I discovered, lurking within my thoughts, hidden deep within my unconscious mind, my familiar fear of failure. I believe that part of my role as a father is to help ensure my children's future success. I believe that I need to convey certain lessons and principles to help them make good decisions that lead to a safe and fulfilling life. I think this is a good thing, and I stand by this role.

But my daughter didn't always want to take my advice or absorb my principles on my timetable. The more she resisted what I tried to share with her, the more anxious I became about her possible downfall or failure as an adult, and the more anxious I got about this, the more anxious I became about my own failure as a father. My anger at her grew and intensified as I made desperate efforts to stave off the possibility of failure that I would have to face as a father if she didn't live up to my expectations of success in her own life. This was at the root of my anger. I was not concerned about what other people might think about her, or what other people might think about my daughter and me if she "failed" as a person. I was frightened that my inadequacy as a parent might show up and be telegraphed to my identity and my sense of competence.

Of course, I know she will be an awesome adult. She's an awesome child. Once I could identify, label, and articulate my deepest concern and anxiety, I was able to change my experience with my daughter. The gift of awareness is choice, and choices provide opportunity for multiple paths and alternate outcomes. Now I choose to relate and connect with my daughter in a more direct and intimate way. I choose to continue to help her develop and refine life skills, but in a more measured and less anxious manner.

14

CULTIVATING COURAGE

Mike was a respected leader in the biotech world who didn't realize how large a role fear played in his life. As an entrepreneur, he earned money through taking risks and demonstrating initiative; not taking initiative and risks felt unnatural to Mike. As a result of his leadership, his business grew in revenue, head count, and process complexity. Now the business growth and formalized structures demanded a more deliberate approach to resource allocation and decision making; strategy and focus became as important as risk and initiative. Mike felt hemmed in by his very success, anxious that he could not be his "natural self" anymore. In one of our conversations, as he experienced a particularly strong wave of frustration, Mike identified and acknowledged his fear: he felt afraid of missing out on opportunities.

Mike's "natural self" was fast-paced and explosive. He leaped at opportunities and felt fulfilled when striking out into new territories, ideas, and ventures. It had become evident, though, that his opportunistic orientation generated tension in the organization: ongoing projects were interrupted, teams were broken apart and reconstituted, and budgets were changed. Feelings of uncertainty fanned employee anxiety, and rumors about Mike's decisions circulated. Mike, in turn, shared how agitated he felt at what he perceived as small-mindedness and lack of courage on the part of his executive team. Mike didn't conceive that his anxiety might be coloring his perception; rather he determined that "they" were doing something wrong.

In *Good to Great: Why Some Companies Make the Leap . . . and Others Don't*, Jim Collins conveys that great leaders are able to look out the window and assign credit where credit is due, and to look in the mirror and accept personal accountability when necessary. Mike's success brought him to such a juncture. One path led to stepping up to his heroic journey and making some changes in order to meet the changing needs of his business; the other path rejected the call for change and continued commitment to momentum and established habits. Mike chose to embrace leadership responsibility and accountability—he looked in the mirror of his experience and recognized that his discomfort and anxiety about being "boxed in" were negatively affecting the company. Admitting that his strengths were contributing to organizational weakness was bitter medicine. He had, after all, orchestrated the growth to date. The evidence, though, was compelling. Mike needed to amend his approach or risk eroding his organization.

Mike elected to squarely face his reflection and accept the challenge of adapting his leadership in order to serve his people and mission. To support his decision, Mike and I met monthly in order to accelerate his results through examining and refining his decision making and judgment calls. In the warm months, we spent our two-hour meetings hiking rather than sitting in the office, and during one of our hiking conversations Mike spoke plainly about his anxiousness. His tone was measured and his typically driven energy was replaced with a palpable density of concern. He realized that he had to cultivate his courage in order to face his own reflection in the mirror of experience.

What Is Courage?

Courage is walking toward what you'd rather run away from; it's an aptitude for doing something that frightens you. Courage is *not* the absence of fear or anxiety—courage can only arise when fear and anxiousness have taken root. Being human means to experience fear and anxiety, but the triggers that invoke

> *Courage is walking toward what you'd rather run away from; it's an aptitude for doing something that frightens you.*

them—threatening events or perceptions—differ. While skydiving might terrify one person, it could bring great pleasure to another. I enjoy public speaking, but making a presentation in public is the number one fear reported by people in the United States. Some people are prone to fear of failure, while their neighbors might feel burdened by fear of success. Regardless of our individual mental and emotional patterns, we all experience fear and anxiety. The hero's journey of leadership is wrought with uncertainty and challenge, a fertile ground in which the seeds of fear and anxiety can take root. As a leader you must cultivate, grow, and strengthen your capacity for courage.

Growing up and functioning in society require that we learn to navigate through and around our fears and anxieties. We can nurture and cultivate our courage; we can strengthen and condition our courage muscle. Like developing a graceful golf swing or mastering financial statements, we can learn and practice courage.

Learning to be courageous requires repetition, feedback, and patience. The challenge for cultivating courage, though, is that we have to unlearn our outdated and ineffective protection strategies and replace them with effective ones. Unlearning requires effort. For instance, I learned to drive in South Africa, with the steering wheel on the right side of the car, so when I moved to the States I had to unlearn my driving habits and learn how to drive with the wheel on the left. It felt counterintuitive and awkward. The skills I'm about to describe may feel counterintuitive and awkward, since our "intuitive" skills typically work to deny, dismiss, or distract our minds from our fear. You can begin to cultivate courage by developing three foundational skills: feel, face, and embrace.

Feel

Contrary to much of what we've been taught, cultivating courage does not begin with an intellectual process—it's actually the second step. The anxiety and fear that arise while driving for results and facing the inevitability of uncertainty are mental ones. Your mind, your intellectual process, is the source of the anxiety and fear and is responsible for its perpetuation. Any effort to rationalize your way out, to logically understand and quell your anxiety and fear, is unsustainable. Simply put, we cannot think our way to courage. Thoughts become expressed and experienced in the body in physical sensations as the result of two opposing and complementary systems that work to excite and calm us: the sympathetic and parasympathetic. The parasympathetic nervous system involves mellowing functions, while the sympathetic nervous system responds to stress and to fight-or-flight triggers with some automatic and fairly predictable reactions: pupils dilate, heart muscles contract with more force and frequency, bronchioles in the lungs expand, sweat glands activate, digestion slows, and kidneys work harder. These physiological actions are initiated by the brain. Your thoughts and perceptions, when colored in shades of fear, awaken the sympathetic system.

Unfortunately, while our inner monologue can quickly escalate our stress response, talking ourselves down is not enough. When attempting to enter a state of calm in the midst of fear, words—internal conversation—are just part of the process. At the door to the calm place in your mind stand mental guard dogs trained to keep things familiar and safe; once these dogs get excited, they begin to growl and bark. Attempting to soothe them with positive self-talk might get you a nasty bite of continuous anxiety. However, turning your attention to the physiology of the anxiety opens a hidden door past the guard dogs. Feeling, the first step in cultivating courage, begins with collecting and exploring sensory data: physiological, muscular, and chemical. Before trying to talk your fear away, before you attempt to influence the fear, you have to relate to it more directly. Connecting and staying present with your fear means paying attention to it, noticing how it looks and feels in your body.

You can talk yourself into a calmer state, but you have to time the effort correctly. Consider that what we feel disturbed by is the physical state of fear: the palpitating heart, sweaty palms, shortness of breath, upset gut, and shoulder tension that are the symptoms of fear. It's an act of courage to simply acknowledge this terrible discomfort. As President Franklin D. Roosevelt said, "So, first of all, let me assert my firm belief that the only thing we have to fear is fear itself—nameless, unreasoning, unjustified terror which paralyzes needed efforts to convert retreat into advance." Remaining present and connected to your body and your sensations affects your relationship with the experience; by allowing yourself to feel your fear, you shape your relationship to that fear. Just like a relationship with a person depends on connection and bonding, so does your relationship with fear. When you have a close relationship, you can exert influence. My wife has a powerful influence over me, whereas our office supply vendor has practically no ability to change my mind.

While I was facilitating an executive team retreat, our discussion turned to an upcoming layoff. I asked the executives to focus on the aspect of the layoff that caused them anxiety: a project, client, team dynamic, career issue, or personal situation. It took the leaders just minutes to identify their anxiety-inducing elements, and as soon as they named their anxiety, they rushed to rationalize and explain their reasons for it, and to declare a decisive action to relieve them of the discomfort. They were physically uncomfortable and wanted the exercise to stop. Yet rushing to a decision to alleviate the discomfort of anxiety is not the mark of a heroic leader. Sometimes, serving the organization with good judgment and clear decision making require us to transcend our anxiousness and grow in our awareness of discomfort.

In order to arrive at workable solutions, the executives had to loosen the grip that anxiety held on their thinking. They had to infuse themselves with courage, which meant first feeling their fear. We turned to uncover personal data that existed at the sensory level, and they were willing to cultivate courage and remained alert to their physical experience in their state of anxiety. Here are some of the physiological symptoms of fear they shared:

- Clammy hands
- Increased heart rate
- Dry mouth
- Muscle tension in the neck, shoulders, low back, arms, and hands
- Headache—pulsing in the temples, concentric pressure around the scalp
- Stomach in knots—nausea, stomach cramping
- Fatigue—loss of energy, sleepiness, exhaustion

These are common symptoms of fear. In times of stress and anxiety, streams of sensations run through our bodies. Recognizing and exploring these sensations is an act of bravery, because it's a choice to embrace the discomfort we'd rather reject, ignore, or deny. The power of this choice is not in the suffering; it's in the gift of mitigating the fear. We feed the fear—the anxious thoughts about an impending calamity—with our internal conversations. Getting into a shouting match with our own thoughts delivers more angst, not less. Counterintuitive to most of us, turning our attention toward the sensations of fear pulls energy and focus away from the discussion. Engaging our attention in observation and feeling disengages our attention from the internal monologue and, consequently, drains it of its relevancy and urgency. In other words, stepping out of the discussion in our head stops the discussion.

Face

The first skill, *feel*, provides rich data about your anxiety and creates a relationship with it. The next skill, *face*, adds more intimacy and influence in your relationship to your fear. Jen, a director at a geotechnical engineering firm, had successfully applied the first step. Jen was furious at one of her peers, a director named Peter: the way he managed his department (mismanaged, if you asked Jen) caused additional work for her department. As peers on the leadership team, Jen didn't have the authority to discipline Peter, and she felt so angry she could barely look at him, let alone talk to him. Peter was a know-it-all who didn't take advice well and took criticism even worse. Jen's frustration grew from anger to resentment to fury. She lost sleep over her anger, devised work-arounds to avoid Peter, and, most hurtful to her, hurt her family with her foul mood.

There were two concurrent conversations that needed to happen: a conversation between Jen and Peter, as well as a conversation between Jen and herself. Interpersonal communication colored by duress and conflict almost certainly leads to poor outcomes, so the wisest first choice for Jen was to have a conversation with herself in order to establish a level-headed approach for her conversation with Peter. As she embraced her heroic journey, Jen understood that fear fed her anger. She expected Peter to understand the impact of his behavior, and there was a higher likelihood of success if Jen communicated from a place of centered power rather than agitated accusation. Jen had to face her fear.

To "face" something is to look at it and, as a result, to know and understand it. Jen, by facing her anger, could understand it and become empowered to make choices that differed from her out-moded habits. Jen began by feeling her anger. Feeling, as described above, has nothing to do with wallowing in anger or succumbing to an internal conversation of self-pity. Feeling her anger meant that Jen turned her attention to the physiological sensations that arose when she became angry.

Jen had the opportunity to practice her courage skills on a morn-ing in late February as she prepared the month-end reports. To her chagrin, she had to call Peter for some critical reporting data, and in the span of a seven-minute conversation, Peter's bullheaded lack of cooperation soured Jen's mood and awakened her anger. She hung up the phone, pushed her chair back from her desk, closed her eyes, and concentrated on her physical data.

Jen felt the flush of heat in her face and neck. She felt her blood pressure elevate and tension press the backs of her eyeballs as her heart rate accelerated. She felt her shoulder muscles tighten up. She felt a turning and discomfort in her belly. She knew that in order to avoid the temptation of being drawn into the vortex of her thoughts, she had to alternate her attention between the physiological sensations, her breathing, and the sounds of the space around her. We need practice to learn how to separate observation from story making. The habit of justifying her anger and ruminating over Peter's stupidity could quickly overrun her new practices of feeling and facing.

Facing your fear requires that you first attend to objective observa-tion of real-time physical experience, and then begin to label your thoughts. When we label files or folders, for example, we give them order and context. Labeling means noting and naming. By facing that which we'd rather be distracted from, we discover its nature—its qualities and components. Jen's inner monologue was a driving narrative that unleashed chemical activity in her brain and throughout her body. By disentangling herself momentarily from the story line and attending to the reality of her physical experience and the actual world around her, Jen could begin to assert order and give context to the main themes of her internal story.

Labeling can be as simple as using descriptive words. Jen articulated inwardly what she thought and felt in relation to Peter: angry, unfair, roadblock, idiot, mad, wasting time, frustrating, holding me back, team breaker. Labeling naturally turns from simple or single-word labels to observations of basic themes in the story. Jen transitioned to more complete elements in her thoughts: "I'm anxious about getting these reports in on time; I'm afraid of looking like an idiot; my team will suffer because of his behavior; this is out of control; if I can't accomplish my goals, then my career's on hold."

Eventually, by persisting with labeling your inner experience, the facing skill turns to deductive understanding. The interpretation of our collective labels reveals a pattern of familiar story lines, of thoughts we believe as true for years and years. Labeling reveals our believed thoughts. These believed thoughts work as the gear wheels that turn the motor of our anxiety. As Jen articulated her believed thoughts, she began to recognize the fear that fed the energy of her anger. "I'm going to fall short; because my team won't make it they will think that I lack vision and control; if my reports are late and inadequate, they will bust me for being a phony; I was promoted by chance and this will only prove it." While Peter's behavior was inexcusable, Jen's anger emanated from her fear of failure and inadequacy. She'd have to embrace this fear to continue her hero's journey.

Through feeling the embodied reality of your experience, you open the door to facing and recognizing the driving forces of your fear. Through facing and naming your faulty, but well-rehearsed and deeply ingrained believed thoughts, you loosen their iron grip on your thinking. As long as your believed thoughts remain hidden in your mind, they act as quiet provocateurs in the machinery of your decision making. Articulating them diminishes their ability to affect your decisions and choices. Entering into dialogue with your actual physical sensations and understanding the deeper roots of what causes your fear gives you a clear space within which to make decisions and from which to take action.

Embrace

Feeling and facing fear are two of the three fundamental skills for cultivating courage—a cultivation that comes to completion with the skill of learning to *embrace* fear. To embrace means "to touch, to hold, to enter into close personal connection with the object." In order to embrace my wife or my children, I have to be open and vulnerable, available for connection.

Similarly, to embrace your fear or anxiety, you must be open and willing to doing so. When you feel frightened, you contract into safety; embracing, by contrast, means reaching out and expanding. This is not a discussion about destroying your fear, or eliminating that which triggers your anxiety; my effort to eradicate my fear of heights by skydiving was futile. I've jumped out of planes, and to this day my stomach lurches in glass elevators. Feeling (firsthand contact with your physical reality) and facing (recognizing and understanding your mental state) begin the process that leads to embracing.

Fear is the gatekeeper to power. When we cower before our fear, we surrender our energy. Anxiousness manifests as fatigue and foggy thinking. Leadership is connected with action and forward motion, and as a leader on a hero's journey you must face the dragon of your fear with a sword of skillful mind, the mind of understanding and wisdom.

Jen effectively catalogued her fear of failure through feeling and facing her anger at Peter. It was time to embrace her fear, to counteract her contraction and withdrawal, and to step out and forward. But which aspect of her experience was she to embrace? Was she to move toward engaging Peter? Was she to move toward embracing her fear of failure? One course was interpersonal (between two people) and the other was intrapersonal (within herself). Did Peter have to cooperate with Jen in order for her to successfully embrace her anxiety?

If Jen required Peter's cooperation, then her experiment was bound to fail. And, Jen wondered, how much did she have to embrace her fear? Was holding hands with fear sufficient? Or did she have to lock arms with it? Or was a full body hug with fear the right amount? Facing and feeling take place in the personal chambers of individual observation, but embracing can be more visible and interactive. Jen identified two friends she could confide in and safely share her insights and personal discoveries; she learned that articulating her inner experience provided her new perspectives—just hearing the way she described her experience out loud changed the way she understood it. Jen's first attempts at articulating her anxiety and admitting her fear of failure were not effective. The conversation quickly slid from the high intention of planning action to the tabloid level of griping and commiserating. Jen learned to wisely choose her discussion partners, and she trusted that these two friends could listen and remain curious rather than judgmental.

Articulating is one part of embracing, planning is another. A plan can be detailed and nuanced, or it can be simple and quick. Jen planned to keep her fear of failure in the forefront of her mind and to practice self-rescue (see chapter 15). She planned to challenge her fear by stepping forward 20 percent more than she would have historically and by dealing with Peter's controlling behavior in real time.

Our ego, our sense of separate identity, has a basic mood of fear. We have, therefore, endless opportunities to cultivate courage. The skills of feeling, facing, and embracing allow you to activate a pause button that halts the momentum of outdated believed thoughts and fear-based reactivity. In the space between stimulus and response lies our humanity—our gift of creation and compassion. Pausing creates space into which we can introduce new behaviors and self-care. Jen learned to manage Peter from a different angle by pausing her established pattern: when Peter started his aggressive song and dance, Jen turned her awareness to her physical sensations and she slowed her mental train from going toward anger and fear. With practice, she could discern the themes of her inner monologue and was surprised at how quickly she grasped the purpose of her mental chatter—to stay small and safe. With this initial success, she committed to manifesting her insights through action and stepping at least 20 percent into the realm of discomfort, toward her fear and anxiety.

You can cultivate your courage by deliberately practicing the sequence of feeling, facing, and embracing. Begin with attending to physical sensations and body states, continue with labeling and naming your thoughts and beliefs, and, finally, step toward what your fear would have you move away from.

15

COURAGE AND SELF-RESCUE

C hoosing to be courageous in a moment of fear is an act of self-rescue. The amygdala in our lizard brain reacts one hundred times faster than the rational aspect of our neocortex does. Choosing to be your own rescuer in the face of fear or perceived danger is an act of courage; it is an act of human development and maturity, and a critical differentiator of effective leaders.

Self-rescue for a leader on the hero's journey is adapted from my experience in the ocean. I was sixteen years old when I was introduced to scuba diving in the Red Sea, and I was immediately hooked; by age twenty-two, I completed all the training and testing needed to become a scuba diving instructor. Of all the certification courses I took, rescue diving was particularly demanding. Most diving trouble and accidents result from poor decision making, not faulty equipment or bad conditions. Of course, when conditions are challenging, and when stress abounds, we are pushed to the edge of our training, and that's the time when skill and repetition offer significant advantages in scuba diving just as in leading. The critical first step in adverse underwater conditions is self-rescue, and it's the same in anxiety- and fear-provoking leadership situations. A panicked diver increases the chances of an accident, and a panicked leader increases the chances of poor decision making, which might also carry dangerous consequences.

To effectively provide rescues in the water, the rescuer has to keep a level head. It's frightening to see a diver floating motionless on the surface, or to find an unresponsive diver underwater, or to discover a diver struggling to free himself from being trapped in an underwater wreck. Effective rescue divers learn to quell their panic. My instructor, Bill Buchwald, drew on his experience as a marine and treated his students like soldiers, contending that the harder and more stressful our rescue training scenarios, the better we'd respond during an actual incident. Bill insisted that we demonstrate a memorable and simple formula whether hauling an unconscious diver on the surface or trying to tame a panicked and thrashing diver on the sea floor.

The formula for self-rescue is: stop, breathe, choose, and act. This works to manage an anxious or fearful trigger whether you're clad in a neoprene diving suit or a wool business suit. This formula works especially well when you apply the fundamental skills of feel, face, and embrace. Following the formula of stopping, breathing, choosing, and acting is a real-time application that empowers you to be courageous.

Stop

The cardinal rule of rescuing a diver is to not make a bad situation worse. Stopping, even for the briefest moment, disrupts momentum. When I feel the crawling fingers of fear climbing up my spine, I stop and focus on relaxing my shoulders and releasing my facial muscles. Fear wants to turn us into mechanical objects that act from impulse and instinct. Choosing to stop is an act of purposeful self-control that may not directly improve the situation, but it will prevent the situation from escalating. Remember, the gap between stimulus and response contains our humanity. Stopping our instinctive, habitual, or mechanical activity is a commitment to that gap, a commitment to our humanity.

Self-Rescue Steps

STOP
Pause the process

BREATHE
Inhale & exhale

CHOOSE
Review your options

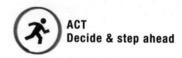
ACT
Decide & step ahead

Just imagine pressing the pause button on your system. It takes effort. It takes awareness. It takes caring. It takes consideration. Stopping—desisting from adding fuel to the fire of fear—is the act of a leader on a hero's journey. It requires surmounting your impulsive urges and asserting your will to refrain. Consider these situations for stopping:

- Refrain from making sarcastic comments that are intended to hurt someone.

- Refrain from running away and avoiding a situation or person.

- Refrain from hiding in busyness, TV, food, games, or alcohol.

- Refrain from compensating by exerting more control and restriction.

- Refrain from name-calling and blaming.

- Refrain from immediately responding to an anger-inducing email.

- Refrain from escalating anger as a cover-up for fear.

Stopping or refraining is not an act of cowardice; rather, it's an act of self-rescue. When fear or anger build up in your mind and body, stopping and counting to ten is a fundamental act of emotional intelligence. If you do not stop, then you will likely slide into actions that do not serve you, might scare your team, and could diminish your trustworthiness as a leader.

Breathe

In medical terms, shock is an emergency in which the organs and tissues of the body don't receive an adequate flow of blood. This depressed

blood flow deprives the organs and tissues of oxygen and allo...
buildup of waste products. Poor blood flow is the initiating factor in
shock, but lack of oxygen is the problem state. The physiology of fear
and anxiety can imitate a state of shock because—when caught in anxiety—your breathing turns shallow and quick, negatively impacting body
tissue from oxygen depletion and directly diminishing your thinking.
The brain is fueled by just two substances: glucose and oxygen. Shallow
breathing compromises oxygen flow to the brain, and your thinking
turns slow and fuzzy. Fortunately, anxiety-based "shock" isn't associated
with blood loss. Reoxygenating your body and mind can take place with
just a few deep breaths.

Here are a few simple breathing tips for reoxygenating your system:

- Breathe in slowly and deeply through your nose. Relax
  your shoulders and keep them down. Imagine your belly is
  a balloon and inflate it as you breathe. If you place a hand
  on your belly, you can feel its inflation and deflation.

- Exhale slowly through your mouth. As you blow air out,
  purse your lips slightly, but keep tongue and jaw soft
  and relaxed. You may hear a soft "whooshing" sound
  as you exhale. Learn to listen for that sound of the
  exhalation and to associate it with relaxation.

- Repeat this breathing exercise for just three minutes.
  Make your outgoing breath as long and smooth as you
  can. The outbreath is the key to relaxation, so give it
  your full attention and practice breathing out in long,
  slow, controlled breaths. You will quickly feel the benefit.

Choose

Stopping and refraining gives you space and time, and breathing reori-
ents you to real-time and real-world experience. When you become
self-possessed, you can act deliberately rather than reactively. Having

paused and reoxygenated, you can focus your mind on the situation at hand. In rescue diving, we have to quickly survey the situation, analyze the causes and possible consequences, and decide whether to go up or down, closer or farther—this is a gift of the neocortex, the complex human brain. Leaders who traverse the hero's journey make choices with their minds and hearts, not just their impulses.

To choose is to select the most appropriate course of action for the situation at hand after rejecting alternatives. Choice for leaders on the hero's journey requires selecting behaviors that benefit others, not just yourself. To help you choose, ask yourself, "What am I really afraid of in this moment?" Use the question to dive below the reactive level of your defensive ego. Are you activated and triggered by fear of failure, powerlessness, rejection, or humiliation? When you can name the actual driver of your fear and anxiety, you can begin to tame it.

Act

Finally, after intentionally pausing, refreshing the mind and body through breathing, and choosing a decision, it is time for purposeful engagement. While fear-induced adrenalin is still flowing through the blood, self-rescue means taking action, and the entire process might last just a few moments; certainly in rescue diving it does. But the actions of a focused mind are inevitably superior to the actions of a reactive mind.

Acting intentionally, with purpose and forethought, is a courageous display of leadership. Reacting is habit or instinct driven, while acting is choice and awareness driven. Courage means making the choice to willingly engage what you'd rather walk away from. In order to choose, to select your response and not merely capitulate to scripted conditioning, you have to practice courage.

Courage Is Not an Option

Writers, educators, and teachers throughout time have distilled the essence of superior leadership. The teachings are rich and varied, and often contradictory. This is no mistake, but a reflection of the complex nature of leadership, a topic further complicated by the varied and complex desires of followers.

How you define superior leadership depends on your style, point of view, education, experience, maturity, situation, and culture. Writers on the subject are also shaped by these same forces. Some will insist that great leaders are bold and spontaneous; others will claim that greatness emerges from being reasoned and reflective. Are great leaders independent or inclusive decision makers, emotional or rational, humble or bold? The list of leadership characteristics is so rich and paradoxical that I often hear, "So how exactly do I begin this journey?" Fortunately, there is a clear starting point in part I, Focus: What Am I Creating? But to journey beyond the starting point, one leadership virtue informs and strengthens all others: courage.

> *In the absence of courage, growth and innovation evaporate, and with them effective leadership.*

Aristotle named courage the first virtue because it makes all other virtues possible. Leadership is a hero's journey—it is boldness of vision and action, willingness to face risk and sacrifice, and commitment to serve and share. Leadership takes courage. Leading depends on innovating and growth, and both of these dry up in the absence of courage. Innovation requires a departure from the known and familiar and the courage to strike out past habit and tradition; it requires the courage to change and transform. Growth requires persistence in the face of failure and disheartenment and the courage to incorporate feedback and initiate change.

In the absence of courage, growth and innovation evaporate, and with them effective leadership. Fortunately, courage is both learnable and teachable. Equally as fortunate, courage is a human virtue available to everyone at any time—each human being has the capacity for courage. Leadership as a hero's journey has little to do with skydiving or sailing single-handedly across the Atlantic.

Leaders on the hero's journey muster up courage in expression, courage in relationship, and courage in action. Courage in expression refers to the courage to speak up, provide tough feedback, share unpopular and challenging opinions, and bring up difficult issues. Courage in relationship means that you trust others, have confidence and faith in people, begin to let go of the need to control all situations, and remain open to feedback and direction. Finally, courage in action refers to the courage of ideas and deeds, the willingness to strike out and do something different, to pursue ground-breaking efforts, and step outside of your comfort zone.

Again: courage is not the absence of fear; rather, fear provides the opportunity for courage. The good news is that you have the capacity to be courageous; the bad news is you can't eliminate fear. Once you accept the fallacy of fearlessness, you can begin to earnestly cultivate your courage. As an educator, coach, and adviser, I feel passionate about helping leaders and organizations become more courageous, and I feel equally passionate about continuing to find the growing edge of my own courage. My clients have proven beyond doubt that when leaders consciously tackle their fear and cultivate their courage, the entire enterprise operates with more courage.

Your job as a leader is to *en*courage your people, to fill them with courage. By practicing courage yourself, the bravery you muster becomes multiplied through your teams and collaborators. It is your job to cultivate courage in your people so that they initiate more complex projects, deal more directly with change, and speak up more willingly about important issues. In short, courageous workers try more, trust more, tell more, and accomplish more.

PART III

GRIT
What Am I Sustaining?

Your leadership journey is initiated by the vision of focus and enabled by courage. Achievements, though, depend on your grit, your persistent effort and action—without action, vision is mere hallucination. Grit means passionately persevering toward long-term goals. At some point on your journey, enthusiasm and motivation will wane and weaken; they may even evaporate for a while. Grit is the virtue that fills the vacuum. Your ability to press on and remain dedicated when you're fatigued, discouraged, and disillusioned is your expression of grit.

Grit is the most reliable predictor of achievement, and it can be developed and strengthened. In part III, we delve into understanding the elements of grit: discipline, determination, and perseverance. Self-discipline is ineffective and unsustainable when applied rigidly and inflexibly, and your capacity to remain disciplined emanates from your intelligent application of choices and discernment. We need to understand how to build that virtue and what gets in its way. Effective leaders know how and when to be self-disciplined.

16

WHAT AM I SUSTAINING?

Writing this part of the book was like hitting a wall. Ironically so, because it examines and explains *perseverance*, the ability to persist in the face of disheartenment and challenge. Strangely, I found it difficult and frustrating to push through and capture the ideas that I have practiced and taught for twenty years!

Perseverance—*grit*—is about remaining inspired. It is about being "fired up," "burning the candle at both ends," "having a fire in the belly," "being hot on the trail," and countless other expressions that denote heat and flame. This part is about the decisions we make moment to moment that consciously commit us to our purpose. It means persisting toward a vision or goal despite our emotions, body, and mind trying to pull us in other directions.

As I found myself struggling to tackle this part, I considered that perhaps it was poetic justice. Could it be true that we teach what we need to learn the most? When I sat at my desk to write, I felt heaviness in my belly, fuzziness in my head, slight pressure in my chest—all telltale signs of emotional resistance. I considered that perhaps I have to earn the right to write eloquently about the challenge of perseverance through experience.

Developing the muscle of perseverance in one area does not mean that it will automatically translate to other areas. For instance, fast running is my primary exercise; I run about four miles most days. Yet when I swim laps in a pool, I get winded pretty quickly. While my physical conditioning is good, different exercise routines require the use of different muscle groups, and it's the same with perseverance. The kind of muscle required to start and grow a business differs from the muscle required to persevere through writing a book.

The Comfort Zone

In previous parts, I've referred to the comfort zone, asserting that staying in our comfort zone is not one of the attributes of leadership. Recall that leadership derives from the Anglo-Saxon word *lithan*, meaning "to travel, to go," especially on a journey that isn't a guided tour of a well-mapped destination, but a departure from the known and familiar toward new horizons of achievement. Your task as a leader is to guide people on unfamiliar and uncertain expeditions toward a desirable shared vision. When Herb Kelleher began Southwest Airlines, he conceived of a different way—a market changing way—to operate an airline. By combining necessity with innovation, his team formed new and unfamiliar methods to operate their fleet, finances, people, and customers' experiences. Forty years later, Southwest Airlines continues to make a profit quarter after quarter.

> *A leadership journey isn't a guided tour of a well-mapped destination, but a departure from the known and familiar toward new horizons of achievement.*

Kelleher and his team departed from the well-known and comfortable and embarked on a journey across three zones of experience: comfort, growth, and panic. The comfort zone is so called because it is familiar, known, rehearsed, and effortless; this zone is predictable and habitual. This is not a bad thing: habits are efficiency patterns. If it weren't for habits, we'd feel even more stressed than we are now, as we'd have to consciously think about each and every action, from driving to brushing our teeth to walking. I'm quite happy that I can drive my car with near effortlessness, awakening to my senses when something out of the ordinary happens, like a car swerving in front of me on the freeway. I feel grateful for my regular exercise routine, which has been hard-won over the years. Habits work as evolutionary shortcuts to getting things done quickly and effortlessly; they reduce the amount of energy required to think and process information.

Thinking takes energy. While a typical brain accounts for approximately 2 percent of a person's body weight, it consumes about 20 percent of the energy we expend at rest, and even more energy when we apply

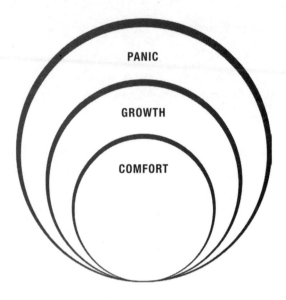

The Three Zones

the higher functions of problem solving, planning, visualizing, making decisions, and learning—in other words, *leading*. The energetic cost of these higher cognitive functions was evident when a client asked me to facilitate an emergency executive team meeting. The client convened the gathering because the firm's revenue was suddenly and unexpectedly cut in half, slashed as a result of its largest client going bankrupt. Upon running the new numbers, the client discovered that it had three months before it ran out of cash, so the team rallied to the challenge and we spent thirteen hours thinking through the crisis, analyzing the situation, identifying alternatives, and planning a solution. Even though I hadn't had any physical exercise that day, I felt famished and exhausted, as though I had run a race. Intensive thinking will do that.

Our bodies and minds strive for *homeostasis*, seeking to maintain a condition of internal balance or equilibrium even when faced with external changes—we're designed to preserve and direct our energy to optimize our survival and health. When I ask leaders to prioritize things they would like more of, energy tops the list above time and money because leading is an energy-intensive function—it is a marathon of higher-cognitive functions. We've developed the comfort zone as a way to maintain energy and ensure homeostasis. It's part of our self-preservation process, an evolutionary wisdom that serves our survival and wellness.

There are drawbacks to being in the comfort zone, though. Besides the fact that learning stops, the comfort zone also lacks innovation, breeds fighting over fixed resources, is devoid of enthusiasm, and makes it difficult to attract ambitious talent. The comfort zone is practiced, familiar, automatic, and predictable. As a leader, your role is to usher your organization toward growth, increased value, adaptability, and efficiency. Your work is to guide your organization toward a desirable shared vision, one that reaches beyond the familiar, and outside the recognizable boundaries of the comfort zone. You are promoted, and promote others in turn, by leading the organization from the comfort zone to the growth zone.

The Growth Zone

The layer of experience beyond the comfort zone is the growth zone. This zone is also the unknown: the unfamiliar, unrehearsed, and unpracticed. It is the realm from which you expand and evolve.

As a leader on the hero's journey, you must venture past the comfort zone and into the growth zone. You may not like it, but you have to commit to it. Leaders are on a quest, an expedition with other people. If you're on a quest by yourself, you're not leading—you're adventuring. An adventurer turns into a leader when he takes on responsibility to and for others. First and foremost is your willingness to leave *your* comfort zone, but being a leader means you'll also spend time and energy encouraging, cajoling, inviting, rewarding, and inspiring your people to leave *their* comfort zones.

The Learning Curve

Moving into growth can feel awkward, messy, and fraught with uncertainty and learning. Fortunately, the learning curve—how we improve performance over time—is a common experience for any person who engages in learning.

Researchers have identified four stages of learning that occur in ascending order: (1) unconscious incompetent, (2) conscious incompetent, (3) conscious competent, and (4) unconscious competent. In Stage 1, the unconscious incompetent is naive. ("I don't know that I don't know how to do this.") In Stage 2, the conscious incompetent learner moves from ignorance to awareness of her limited competence. ("I know that I don't know how to do this.") This beginning learner stage is frustrating, and the place where people form the most negative self-judgments. This is also the stage when most people give up, and when existing habits are challenged and attempt to reassert themselves. Stage 3 is the conscious competent learner. ("I know that I know how to do this.") While this learning stage is easier than the second stage, it is still marked by discomfort and self-consciousness. In Stage 3, we form new habits, but they have yet to become efficient. In Stage 4, the unconscious competent practitioner reaches expertise; she performs her functions as second nature. ("Really, you say I did this well? I didn't even think about it!") The fourth stage of learning occurs when

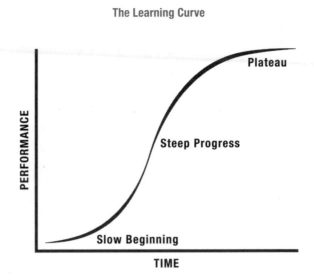

The Learning Curve

a new skill has become a natural part of us; we don't have to think about it.

Learning to stretch the boundary of the comfort zone is part of acquiring leadership maturity and wisdom. Sometimes, though, you might push too far or too quickly, and you reach beyond the growth zone and into the panic zone.

The Panic Zone

If you press too far past the growth zone, you will step into the electric, and sometimes shocking, panic zone. This zone is intensely stressful and has a tendency to shut down the higher cognitive functions. The growth zone includes stress, but not to the point of panic. Research has unequivocally demonstrated the costs of spending too much time in the panic zone: perpetual stress damages the heart and blood vessels, and long-term production of high levels of cortisol and epinephrine (stress hormones) age the body and mind and cause breakdown.

If you push too hard, you will send your people into the panic zone, and they will turn from stressed and excited to stressed and defensive. I've had bosses catapult me right over the border of the growth zone into the panic zone. One told me, "Eric, I'd like you to spearhead this new project and have it completed before the end of the quarter. This is a game changer. But don't let up on the two key projects you've been focused on; they're really moving along well now." My response to his request was to rush headlong into feverishly calculating how to pull off another major project when my team and I were already stretched beyond our resources and capacity. The panic zone was not a good place for us if we were going to succeed, and it was my job as the leader to find my way back to the growth zone and lead my team back there with me, even with the added project. This required that I weigh my decisions very carefully; it required self-discipline.

17

SELF-DISCIPLINE

iscipline shares the same linguistic origin as *disciple*, which is significant as they both point to an attitude of learning. Discipline, rather than being constricting, is an approach centered in growth and development, but what do you learn through the act of discipline? First and foremost, you discover your boundaries of ability, will, and energy. By applying the effort of discipline, you become intimately cognizant of your talents, mental models, and limits. Discipline, in many ways, is an exploration of limits; in fact, if something doesn't push us to our limit, it doesn't require discipline.

Discipline, for a leader, is an application of deliberate practice aimed at outperforming past experience and beliefs. By applying yourself—by making a deliberate effort to work against the forces of habit—you learn where your limits lie. Even more interestingly, the effort of discipline affords us the opportunity to expand our belief limits and to reach beyond our comfort zone. As we've discussed, leadership lies in stretching beyond the boundaries of the familiar, "pushing the envelope," so to speak. Leaders produce results, and they do so by successfully guiding their teams past the edges of their collective belief system and experiences to reveal new ability, resources, application, and deliverables. Those leaders who have accomplished admirable results—financial, societal, or spiritual—have learned to discipline themselves, and move beyond their comfort zone.

Discipline isn't a transactional experience; it isn't a onetime application that fulfills its purpose and is then tossed aside; rather, it's an attitude, an approach, a trait common to leaders who are on a hero's journey. As such, it remains a lifelong process. Before we venture too far afield, though, it's important to mention that discipline is not the same as being inflexible or dogmatic. Think about your leadership, and you'll recognize that you often operate in the realm of paradox: you have to appreciate the nuances of gray over the comfort of black and white. Your competitive advantage arises when you effectively combine discipline of intention and spontaneity of execution. By setting a clear intention—focus—you set your purpose, articulate a reason, and establish a goal. It is the clarity of your purpose that provides context for your choices, which are the practical part of discipline. Discipline isn't anything more than making choices. If I say that I am going to exercise to build my strength and endurance, then my schedule will reflect my intention when it shows that I've blocked off exercise time from five to six thirty. When five o'clock rolls around, I have to choose whether to follow through on my intention or do something else. Choosing to do something other than my stated intention demonstrates a lack of discipline.

As stated, discipline comes from choices. By accumulating a series of choices, we move along a consistent (although not necessarily linear) path toward our desired outcome. Discipline is a dynamic, deliberate, and continuous practice of staying in contact with the intention that we have declared.

Having lived in San Diego for a couple of decades, I recognize that discipline resembles surfing. You paddle hard and fast to get to the front edge of the wave—that's the aspect of discipline that requires energy and hard work, to swim past the swell of our habits. Next, surfing requires timing and balance. You don't accomplish surfing by the speed with which you paddle to catch the wave, but by the ability to time the surge of energy flowing beneath you and align your board with the wave's power. Discipline, like surfing, is a continuous series of choices (small or large) that allows you to remain on the edge of the wave, standing on your board, focusing your intent on the ride and on the beach in front of you. Surfing requires that you stay attuned to the dynamic force—leaning forward to accelerate, leaning back when you get ahead of the force, swaying left or right to go with the roll of the wave so that you stay with that force.

In leading, the wave that you're catching is the rising power of learning and growth. The power of learning accelerates your leadership results.

In fact, John F. Kennedy, in a speech prepared for delivery in Dallas the day of his assassination (November 22, 1963), said that leadership and learning are indispensable to each other. Your developmental edge might be learning to think strategically, communicate effectively, acquiring financial savvy, or team building. Whatever force arises, whatever wave we try to ride, requires significant attention in the moment-to-moment series of real-time choices if we want to ride the wave to shore. The surfer's reward is a sense of flow—the continuous effort yields a transcendent experience of connection, one that many surfers refer to as a spiritual experience. And so it is, too, when we make continuous deliberate choices to connect with the force that we are attempting to master in leadership: we arrive at a sense of flow, an easy and effective competency in the aspect of our choosing.

The choices we make toward our focus are for the best. Although we might fear failing or worry that what we decide to do will take us down the wrong path, if we approach leadership as a series of learning experiences, we will see that even the seemingly bad choices have the potential to lead to positive outcomes. So often we think of leading as being linear—one decision following the next. In reality, leadership is much more organic, and realizing this makes it easier for us to engage in the process. Recognizing that your choices are always positive will strengthen your resolve and trust that things will work out for the best.

In their effort to stretch beyond the comfort zone, leaders, like surfers, never stray too far from fear, uncertainty, and doubt. Nor do they wander too far from feelings of joy, excitement, and clarity. When there is an internal focus on the benefit of making good choices, there is motivation toward the goal, and it is easier to stay disciplined.

One school of thought advocates that it is easier to practice discipline when you are driven to avoid something. A peer of mine used to threaten his team members that he would publically humiliate them if they missed their deadlines, but this so-called discipline was actually avoidance of punishment. It was short-lived behavior modification and could be maintained only in the presence of a punitive figure—a parent, a boss, or some form of threatening overseer. Results achieved through a fear-based disciplinarian approach only replicate when there is another threat of punishment, so the discipline that arises from wanting to avoid something—like being fired, rejected, or hurt—doesn't fall into the same category as growth-oriented motivation. It is survival oriented.

Disciplining the Self

Interestingly, leaders who report having a lot of self-discipline are the ones most eager to enhance their discipline. Those who admittedly possess modest amounts of self-discipline seem satisfied with the discipline at their disposal. Self-discipline is not the only predictor of personal success, but it is one of the critical factors. Self-discipline, self-control, and self-regulation are all variations of grit integral to its application to life, leadership, and personal evolution.

In the context of leadership as a hero's journey, focus, "What am I creating?" provides the spark that ignites our fire. But fire doesn't burn without fuel. The fuel that continues to feed our fire is our passion. As the fire burns, you need to fan it with perseverance, and the attribute that lies at the center of perseverance is self-discipline.

> *In reality, there is no such thing as long-term discipline. Discipline happens in the moment—in the instant when we make a choice.*

Is there such a thing as long-term discipline? I've looked at people's lives, at leaders who have achieved wonderful results, and marveled at the degree of self-discipline that they've been able to apply through difficulty, disheartenment, and boredom. How have they accomplished this? Where do leaders find the ability to press on in a given direction in the face of great resistance, or in the cold, clammy presence of pervasive uncertainty? Two of the major contributors to this consistency are focus and courage, which we've already discussed, but they are insufficient without self-discipline.

In reality, there is no such thing as long-term discipline. Discipline happens in the moment—in the instant when we make a choice. Choice by choice, decision by decision, we build the critical mass called self-discipline. When my focus is clear, my decisions become a calculation of distance: Is this decision taking me closer to or further away from my stated intention?

Carl, a fifty-one-year-old VP of operations, realized that he would get better leadership results by genuinely listening to his executive team. He decided, therefore, to become a disciple of curiosity—he set as a clear goal for himself to practice curiosity by becoming an expert listener. Becoming an expert listener did not negate or minimize his intense drive for results, his opinionated presence, or his strong directive nature; becoming an expert listener meant adding another aspect or tool to his repertoire of leadership skills. While Carl struggled mightily against his well-established habit of telling rather than listening (in the belief that he was adding value to every conversation by improving on what he was told), he was genuinely committed to becoming an expert listener.

Carl set a clear intention (focus) to become a skilled listener. In every interaction and conversation he compared his behavior to his intention, and soon he amassed a treasure trove of data about his behavior. Carl started applying his self-discipline as he applied his choice to listen well during calm conversations. He began with easy situations in which he practiced overriding his habit of not listening.

Thinking back to our earlier discussion about habits, you'll remember that shifting them requires self-discipline. Over the years, I have heard that a new habit can be formed in three or four weeks. This factoid has caused heartburn and frustration for me as I have labored to form new helpful and healthful habits. Moreover, over the course of thousands of coaching conversations with clients, I have yet to find a single person that has implemented new and effective habits in twenty-eight days! Habits that we'd like to deliberately establish—behavioral goals for ourselves—must form new neural pathways while simultaneously overriding existing neural pathways. Adult habit formation requires more time, energy, and repetition than child habit formation, because as we update or change a pattern, we concurrently unwind an old habit. Children's minds, on the other hand, are just creating new habits.

Carl, in his quest to become an expert listener, spent more than a year practicing new skills of asking questions, pausing to reflect, and being curious. Concurrently, he became much more aware of his habitual pattern of cutting people off, rushing to closure, and turning away in mid-conversation. It was not enough for Carl to just apply the new skills; doing so did not preclude his old habits. Rather, he had to notice and deliberately refrain from his old habits, even as he practiced his new skills.

Decision Fatigue

Self-discipline is an integral characteristic of success and the hero's journey. It is also mentally and emotionally exhausting; we struggle with mixed intentions and impulses that pull and push us in various directions. James, a director of IT in an established technology consultancy, is an example of this struggle: at thirty-four years of age, he realized that he must diversify his leadership skills and behaviors. Specifically, he wanted to become an effective coach to his people to complement his directive and problem-solving skills. In the past, as coaching opportunities emerged, James relied on familiar problem solving rather than the unfamiliar practice of coaching. There were multiple coaching opportunities: questions from seasoned employees, project reviews, guiding trouble-shooting discussions, staff developmental dialogues, and individual career discussions. However, James felt compelled to appear strong and in command, as he couldn't bear the learning curve demands of temporary incompetence.

Besides mixed intentions, there is a "mental software" barrier to discipline—decision fatigue. We find self-discipline challenging because of the mental energy required to make a decision—the energy that's drained when you have to vigilantly avoid temptations and stay on an intentional course. As a leader you strive to do the right thing. The "right thing" is a constant calculation—spend money on X or Y, give time to A or B, pay attention to 1 or 2, and so on. In the best-case scenarios, you face a simple choice between two options. Many critical decisions, however, are much more complex, demanding selection from multiple options. Even more challenging are the choices that you have to make among shades of options: A, B, C, and D are all poor choices, but which one is the least poor?

Psychologist Roy Baumeister coined the term *decision fatigue* in the course of conducting research on a phenomenon called *ego depletion*. Decision fatigue sheds light on why otherwise levelheaded leaders sometimes make obviously unwise, even foolish, decisions. Why do well-meaning leaders splurge on office activities, lose their tempers at the end of the week, agree to frivolous project ideas, or commit to expensive vendor contracts? One reason they make these poor decisions has to do with depleted mental energy—thinking demands energy, and decision making is the most costly of mental expenditures. Regardless of a leader's level of intelligence, education, or even practice, making decisions one after another exacts a biological and mechanical price. Compounding this challenge is the fact that we're often oblivious to the signs of mental fatigue.

As your choices pile up over the course of a day, each choice exacts a toll of energy. When you exercise your muscles, each successive repetition is harder; my tenth push-up is more exhausting than my first because of the cumulative effort. Similarly, each mental act of deciding is exponentially more difficult and depleting. The brain, oriented as it is toward the equilibrium of homeostasis, works harder with each successive choice. Executives responsible for implementing decisions and plans live under constant pressure and mental energy drain; our brains attempt to relieve this strain by finding and following the path of least resistance.

When decision fatigue sets in and the strain of choice making begins to threaten our energy reserves, the brain attempts to preserve energy through its own version of fight or flight. The fight response manifests as carelessness—an uncalculated reaction or decision with no consideration of consequences or impact. The flight response plays out as inaction—a form of escape from deciding or choosing which, in the long run, can bring to bear the laws of compounding interest, meaning greater problems down the road.

Unfortunately, we do not come into the world with a user's manual for the brain. Fortunately, there is evidence from millennia of study and exploration about how to reverse decision fatigue and grow in discipline. There is a path toward improving grit. But before we turn to that path, we must take a deeper look at grit.

Grit Survey

The hero's journey is a quest filled with challenges and problem solving, resulting in a meaningful prize. It is a pursuit of success and the ability to produce results. Successful leaders guide a community through uncertainty toward a desirable shared vision. What, then, is the single trait that separates successful from unsuccessful people?

Dr. Martin Seligman has researched aspects of this very question since the 1960s. Seligman's early work led him to describe a state he called *learned helplessness*. Learned helplessness refers to a psychological condition in which a person has learned to behave helplessly in a particular situation, usually after experiencing some inability—either perceived or real—to avoid an adverse situation. This condition contrasts sharply to the heroic mind-set.

Seligman's research then turned to understanding optimism, the opposite of learned helplessness. His results led to the codification of a field of psychological study now referred to as Positive Psychology. In his 2012 book *Flourish*, Seligman uses the acronym PERMA to describe the five essential elements for experiencing lasting well-being:

- Positive emotion: focusing on gratitude by writing down at day's end three things that went well, and why

- Engagement: becoming immersed in work and using your strengths to perform daily tasks

- Relationships: honoring your nature as a "social being" and forming relationships that matter

- Meaning: serving a cause and belonging to something bigger than yourself

- Achievement: committing to bettering yourself and recognizing that determination counts for more than IQ

Dr. Angela Duckworth was a student of Seligman's at the University of Pennsylvania. She focused her attentions on achievement—one aspect of positive psychology and PERMA—and attempted to answer the question: What is the single trait that separates successful from unsuccessful people? Duckworth and her colleagues focused on a recognizable group of high achievers—incoming cadets at West Point Academy. In order to gain admission to West Point, candidates must apply directly and receive a nomination from a US senator or representative. The cadets are officers in training. Of the approximately thirteen hundred cadets who enter the academy each July, about one thousand graduate.

West Point holds a vested interest in quickly determining which cadets will succeed enough to become officers, and the academy has spent millions of dollars on decades of research developing a comprehensive battery of tests that will predict success. They created the Whole Candidate Score, which combines academic grades, a gauge of physical fitness, and a Leadership Potential Score to discern which cadets are most likely to make it through the demands of West Point and become a successful army officer.

Duckworth's research led her to the conclusion that the greatest predictor of success was *grit*, a combination of perseverance and passion for long-term goals. Duckworth and her colleagues formulated a twelve-item Grit Questionnaire, which they administered to the West Point cadets alongside their Whole Candidate Score tests. It surprised the West Point brass to learn that the Grit Questionnaire predicted success and failure more accurately than the academy's battery of tests did.

Grit, or the passion and perseverance for long-term goals, is also the greatest predictor of success and a core virtue of leaders on the hero's journey. As leaders, we constantly teeter between feeling fired up and getting burned out. When I feel fired up, it's easy to face challenges and push through expected and surprising barriers; I require perseverance, however, when I edge toward the burned-out pole of the spectrum. When I have lots of energy and a clear sense of commitment, I merely have to persist. But I have to persevere when I become bored, disheartened, or disillusioned.

Perseverance is characterized by a lack of enthusiasm. When you don't feel in the mood and become uninspired—that's when you need perseverance. When you feel enthusiastic and excited, your motivation carries you on a wave of endorphins that make the task easy and attractive. The hallmark of perseverance is, "I just don't feel like doing it, but I do it anyway!" I focus on my intention and what I choose to do in spite of my mental fatigue and physical discomfort; rather than avoiding or forgetting about it, I commit myself. That's perseverance.

Sustained change requires sustained effort. Leaders resemble chemists trying to formulate a new prescription: the formula they create is neither quick to arrive nor without effort to complete. If work outcomes would happen on their own, they would not require leadership. However, rather than results happening spontaneously, we accomplish them in the face of difficulty, challenge, and constant disruptions. Your self-discipline places commitment above comfort. Because leadership is an act of service, your self-discipline is a servant leaders' primal contribution to the community.

PERSEVERANCE AND ITS BARRIERS

When I lived in South Africa in the 1980s, Kentucky Fried Chicken (now KFC) was the great American import. In my neighborhood, KFC was the only fast-food restaurant. KFC almost didn't make it beyond the idea stage; its beginning is an object lesson in perseverance. The famed Colonel Sanders retired from his single-location restaurant when he was sixty-five years old, but he was still passionate about his special chicken recipe, and he realized that there was value and contribution in selling it to restaurant chains. However, his attempts were not well received—over the course of two years, Colonel Sanders was rejected by 1,009 owners before he accumulated a following. After two years, six hundred restaurants contracted to buy and use his recipe. I cringe at the idea of being rejected one thousand times! But Colonel Sanders persevered in the face of challenge, disheartenment, and disillusionment.

Perseverance is the trait of leaders who fundamentally grasp that commitment to the vision is itself reason enough to press on, even when the mind is numb and the heart is heavy.

Another American cultural icon—Disneyland—barely made it into existence. My kids love to go to Disneyland. My wife loves to go to Disneyland. New York Giants quarterback Phil Simms, upon winning the Super Bowl in 1987, turned to the camera, grinned broadly, and declared, "I'm going to Disney World!" Whether you are a domestic or foreign tourist, visiting Disneyland is a must, and yet, Walt Disney, in spite of his successes in movies, fought tooth and nail to convince investors to loan him the money for Disneyland. Amazingly, banks turned down Walt Disney 302 times as they believed his idea for a massive theme park was ridiculous. Disney was a visionary; his leadership closely follows the arc of the hero's journey—he persevered and followed his vision.

Perseverance is the trait of leaders who fundamentally grasp that commitment to the vision is itself reason enough to press on, even when the mind is numb and the heart is heavy.

Why Should We Persevere?

All great masters are chiefly distinguished by the power of adding a second, a third, and perhaps a fourth step in a continuous line. Many a man has taken the first step. With every additional step you enhance immensely the value of your first.   RALPH WALDO EMERSON

There are stories of perseverance in every aspect of life: Colonel Sanders and Walt Disney persevered in business, and the Greek epic poet, Homer, wrote of Odysseus's twenty-year journey of perseverance to return home from the Trojan War. Regardless of the setting, perseverance defines the human experience marked by goal orientation and a desire to reach a destination different and better than our current state. If accomplishing a goal were as simple as merely declaring it, then each and every one of us who ever declared a goal would be content with our success. In reality, achieving significant accomplishments requires focus, effort, and commitment. Perseverance demonstrates and springs from commitment.

Just one year into my undergraduate career, I received a letter from the university informing me that I was disenrolled; they were kicking me out. The letter declared that a 0.2 GPA did not demonstrate a sincere commitment to remaining one of the university's students. They were right. I did not have a sincere commitment to being a student; I was committed to having fun. The letter fell on my consciousness like a bucket of ice water dumped on a sleeping person—it woke me up and I began to deliberately examine what I wanted to accomplish. What was my goal? What was I committed to? Fear, anger, and humiliation swatted at my unfocused mind and cleared away the cobwebs of misdirection. After a period of forced introspection, I emerged intensely focused on wanting to accomplish my degree and graduate from college; I became committed to my education and my future.

Graduating from college is more a test of endurance than intelligence. Some classes and subjects are more intellectually challenging than others. Statistics challenged me in ways that history didn't. The real test was sticking to the schedule, doing homework, and studying day after day, night after night. I particularly found it difficult to study when compelling temptations swirled all around me, and I found it challenging to slog through months of applying myself when my motivation had fizzled and I had to stay the course. The university allowed me to retake five classes that marred my record to erase the grades that reflected my initial year of distraction. Sitting through an entire semester's worth of work, knowing that I had squandered all that time, was difficult and frustrating, but I knew that tremendous effort must go into repairing bad choices, poor judgment, and slack behavior.

I eventually graduated with good grades. Today, my professional circle is mostly filled with college graduates. Colleagues come in all varieties of styles, colors, and abilities, but they share one trait: they learned to persevere. Along their journey they developed the ability to stick to a plan and consider their goal as a key factor in their moment-to-moment decisions and choices. University degrees, for the most part, don't require genius; rather, they demand an ability to stick to a plan and accomplish a series of difficult tasks. To most hiring managers, the value of a university degree is the demonstration of grit more than the candidate's particular major; knowing that a person committed to a long-range goal speaks volumes about their perseverance. Of course, this is not the only measure or proof of perseverance. My father never went to college, and he's one of the most intelligent and persevering men I've ever known. Bill Gates, Steve Jobs, Lady Gaga, Tiger Woods, Mark Zuckerberg, and Tom Hanks all dropped out of college to pursue their careers—they may not have completed their classes, but they mastered perseverance, nevertheless.

We need perseverance because we will invariably encounter fatigue, disheartenment, confusion, and uncertainty on our journey to accomplish our goal. Perseverance might act as the final tether connecting us to our passion and commitment.

Leadership means that we willingly plant a tree under whose shade we may never sit. Perseverance is the ability to commit to the long haul. Passion or opportunity might begin the hero's journey, but these initiating factors cannot in themselves sustain the journey. The originating burst of energy that sets you on the path toward accomplishing results eventually fades; unfortunately, it usually does so long before the journey ends. To that end, perseverance is one of the critical forces that you need to carry you through to completion.

Barriers to Perseverance

Grit is a capacity that can be learned and honed. But before we discuss how to enhance your grit, we must understand what gets in the way of it. Grittiness is a determination to climb over walls on the path and to tackle obstacles as they appear. Randy Pausch worked as a computer science professor at Carnegie Mellon University when he received a diagnosis of terminal pancreatic cancer in August 2007. When doctors told him he had three to six months of good health left, he wrote and presented an inspirational talk titled "The Last Lecture: Really Achieving Your Childhood Dreams." He then coauthored a book on the same theme that became a wildly popular bestseller. Pausch died in July 2008.

In his book Pausch wrote, "The brick walls are there for a reason. The brick walls are not there to keep us out. The brick walls are there to give us a chance to show how badly we want something. Because the brick walls are there to stop the people who don't want it badly enough. They're there to stop the other people."

Setting out on a journey toward a desirable vision invokes both joy and challenge. Brick walls of various sizes and styles stand along the path to achievement. Grit—passion and perseverance for the long-term goal—accompanies the other virtues of leadership on a hero's journey—focus and courage—as your commitment is tested while you march toward your desired results.

Your leadership is distinguished by the ability to look toward the distant horizon and remain fixed on that destination as you take steps in the here and now. Leaders with grit approach accomplishment of results as a marathon, not a sprint—a leader's advantage is perseverance and endurance. While disheartenment, boredom, or frustration might tempt some to stop or change direction, the leader with grit stays the course.

Brick walls—or barriers on the journey—come in two basic types: external and internal. External barriers come from the environment and circumstances: social trends, competition and substitution, economic trends, ecological influences, politics and regulatory forces, technology, industry rules and norms, supplier relations, and customers. Internal barriers are personal; they arise from mental bricks, fashioned from our beliefs, thoughts, and feelings. They include inertia, procrastination, laziness, self-negation, discouragement, and overwhelm.

We formulate strategic and operational plans to clarify our desired end states and to identify steps to overcome the inevitable external barriers along the way. Often, though, we miss these plans because of internal barriers. Even the most elegant strategic objective will be poorly implemented when you or your team are blocked by your inner barricade. For this reason, prepare yourself by knowing about commonly occurring internal barriers—knowledge is power, but only when it leads to understanding and blossoms as wisdom.

Inertia—I Can't Stop Myself

Never underestimate the addictive power of comfort: obvious physical comforts like a comfy couch, an expensive mattress, a good pair of shoes, and tasty foods; emotional comforts such as being surrounded by friends and family who are safe and fun; and less obvious comforts like lack of strife and familiarity. Familiarity is a funny creature—it doesn't always guarantee or imply pleasantness. For example, years ago, I worked for a nasty boss. As a manager, he was downright abusive, but I stayed at the job because the stability appealed to me more than the uncomfortable change of interviewing and selling myself to a new company.

Inertia is our tendency to keep doing what we've been doing. It takes less energy to do what we've always done, even if it's unsatisfying or even harmful. Inertia—unconscious and habitual—is the opposite of perseverance, as perseverance is intentional and purposeful. Inertia, in physics, refers to the tendency of an object to stay in a state of motion or rest until another force acts on it. When setting a goal, you introduce a new force that disrupts the inertia of your mental habit pattern.

Committing to a goal challenges our habitual patterns. When I set out to do something differently than I have done before, I have to behave differently than I have behaved in the past. If I succumb to believing that I can't stop doing what I'm doing, then I will not be able to redirect my resources and efforts toward my goal or aspiration. In that case, inertia will script a future that is a predictable extension of the past.

Albert Einstein is credited with saying, "Insanity is doing the same thing over and over and expecting different results." That's inertia. It's a little slice of insanity. Discipline and steadfastness are synonyms for grit and perseverance, but they are *not* synonyms for inertia.

Sometimes we don't notice perseverance right away. Consider this example of what might seem like inertia—lack of purposeful change—but is in fact grit: Tanya, the district manager of five tanning salons, has lost money with her newest store for five months, and her peers strongly believe that the store won't succeed. Tanya, however, trusts her instincts and the store's manager and perseveres in coaching and supporting them. This is not inertia, apathy, inaction, or lethargy (all synonyms for inertia)—inertia is reactive and disengaged, but Tanya is proactive while remaining focused on her vision.

Procrastination—I Have Plenty of Time

In my twenties I was blessed with inexhaustible energy and believed I could conquer the world; I probably could have. The problem was that I thought I had all the time in the world to get everything done, so I put things off. I procrastinated. Procrastination comes from the Latin *procrastinationem*, "a putting off" (*pro*, meaning "forward," and *crastinus*, "belonging to tomorrow"). Procrastinating is not the same as waiting or practicing patience. Patience is a deliberate exercise of self-control, and Tanya acted patiently with her store managers while her boss and peers urged her to close the store, to take immediate action. Yet Tanya believed that waiting and persevering with her plan was a better approach. Waiting acts as a form of perseverance: pausing for knowledge, for team members to understand a new idea, or for returns on an expensive investment. Procrastination means to put something off—it's a choice often made at the edge of conscious thinking. There are two primary reasons for procrastination: avoiding discomfort and faulty thinking.

Procrastination can mask anxiety, doubt, or lack of faith. Procrastination can be avoidance—evading something undesirable or scary that you know needs to be done. I remember a conversation about procrastination with a client named Rachael, who had been promoted to director just two months before our meeting. While she worked in the same health care organization for a dozen years, she was promoted into a role overseeing many of her former peers, and when Rachael's new team came up for their annual reviews, she put it off. Even though she knew the process, forms, timing, and skill of reviews, she felt anxious and tense about giving them, and this discomfort led to her delaying, evading, and deprioritizing the task.

On the other hand, the faulty thinking path to procrastination refers to a misconception of time, specifically a notion of infinite time. Sometimes we convince ourselves that there's still plenty of time to accomplish our goals, to bring into reality that which we desire. But is there?

Fifty-year-olds can procrastinate just as expertly as twenty-year-olds. That's because it is not our age that determines faulty thinking, but misperception. Stewart was a charismatic and energetic CEO who had a knack for attracting and retaining smart and driven professionals. He was such a skillful salesman and ambassador that people wanted to be around him and customers wanted to do business with him, but Stewart deeply disliked getting "bogged down" in the financial management of his business. He had taken accounting classes in college and knew how to read financial statements, and he wanted to get better at using financial data in decision making; he even set a goal in our executive coaching process to become more financially savvy. Yet month after month, Stewart put off reviewing the financials, thinking he had plenty of time, a delusion that was shredded by his banker; he received a call that the firm's accounts receivable credit line was about to be reduced. His first reaction was surprise, which was then quickly followed by anger and fear as 60 percent of the company's payroll was carried by this credit line.

Stewart had not persevered toward his desire to master finances. He had procrastinated. He thought that his strong interpersonal skills would compensate for his lack of financial skills, and he believed that given enough time he would prove that his approach was valid. Stewart chose to put off the awkwardness of the learning curve and to spend his time strengthening relationships. Because he delayed the effort of reviewing the balance sheets with his controller, he jeopardized his company's credit. Stewart experienced the interesting paradox of leading: on the one hand, there is plenty of time, but on the other hand, there is no time at all.

At our Zendo (Zen meditation center) we recite a short verse at the end of the daily sitting meditation. It speaks to the awareness of procrastination:

> Time swiftly passes by, and with it, our only chance.
> Each of us must aspire to awaken.
> Be aware.
> Appreciate this precious life.

Discouragement—This Is Just Too Hard!

Joan felt discouraged. As president of a (previously) fast-growth company, she was accustomed to the challenges of expansion. However, the company had been hit with three years of 6 percent downslide in revenues, and her strategy to return to profitability wasn't working. Customers failed to demonstrate the loyalty they once had, competitors gained market share, and her senior managers displayed signs of wear and tear—they resorted to power grabbing, blaming, fault finding, sarcasm, and micromanaging. Joan knew in her heart that the strategy they'd chosen was the right one, but they needed more time and investment to make it work.

Discouragement began to overtake Joan's otherwise optimistic mind-set; protracted shortfall gnawed at her will to persist. To be *discouraged* literally means to feel "deprived of courage, hope, or confidence." Courage means having the heart to tackle fear and being discouraged means losing heart. Leadership is the spirit of growth and expedition, and being discouraged is being dispirited. As Joan's courage and spirit waned, her grit slipped.

As a leader you are measured by the results you help create. You are evaluated by the levers you pull in different aspects of work, levers that shape and influence outcomes. Culture, relationships, supply chain, financial management, innovation, and strategic focus all serve as means to an end—contributing factors to successful outcomes. As a leader, your attention points forward, and things regularly take longer than expected. Discouragement takes root in the maddening breach between efforts and outcome; it often results in an impulsive lurch toward the tried and true—toward the past.

Joan's team wanted success. They wearied of succumbing to the market; they impulsively looked to the past and tried to convince Joan to resuscitate old programs and processes that had once worked to drive sales.

Perseverance means to persist in the face of discouragement. The dark mood that typifies discouragement clings like gummy tar that traps hope and ambition; straining against discouragement demands energy and conviction—the very elements that discouragement siphons away. There are times when the end seems impossible to attain, and our inner conversation turns against us. We lose heart; we lose courage. I've felt it. Joan felt it. Every leader I've ever spoken with, every man and woman who has catalyzed change and accomplished beneficial results, has felt it. The journey of leading differs from a tourist outing precisely because of discouragement. When optimism, hope, and confidence retreat to the far edge of awareness and discouragement takes center stage, you are treading the leadership path.

Laziness—It Takes Too Much Energy

Laziness is a reluctance to take action, despite having the ability to do so. I have a lazy streak. I feel its regular tugging, beckoning me to slow down, to stop investing time, energy, and effort. My laziness got the better of me in elementary school as I avoided the effort required for homework and study; consequently—and in spite of my intelligence—I earned mediocre grades through high school. It wasn't until my second year of college that I discovered my grit. In fact, as mentioned previously, it took being kicked out of college to awaken my grit.

Laziness has played a role in human behavior throughout history. Aesop's fable from about 600 BCE about the ant and the grasshopper is a story about laziness: The grasshopper spent his summer singing and playing while the ant meticulously worked to store food for the coming winter. When the cold arrived, the starving grasshopper begged the ant for food. The ant admonished him for singing through the summer and told him to dance through the winter.

Modern life is particularly conducive to laziness. We have laws for safety, machines for expedience, technology for innovation, and power to light our lives and defy nature's cycles and rhythms. Our ancestors lived in a world of immediacy. Our ancestral families were compelled by predators and environment, by fear, and by the forces of nature. They didn't have to invest in thinking about long-range issues, scenario forecasting, or strategic planning—they operated and lived in the immediacy of reactions. They could neither store food in their refrigerator nor become obese from lack of exercise. They had few choices. Laziness is an exacerbated problem of modern life; it is an exercise of poor decision making and choosing.

There are three kinds of laziness: laziness of exertion, laziness of thought, and laziness of perspective. Laziness of exertion plays out as not wanting to put forth effort; we don't want to exert ourselves. We'd rather stay the course on an old decision than make the effort to imagine and commit to an untested plan. Leadership, as I've mentioned again and again, is an energy-intensive role. Your leadership responsibility demands that you energize your people, projects, and plans. Sometimes the seduction of laziness, of not putting forth energy and effort, can be quite compelling. One way to avoid the seduction of laziness is to preempt it with relaxation; relaxing is an intentional choice, while laziness is a capitulation.

Laziness of thought refers to a lack of effort to change our self-defeating and outdated ego chatter. "I can't do this. Other people can lead. Other people can be strategic. Other people can be engaging and inspiring; they can be strong and decisive in difficult situations, but I can't. I'm just not good enough." Or, alternatively, "I'm always an operational person," "I've never been able to stick with things very long term," or "I've always failed, and I'm bound to fail again." This kind of thinking is lazy if you're not willing to invest the energy and effort to challenge and rewrite these thought scripts.

Laziness of perspective means that we give chase to the urgent at the cost of attending to the important. We can easily fill our time by staying busy, and some leaders confuse busyness with accomplishment; they feel virtuous by keeping busy. This type of laziness doesn't feel lazy at all, but it's actually a form of escape. Constant reactive busyness is a laziness of perspective as it replaces near-term needs for long-term responsibility. Laziness of perspective avoids the demands of leadership that include tending a long-term vision, forging and maintaining relationships, making difficult decisions, and engaging with subtle aspects of organizational culture and efficiency.

Lazy means "not inclined to work, not interested in putting forth effort." It has its place. For instance, several years ago I decided that I would make Saturday my lazy day. The amount of effort and thought that I exert in a typical workday is quite fatiguing. I discovered that when I have a day set aside for nonproductive activity, I feel better over the course of the week that follows. I love my lazy Saturdays. My kids love lazy Saturdays, too.

Leadership costs energy; decisions and plans require that energy. Teams and stakeholders require reenergizing. Brands need refreshing. To fulfill your leadership responsibility, you must expend energy at every turn; countless leaders have told me that they value energy more than time and money. Grit—perseverance toward a long-term goal—requires energy. In order to stay the course, you need to be reenergized. It's paradoxical that to maintain your energy, you have to relax and refresh, so you have to be a little lazy. But be aware of the difference between relaxation (intentional laziness) and avoidance (habitual laziness).

Multitasking—I Want to Do It All Now

My wife prides herself on being a master multitasker. Her proof is quite compelling: she concurrently earned a doctoral degree while competing in triathlons and placing her writing in professional publications. At home, she is a master of what we call "kitchen aerobics"—organizing dinner while simultaneously returning dishes to their places and planning and executing two different lunches for the next school day. While this is compelling evidence, it isn't really proof. Her academic and athletic accomplishments happened in parallel, not simultaneously. In other words, she achieved disparate things, but they were projects that got done in discrete chunks of time; she wasn't writing her dissertation while swimming. Multitasking works for simple tasks, for those that require minimal cognitive effort like kitchen aerobics. However, when my wife engages higher cognitive functions such as problem solving, creativity, and analysis, she must focus on one complex task at a time. We can't juggle complex cognitive functions simultaneously.

For example, my wife and I like to walk around our neighborhood reservoir, Lake Murray. I remember one particular walk we shared about two months after our oldest daughter was born. On that day, we were walking at a fast clip; my wife pushed the stroller while chewing gum and discussing mundane facts about our past week. As we turned a bend, I brought up an important question about our investments. This new topic shifted our conversation from the familiar exploration of schedules and logistics to the complex process of decision making—exploring options, analyzing, and calculating degrees of uncertainty. As my wife turned her remarkable cognitive powers toward that question, I immediately noticed three things: her pace slowed, her shoulders tightened, and she stopped chewing the gum. My wife—a doctor of psychology, a graduate school professor, and an accomplished triathlete—could not think intensely and chew gum at the same time.

Multitasking generates overwhelm, not mastery. By attempting to juggle a myriad of tasks, we get pulled in multiple directions, sometimes canceling out our efforts. Perseverance is a long-term path to our goals, and multitasking forges various small trails away from the path. It disrupts the journey to results. Multitasking is especially disruptive to the application of higher cognitive skills of leadership—analyzing, planning, and prioritizing—that are critical because they work as the building blocks for decision making. Making decisions is the great contribution of leaders, in general, and of executives, in particular.

Dr. Roy Baumeister of Florida State University has focused much research on decisions and the perseverance of discipline. He asserts that self-control acts as a central function of character and an important key to success in life. Baumeister says that the exertion of self-control—deciding again and again to stay on course—appears to depend on a limited resource. Just as a muscle gets tired from exertion, decisions of self-control cause short-term impairments in subsequent self-control, even on unrelated tasks.

The price of multitasking is reduced decision effectiveness. Research demonstrates that decision fatigue affects us in all domains: eating, drinking, spending, and relationships. Critical for leadership, decision fatigue also negatively impacts intelligent thought, decision making, and interpersonal behavior. You must responsibly apply these leadership dimensions, and multitasking causes you to lose sight of your driving purpose and the clarity of your vision and mission.

Self-Negation—I'm Not Good Enough

When was the last time you thought, "I'm not good enough" or your own version of that thought? You may think to yourself that you are not _____ enough. Fill in the blank with: smart, fast, strategic, charming, decisive, attractive, considerate, competitive, analytical, authoritative, creative, worldly, educated, disciplined, or whatever else fits. Our internal self-critical voice drills away at our mind; our self-negating inner monologue drains our resolve when we most need to press through challenge and difficulty. Self-critical thoughts act as mental termites that burrow into our thinking and eat away the core strength of our psyche.

"I'm not good enough" expresses our fear of inadequacy. This universal feeling forms in early childhood. Somewhere around age two, toddlers develop a sense of personal control over physical skills and a sense of independence. Success leads to feelings of autonomy; failure breeds feelings of shame and doubt. This independence also introduces a realization of the separate self—newly independent of the mother, the child becomes acutely aware of its limitations and of scarce resources. When our young minds begin to grasp that we have limits (we can't reach the toy on that high shelf, we can't change our own diapers, we can't feed ourselves, and so on), our notion of not being adequate enough to meet our needs crystallizes. This inadequacy is neither good nor bad, but it's a fact.

Theologians, philosophers, and psychologists have long addressed this fundamental inadequacy. Christian theology describes the abiding sense of insufficiency as *original sin*. Adam and Eve committed the original sin when they ate an apple from the tree of knowledge against God's wishes; their guilt, we are told, has been passed down throughout time to every generation and every person since then. It is an ongoing repercussion of their transgressions. Zen teachers shine a light on this felt experience, too. In *Being Zen*, Ezra Bayda describes the "anxious quiver in our being." This inner trembling, he writes, remains ever present and responsible for a myriad of behaviors intended to soothe it. He explains how a pattern of beliefs and thoughts focuses particularly on our inadequacy.

Regardless of how we explain the origin of our sense of inadequacy, it is common to all of us. But when this feature is magnified in your attention, when your internal dialogue magnifies faultfinding and inadequacy, it turns into self-criticism. Criticizing the self, just as criticizing another, forms tension and separation; it creates enmity toward the self, and results in a state of detachment. Emotional detachment is a fatal flaw of leadership.

There's an important distinction between criticizing and critiquing. When you objectively critique yourself, you take stock of your strengths and areas for improvement, and you can thereby take valuable steps in your ongoing professional growth. Criticizing yourself, however, is just an aggressive repression that builds tension. A critique manifests as a detailed and unbiased evaluation of something. If you pause and reflect by asking yourself, for example, "What's my critique of how I facilitated the team meeting?" you will gain rich learning and possible improvement. Criticizing yourself just reduces your opinion of yourself. "I was really horrible in that meeting. Brian always does a better job than me." That's not a detailed evaluation; it's an attack on yourself.

When I feel criticized, I reactively want to defend myself. Defending requires that I pull away from the "danger" and shield myself from it. Whether the criticism and negation are external or internal, the reaction is similar: a defended and guarded state. Because leaders accomplish success with and through people, being defended and guarded immediately reduces leadership effectiveness. As your connection and contact dissipate with defensiveness, so does collaboration with your team, customers, and stakeholders.

Perseverance, as we've seen, requires an application of mental, emotional, and physical energy—an expense in the service of leading. We've discussed patterns that get in the way of persevering; now it's time to turn our attention to the patterns that nurture perseverance.

19

BUILDING BLOCKS OF PERSEVERANCE

The hero's journey is fashioned out of challenge, the challenge to arise from being torn down and choosing to express your abilities and intentions. The reward is nothing less than community progress and personal evolution. You earn this reward because you remain on the path and persevere when you feel tempted to give up—your heart is broken and your mind is numb, but you don't give up in bitter resignation.

This might sound idealistic, but it isn't. It's practical. More important, it's an unavoidable reality of the professional and personal journey. When I secluded myself in a mountain cabin for a yearlong meditation retreat, I expected waves

> *The hero's journey is fashioned out of challenge, the challenge to arise from being torn down and choosing to express your abilities and intentions. The reward is nothing less than community progress and personal evolution.*

of great joy and light, clarity and power. Having spent ten years dedicated to both professional accomplishments and meditation practice, I took a sabbatical designed to create a monastic stillness not available to me in the city. I was surprised, therefore—sitting alone day after day, week after week, month after month—that rather than lightness and joy, I first tasted the terribly bitter resin of depression. And I was shocked when depression occasionally bubbled into suicidal fantasies.

At the three-month mark of my seclusion, I hit an emotional low point; I realized that I was miserable, angry, and depressed. What made it so horrible in seclusion was that there was no one or nothing to blame—not my job, girlfriend, parents, friends, boss, or the government. I was 100 percent responsible. The quiet meditation practice in my voluntary solitary confinement stripped away the busyness of daily life, and I became completely attentive to the depths of my feelings for the first time. And the deeper I dove, the more I felt like a worthless worm. All the negative self-talk, all the self-negation, and all the inward animosity began getting the best of me. In the absence of perspective or anyone to dialogue with, I grew convinced that the only sensible course of action was to end it all, to kill myself.

I struggled for my life. On one side of the psychic battlefield was the Goliath of self-denial. On the opposite end of the field was the David of grit—a passionate perseverance for the long-term goal. At one point, Goliath tried to convince me that killing myself would serve society, that removing a selfish, self-centered, perpetual taker who added no value to the world would be the greatest act of kindness I could manifest.

Looking back on it now, I have much more clarity about what happened. I had pushed myself so far out of my comfort zone that I was unable to make sense of anything. What saved me was an abiding belief that I had a purpose, even though I wasn't certain what that purpose was. Practically, though, it was grit that helped me stay the course. By persevering amid the pain and self-negation, I could encourage David to defeat Goliath. The assaults of self-hate rose in waves and eventually spent their energy and dissipated. In such intimate contact with my compelling inner critic, I began to see the fallacy of his argument—the myopic determination that was born from fear, not fact. My gritty perseverance of calm and attention was eventually rewarded with a wider perspective—my life is a construct of paradox. I'm selfish and caring, angry and loving, ambitious and content, fearful and courageous, energetic and lazy. I recognized that living a full life demands grit alongside vision and courage and faith.

Liane Cordes, in her book *The Reflecting Pond: Meditations for Self-Discovery*, said, "Continuous effort—not strength or intelligence—is the key to unlocking and using our potential." While I learned more than I bargained for during my seclusion in the mountains, I was not, in fact, all alone. I was the product of untold hours of contact and care, of relationships that had fashioned and remained with me. Parents and peers, teachers and mentors—all contributed to unlocking my potential. As a leader, your task and challenge is to unlock the potential of your people, your market, and yourself. To do this calls forth your grit, and there are a number of key factors that enhance your grit:

- Gratitude: an ability to recognize and appreciate

- Purpose: a compelling reason for action

- Values: a clarity and focus on what's most important

- Discernment: an ability to make choices aligned with purpose

- Competence: repetitive behaviors to build skill and confidence

- Chunking: subdividing issues and challenges into manageable proportions

- Responsibility: maturely embracing your power and control

Gratitude

Gratitude is a foundational element of grit and of leadership. Gratitude means being thankful, showing appreciation, and returning kindness. Gratitude counterbalances the urge to complain and blame and reinforces the reality of interdependence and accomplishment; when we feel grateful, we appreciate what's already present in our lives, even as we strive for more. Since leading means striving, in the absence of gratitude that reaching can become tense and unsatisfying.

The Zen teacher Roshi John Daido Loori shared this story about gratitude:

Expressing gratitude is transformative, just as transformative as expressing complaint. Imagine two people experimenting for a year: one is asked to spend ten minutes each morning and evening expressing gratitude, while the other is asked to spend the same amount of time practicing complaining. The first person says things like, "I hate my job. I can't stand this house. Why can't I make enough money? My spouse doesn't get along with me. That dog next door never stops barking and I just can't stand this neighborhood." The other is saying things like, "I'm really grateful for the opportunity to work; there are so many people these days who can't even find a job. And I'm sure grateful for my health. What a gorgeous day; I really like this fall breeze." Guaranteed, at the end of that year the person practicing complaining will have deeply reaffirmed all of his negative "stuff," while the one practicing gratitude will be a very grateful person. Expressing gratitude can, indeed, change our way of seeing ourselves and the world.

Gratitude can occur spontaneously, but we can also cultivate it. The more space you make for gratitude through practice, the less room disappointment has to take root. Gratitude is a feeling, and it is also a behavior. When you express your gratitude for others, there arises a sincere desire to give back; appreciation can stimulate a sense of obligation—not a forced obligation or one that is externally imposed, but one internally generated as we recognize how others have supported and cared for us.

Gratitude is the opposite of complaining. It empowers you to care for, appreciate, and embrace the people who make your leadership possible. You can cultivate your gratitude when you consider these principles:

- Gratitude follows focus. If you focus your attention on evidence of gratitude, there will be much to be grateful for. Remember, we don't see the world as it is; we see the world as we are. If you want to find evidence for gratitude, look for it.

- Gratitude is a choice. Sonja Lyubomirsky, a psychology professor and author of *The How of Happiness: A New Approach to Getting the Life You Want*, wrote that external circumstances only account for ten percent of people's happiness. Even if you receive all the things that you want, that would still not ensure your happiness, nor gratitude or appreciation. Gratitude is independent of your life circumstances. Gratitude is an attitude, not a reaction.

- Say it to believe it. In order to cultivate gratitude, begin expressing it. You may not feel it deeply, but expressing gratitude in words and actions actually heightens your personal experience of it. By expressing gratitude in speech and writing you strengthen your discipline in this practice, and, over time, the habit becomes established and natural.

- Competence cultivates confidence. Continuous and deliberate practice turns effort into habit. Regularly practicing and applying gratitude strengthens your gratitude. When we continuously practice gratitude, we begin to take it for granted and feel it spontaneously. Think about the many things in your leadership that you feel grateful about—include relationships, contributions from others, and advantages and opportunities. Identify aspects of your leadership for which you can be thankful, and spend a few moments each evening writing about the things for which you are grateful. Some of the things you feel grateful for might be the same, even as some might be unique to that day.

- The gift of gratitude is perspective. Chris Peterson and Martin Seligman, coauthors of *Character Strengths and Virtues: A Handbook and Classification*, define gratitude as one of twenty-four character strengths recognized all over the world throughout time. Gratitude involves both acknowledging good things that happen—being mindful of present benefits—and recognizing that the sources of goodness lie outside us. Gratitude is a moral emotion acting as a moral barometer ("Someone else has done something good for me"), a moral motive("I will now do good things for others"), and a moral reinforcement ("Remembering good things done for me gives me energy to do good for others").

Purpose

Purpose is the focusing element we need to understand and develop among the building blocks of grit. Grit is a forward-facing principle. Running away from something isn't grit; it's fear. While fear provides a strong motivation to keep running and moving, it drives you from behind as it pushes you along. Grit, on the other hand, magnetizes you toward a long-term objective. Clarity of purpose is a critical element for successfully developing and enhancing your grittiness; this can be something as broad as your life purpose, or a more narrowly defined sense of purpose for your work, team, or project.

Purpose draws from your focus, from your answer to "What am I creating?" In formulating your focus, you keep attention toward the horizon, and in so doing *forward* becomes obvious and easy to press toward. Leadership is a constant vigilance toward the future, toward what's coming, as well as to the present, to what's happening now. Long-term goals feed grit. We persevere when the future plays an active role in moment-to-moment decision making.

I've seen a common pattern among people who are most effective at remaining on purpose. I've coined the acronym FOCUS as a thinking guide that reflects how gritty leaders articulate purpose. FOCUS is a way to concentrate your efforts forward and bring forth the elements that empower grit:

- **F—Fulfilling.** Is your goal fulfilling to you? How does this long-term goal feed your spirit? How does it make you a better person? Beyond the things that we have to do that we find challenging and difficult, how is this work feeding your soul? My job is challenging. It takes lots of attention and energy. Yet I grow and learn and make extremely rich and meaningful connections. I can press through the challenges because my work is fulfilling. My grit—my perseverance for striving to improve professionally—is fed by the fulfillment of being of service, of touching people's lives in a meaningful way.

- **O—Optimistic.** My daughter has a glass on her desk half filled with water. She keeps it there because she wants to be gritty, and gritty folks choose to look at the glass as half full. It's difficult to be gritty when you're pessimistic about your goal in particular or future in general. You can learn and practice optimism, and the optimistic aspect of FOCUS isn't just looking at the world positively, but looking forward and being engaged by the future. Being focused on the goal means that you direct yourself toward it; being optimistic about your goal means that you look forward to it. It's nearly impossible to persevere toward something that you dread.

- **C—Challenging.** Believe it or not, if the purpose is too easy or too ordinary, we lose interest in it. It's paradoxical that grit—stamina and determination in the face of difficulty—is activated by the very presence of challenge and difficulty. Being challenged has a stimulating and energizing effect when the goal is also fulfilling; you strengthen grit when you know that you're working toward something fulfilling and challenging.

- **U—Urgent.** To stay on track with your purpose, it has to entail a sense of urgency. Urgency keeps your intention top of mind and your attention focused. This might sound counterintuitive, as *grit* refers to passion and perseverance for long-term goals. Yet if the long-term goal has no sense of urgency, then it simply languishes in the "would-be-nice-someday" category. When urgency turns to stress, though, it actually consumes the ability to be gritty. What builds purpose for true grit is your continued attention to the urgency of the goal while maintaining a rational detachment from the strain and stress of the deadline.

- **S—Specific.** The final component of FOCUS is that the goal is specific; it's restricted. During strategic planning, I refer to strategy as the "art of exclusion." Being specific means honing in on one defined outcome and ignoring the other possibilities and temptations. Losing weight through diet and exercise can take a while, often longer than we wish, and saying, "I want to lose weight" is fairly useless. But saying "I want to weigh 140 pounds" is specific. "Hiring good talent" is vague; "hiring three experienced trainers" is specific.

Values

Our behaviors, choices, and relationships express our values whether we are conscious of them or not. *Values* are principles that we prize; they appeal to us in a meaningful way. When we articulate our values and keep them near, they provide a direct source of motivation and discernment. Our environments push and pull our leadership choices and behaviors; our clarified values—integrity, respect, trust, or empowerment, for example—orient our leadership toward integration and meaning. When our attitude falters and circumstances henpeck at our resolve, values give us a shot of power to stick with the journey toward change and results.

Your values are the ideas that you hold dear and important; they fuel your perseverance. For my first corporate sales job, I sold copy machines for Lanier/3M. As I drove around my territory, I carried a sample Lanier 6514 copier on a gurney in the back of my pickup. Our selling process was based on demonstrations, and my task was to demonstrate how the copier worked to business owners. I had to walk into businesses uninvited, awe prospective clients by the features and benefits of the copier, and compel them to buy or lease it. This was a tough selling environment, but it could be lucrative for a fresh college graduate. It offered a structured learning of the sales process and was known as a stepping-stone job to getting into pharmaceutical sales—the coveted sales position in 1990.

At thirty-three, Jeff was the oldest salesman in our office, and the only married man with two young children; he was an anomaly among newly minted college graduates. He also earned a comfortable living as the most consistent sales leader. I asked to ride along with Jeff for a day in the field to observe what he did that made him so effective—turned out he had no magical abilities, no secret strategy, and not much charm, either. What Jeff possessed was perseverance and consistency. When I asked him about the source of his inspiration and motivation, he pulled down the visor in his car and showed me a photo of his wife and two kids. The picture was faded from sun and finger pressure. "I value my family more than anything on this planet," Jeff shared with me. "No matter how tired or frustrated I am, they are the reason I do this." Jeff's perseverance was fueled by his values.

Multiple influences shape our values: family and friends, religion and culture, experience and circumstances, education and stories. Perseverance and self-discipline rest on a foundation of values, regardless of their origin. Values fuel our grit and influence our leadership. However, for values to provide motivation, we have to articulate them and keep them current. Courage, for example, is one of my values. I can feel when fear and anxiety take a seat at my mental conference table and attempt a hostile takeover of my decisions. By focusing on courage as a guiding value, I remember what I want to be and how I want to behave; recalling courage reminds me that I want to press on and persevere. And here's a corollary: if what you attempt to do negates your values, you will struggle to persevere. Your energy flows forward when your values support your intention.

Sophisticated assessment tools exist to guide you in uncovering your values, but here is a simple exercise that gets right to the point:

think about your coworkers and bring to mind behaviors that bother or annoy you, make you judgmental, or seem inappropriate. My wife, for example, gets bothered by arrogant and dismissive behavior. I become annoyed and judgmental of people who are late, especially if they have a pattern of arriving late. It also irritates me when people cc everyone in emails that clearly (in my mind) should remain private conversations.

What does getting annoyed and judgmental have to do with values, you might wonder? Well, we are bothered when our values are violated. My wife gets upset when people behave arrogantly in meetings, or when they present a conceited attitude. Regardless of the merits and drawbacks of arrogance, the aversion to arrogance reveals something interesting about my wife's values. When pressed to answer why she feels averse to arrogance, she opines that people should behave modestly, be kind to one another, and not overestimate their own importance. When I ask her to summarize that belief in one word she says, "Humility." My wife believes humility is an important value, and it shapes her perspective, decisions, and relationships.

Here's another example. A few years ago, I was enjoying spicy Thai food with Jon, a good-natured fellow board member who shared with me his frustration with Bruce, another of our board members. Jon recalled with agitation that Bruce sent an email chastising our board president and cc'd it to the entire board. While the email contained valid comments about the president's recent decision, Jon was disturbed that everyone was cc'd. Before we delved into the political pros and cons of making a conversation public, I wanted to understand Jon's belief about etiquette, so I asked him to explain his upset regarding this email. Jon quickly explained that people should always keep in mind the honor of others. He spoke easily and quickly about his belief. The whole cc'ing process dishonors the president, he told me. When I asked him to label which principle had been violated, he said, "Respect." Respect is a key value for Jon, and it directly affects how he relates and behaves.

Your values shape and guide your leadership, just as they shape and guide your grit. By studying yourself, you discern your values and name them. Gritty leaders articulate their values. Your clarified values serve both as guardrails keeping you on the path, and as crutches propping you up when your resolve is sapped and lacking.

Discernment

Discernment refers to your ability to apply good judgment in making choices that bring you closer to your goal. Let's imagine three scenarios where discernment yields discipline and grit.

Scenario 1: It's morning and my alarm clock dutifully chirps at 5:00 a.m. The narcotic effect of sleep clings to my body and mind as the soft sounds of waking nag at my attention. I could reach out my arm from under the covers and hit the seven-minute snooze, or I could pull my body out of bed and start the day as I had planned the night before. In this moment, discernment is called to action.

Scenario 2: It's rush hour. Traffic is jammed up as usual. I'm at risk of running late to my morning meeting, and I hate being late. Suddenly, without any indication, a red van lurches into the lane in front of me. I quickly jam on the brakes and, fortunately, avoid a collision. Unfortunately, I have lost a couple of critical feet in the interminably slow movement toward my inevitable late appearance. My skin starts to tingle with heat, and my internal conversation turns to calling the driver unflattering names as anger arises. This is a moment to call forth my discernment. Will I choose to breathe and dissolve my growing anger, or will I allow the wave of habit to wash over me and shape my behavior?

Scenario 3: I'm enjoying dinner with our division president. She informs me that the largest player in our market has just submitted an intention to buy our company. She tells me this in confidence, and I learn that it will become public knowledge in a week or so. The next day my stockbroker calls me to tell me about an opportunity in one of my funds and to find out what I want to do about it. At the end of the conversation he asks if there are any trades I'd like to execute. Our company is public and about to be greatly valued by the merger; I have the inside scoop for trading. Discernment will shape my choice.

These scenarios, like countless other moments in your leadership journey, require discernment—acuteness of judgment. To discern means to grasp the nature of a situation and to make an appropriate choice. Our journey cannot unfold in a conscious way until we learn to discern; you can be discerning only when your awareness is open and active because to be aware you must choose where to place your attention. In turn, choosing where to place your attention requires discernment.

Grit is a momentary choice as well as a string of choices that accumulate and build momentum. I can choose to stay in bed an extra hour or get up and start my day, but not both. I can choose to react angrily or calmly to a situation, but not both. I can choose to pay attention to my partner in conversation or I can pay attention to my internal dialogue, but not both. Without the application of deliberate choice—discernment—there is no conscious leadership. In fact, we cannot fully utilize our gift of free will until we develop discernment and engage in fully conscious decision making.

Being discerning is the opposite of being reactive and thoughtless. Philosophers and religious teachers emphasize discernment. For instance, Buddhist teachings about the way to enlightenment are based on the notion of the "eightfold noble path." This path entails three categories: *sila* (ethical conduct), *samadhi* (concentration), and *prajna* (wisdom). Buddhism teaches that morality serves as the foundation from which concentration and wisdom emerge. Sila—morality—is a code of ethics and conduct that relies on discernment, on choice. In essence, we can choose acceptable or unacceptable behaviors, and choosing the acceptable ones is equated with morality. Christianity similarly advocates for discernment, as Jesus taught that "no man can serve two masters." We can choose to travel only in one direction at a time.

Discernment and decision making serve another important function of grit. Grit is discipline—nothing less than an accumulation of deliberate and consistent choices that move you toward a desired achievement. Discipline is not a complicated principle. At given junctures we make choices, and if the choices are consistent with my intention, then that is discipline. If my choices vary from my intention, that displays a lack of discipline. Discipline implies consistency, perseverance, determination, will, commitment, and accountability—all foundational requirements for traveling the hero's journey.

Discernment doesn't happen in a vacuum; it requires a context or a measure for comparison. That measure is your focus, the answer to "What am I creating?" In *Alice's Adventures in Wonderland*, Lewis Carroll captures the idea in a conversation between Alice and the Cheshire Cat:

> Alice: Would you tell me, please, which way I ought to go from here?
>
> The Cat: That depends a good deal on where you want to get to.
>
> Alice: I don't much care where.
>
> The Cat: Then it doesn't much matter which way you go.
>
> Alice: . . . so long as I get somewhere.
>
> The Cat: Oh, you're sure to do that, if only you walk long enough.

Competence

I enjoy public speaking in spite of the anxious waves that ripple through me before almost every presentation or keynote. But the anxious waves don't diminish my enjoyment or passion for it, or my audience's enthusiastic response. Speaking is one of my professional strengths. My presentations are inspirational, my style is approachable (even as I challenge my audience to self-reflect and challenge themselves), and my message is practical for leaders. I am making a point here beyond this shameless plug: I like public speaking because I'm good at it, and since I've put in the time and effort and have become strong in the skill, the act itself is rewarding. I do it because I like it. I like doing it because I'm good at it, and I'm good at it because I'm well practiced at it.

Admittedly, I didn't always enjoy public speaking; in fact, it first terrified me. I vividly recall Speech 101, a mandatory class requirement in college—my first assignment was to write and present a five-minute persuasive speech intended to influence my classmates. I spent weeks to prepare that five-minute speech, and I felt sick to my stomach whenever I thought about the upcoming presentation. Even though I no longer remember the speech topic, I easily recall that the entire semester was darkened by that class—for fifteen weeks, fear was my constant companion and panic was close at hand.

So how did I travel from panicking over a five-minute class presentation to enjoying hour-long keynotes? I've become skilled and expert through practice, feedback, mentoring, and coaching. And the reward of competence is confidence. Grit is the effort you must apply in order to climb up the learning curve, to grow in skill and ability, and to achieve competence. In turn, that competence (and the confidence it brings) feeds your grit.

Being gritty, though, is not the same as being stubborn. Stubborn leaders are rigid and unwilling to change their minds; gritty leaders are persevering, determined, and unwilling to capitulate to circumstances or admit defeat when challenged. Choosing grit draws heavily on inner resources, self-confidence, and self-esteem, which, in turn, all relate to competence.

Things that we're good at we like to do, and we're good at things that we've practiced. Marc, for example, was a well-regarded CFO who loved to roll up his sleeves and work with his staff to solve problems. Although Marc was accomplished at solving problems himself, he wasn't well rehearsed at coaching his staff members to become skilled problem solvers in their own right, and because he wasn't a good coach, he didn't like to coach. Consequently, he didn't spend any time coaching his staff. The firm's succession plan, however, required Marc to develop and train a suitable replacement, and Marc's boss, the CEO, insisted that Marc coach two key team members.

I taught Marc the essential elements of applied coaching: setting near-term and midterm goals, using open-ended questions to understand the current situation, thinking collaboratively to identify ways to close the gap between goals and the current situation, and committing to specific next steps. Yet for Marc to adapt his old way, he needed more than an intellectual understanding of the process—he required proficiency that grows from practice and feedback. He needed to get good enough to become confident enough with this skill to regularly incorporate it into his leadership. Competence cultivates confidence and self-esteem.

William James, considered the father of modern psychology, wrote in his 1890 book *Principles of Psychology* that self-esteem was a ratio of successes divided by aspirations. Decades of prolific research and experience show that self-esteem and confidence emerge in the context of achievement through trial and effort. Praise alone, or honor without effort, does not build personal strength. In his book, *The Psychology of Self-Esteem,* Nathaniel Branden said, "Self-esteem has two interrelated aspects: it entails a sense of personal efficacy and a sense of personal worth. It is the integrated sum of self-confidence and self-respect. It is the conviction that one is competent to live and worthy of living." Self-confidence and self-esteem are related to competence. Competence, in turn, grows from practice and grit.

Self-esteem builds from two sides: achieving successes in areas meaningful and important to us, and having significant others recognize us. Competence—the ability to do something proficiently and skillfully—arises from experience, practice, and feedback. Bill Gates, founder of Microsoft, for example, slept six hours per night and never a missed a day at work during the early years of the company. By his own accounts, he grew his competence as an entrepreneur and leader though a gritty application of time and repetition. Gates references hard work as one of the pillars of success that strengthened his self-confidence as a leader and increased his trust in his own judgment and ability.

Grit, therefore, is fueled by self-esteem and self-confidence. We often treat these two terms as synonyms, but they differ in an important way. Self-confidence is situational; it rises and falls in the context of circumstances. For example, when I was promoted to director, I achieved a coveted career goal, and a wave of pride swelled through my body when my boss announced the promotion. I left work that Friday feeling validated and energized. But by Monday morning, my excitement was tinged with concern; I realized that I wasn't sure how to effectively fulfill my new responsibilities. When I arrived at work on Monday, my determination was as robust as ever, but my confidence was shaken as I realized that I was not competent for my new role. There is nothing like being promoted to suddenly make us feel incompetent.

Self-esteem, however, is cumulative; it grows over time and is less susceptible to circumstances. To illustrate the difference between self-confidence and self-esteem, imagine that your psyche is a tree trunk. Self-esteem lies at the core of the trunk, the hard woody center of the tree that grows and expands year after year. Some years the growth is minimal and some years, when conditions are favorable, a thick ring of growth is added. Grit creates those favorable conditions that contribute to the growth of your core self-esteem. In this metaphor, self-confidence is the bark of the tree—the outer layer of the psyche that immediately touches the world and in continual contact with the environment. Sun, wind, birds, and teenagers with pocketknives shape the bark. Similarly, situational influences of work, relationships, and finances touch and shape our self-confidence.

Take Sandy, for example. She is a forty-four-year-old senior product manager who has grown in her leadership effectiveness as time and learning have sharpened her judgment. Her confidence has swelled in line with her competence. Over time, the core of her esteem has grown strong enough that periodic pressures or threats won't hurt her confidence. In fact, a symptom of healthy self-esteem is to accept challenges and rise beyond our competence; challenging ourselves to leave the comfort zone becomes par for the course, where once lurked mostly anxiety. When starting a new and important venture, Sandy reports that her self-confidence runs temporarily low even as her self-esteem remains strong. Gritty leaders draw on their esteem and confidence to press on in the face of challenge, disheartenment, and uncertainty.

Chunking

"Fall down seven times, get up eight," a Chinese proverb teaches us. If you fixate on all seven falls together, you might become despondent at the pattern of collapse, but if you consider each fall as a single event, it's easier to think of it as a momentary setback. That's "chunking"—reducing difficult experiences to smaller, more manageable, events. As a child, whenever I faced a challenge that seemed overwhelming, my dad would ask me, "How do you eat an elephant?" Even though I'd heard this question countless times, I still loved the answer: "One bite at a time." Grit is a passionate and persevering march accomplished one step at a time.

At fifty-two, my friend Shawn has worked as a successful CPA for many years. He was an air force officer, is charming, and is a respected pillar of our community. However, getting his office filing up-to-date and organized stymied him—papers (not client documents, his own papers) piled up on his desk, floor, credenza, chairs . . . everywhere! We laughed at ourselves because we're both so organized in our professional dealings, yet downright overwhelmed by paper. I asked Shawn what he saw in his mind's eye when he thought about the papers piling around him. "It's a mountain of paper bearing down on me, a darn Mount Everest of paper." Shawn readily admitted that when he visualizes this looming and unconquerable mountain, he can practically feel it crushing his will to persevere.

Shawn gave up his attempts to tame the papers when this imaginary mountain grew bigger than his organizational skills. For Shawn to change his behavior and implement a new routine, he had to chunk down the mountain into a manageable dimension. Lao-tzu, a Chinese philosopher, wrote, "The journey of a thousand miles begins with a single step." Goals are made up of subsets, and long-term goals are achieved one step after the other. Chunking breaks down a large commitment into manageable pieces and parts.

Shawn decided to take this approach and shifted his attention from the grand goal of scaling his mountain of paperwork to handling one chunk of the process. He committed to clearing his credenza; he succeeded in this smaller task and felt energized about tackling the floor near the southern window next. Within a week, by addressing his large task a chunk at a time, Shawn had cleared his office. This might seem like a trivial accomplishment for an otherwise accomplished man, but it was the effective application of chunking that enabled Shawn to press on in the face of overwhelm and frustration.

Responsibility

When my gas tank gets low, my car rings a bell and an amber-colored symbol glows on the dashboard to draw my attention to the issue. I used to drive until my fuel tank got as empty as possible before refilling, but a frightening early fatherhood experience changed my pattern. When our daughter was eight weeks old, she was due for an immunization shot. Neither my wife nor I are physicians, and we were aware of the rich debate about the pros and cons of vaccination; both sides cite scientific research as their proof. We wrestled with conflicting data about vaccines and their side effects, as we tried to ferret out the truth about their safety and efficacy. After our research and discussion, we decided that getting the shots was better than rejecting them. As a leader in an organization, you know this decision-making process well and how significant it is to make the best choice in the midst of conflicting data. The decisions you have to make are rarely black and white, and more frequently you have to decide from among multiple—and even competing—options. Sometimes there isn't an ideal option, but still you have to select the one you deem better than the others.

On the day that our daughter received her vaccine shot, we took turns doting over her (yes, even more than usual). Late that same night, I sat on our couch with her bundled in my arms, and I remember marveling at nature and life as I gazed at this beautiful and amazing being. Even as my heart was filled with love and affection, I was also aware of my nagging concern about the possible side effects of the vaccine. As I sat there gazing and worrying, my seven-pound baby suddenly convulsed with two powerful coughs and began to froth at the mouth. Her breathing became labored, and her skin tone changed from pink to blue.

I was not prepared for the shock that gripped me. I pride myself on being dependable in emergencies—I am a trained rescue diver, a diving instructor, and I taught first aid and CPR. Yet the shuddering of my baby girl wiped away my clear thinking like formulas being quickly deleted from a dry erase board. Fortunately, my wife stayed calm and directed me to get in the car and drive to the hospital. When I got in the car and turned the key in the ignition, a little bell rang and a bright-orange symbol flashed on the dashboard indicating that I was practically out of gas. I've never let the tank go below a quarter tank since then. I changed my habit on the spot.

Unpleasant and uncontrollable events and situations happen all the time. Your leadership role requires you to respond to changes that challenge you, your team, and your mission. I chose to give my daughter the vaccine, just as I chose to run low on fuel in the car. While I hated the terrible situation I was in, I had to take responsibility for my actions and, most important, responsibility for my reactions. Being willing to bear the mantle of responsibility is an act of maturity and a significant building block of grit.

Consider this frustrating Monday that began with the dashboard fuel indicator lighting up on my way to an early meeting. As I pulled into the gas station, I felt my frustration percolating. My wife had used my car the night before to drive our daughters to a Girl Scout function, and she ran the car to near empty. In my frustrated inner monologue, I blamed her for ruining my commitment to always have gas in the tank. Then, arriving home after a full day at work, I heard the phone ring and quickly made my way to the phone base by the kitchen—where the wireless receiver was nowhere to be found. I've nagged, threatened, and cajoled my kids to return the phone to the charger, but it wasn't there. As the phone rang and rang, I grew agitated, and I ranted at my kids for being irresponsible. Living and working with people invariably creates conflict; I can't turn everyone into machines that perform exactly as I want and expect. When my ideas and ideals are challenged, the urge to blame comes on swift and strong. Nevertheless, leading requires maturity—accepting responsibility for circumstances.

My frustrations were not over. The next day at work I got a call from a vendor asking to expedite a payment on an invoice that was past due. Yes, I'm in charge of the business, but I don't handle our bookkeeping. My thoughts quickly jumped to find a person to blame. Team members can fall short of our expectations, and unmet expectations are a primary source of frustration for leaders. The urge to blame circumstances, individuals, and teams is strong and instantaneous; blame, however, steals the heroic spirit and retards the power of perseverance. Perseverance is a commitment to your focus, to the question "What am I creating?" To persevere means to choose to apply your effort and energy even as the environment and circumstances challenge you. Blaming, on the other hand, gives power to circumstances.

When you blame, you assign authority to the environment and stop focusing on the power of creating and shaping circumstances; your blaming mind-set gives credence to a state of helplessness and victimization. The empowering question "What am I creating?" is replaced by a disempowering one: "Why is this happening to me?" We don't have the power to single-handedly shape our world, but we do have the power to choose our reactions to circumstances. That's how I followed a path away from the blaming mood and back to the heroic spirit—recalling my focus, practicing my cultivation of courage, and reflecting on my values.

When we blame we attribute fault to someone or something outside of ourselves. When I blame, I absolve myself of responsibility for a situation because blaming negates responsibility and accountability. Of course, people make mistakes and get things wrong; they make wrong choices and act unskillfully. Your role is to coach and teach your people to grow in critical thinking and good judgment. To become an effective leader you have to become skilled at turning mistakes into teaching opportunities and steering clear of blame.

Responsibility is a hallmark of maturity, and mature leaders defy conventional math. In conventional math, 100 percent represents totality. In the instance of the late payment, for example, I could claim that my staff was slightly more responsible for the situation and, therefore, were 60 percent responsible and I was 40 percent responsible.

However, in leadership math, I was 100 percent responsible; my staff was also 100 percent responsible. The nature of maturity is to be accountable, to be dependable, and to take ownership of your choices and behaviors. This mind-set of ownership energizes grit. When I blame, I deny my full responsibility; when I blame, I hand over my power, engagement, and creativity. I bow out of my grittiness and resolve, and become a victim of circumstance.

Blaming is the opposite of responsibility and maturity. Leaders on the hero's journey willingly accept accountability rather than place blame on another person. I could have turned to blaming as a reaction to the situations I described above; doctors to blame for my daughter's convulsions, staff to blame for late payment, and my children to blame for not putting the phone back. However, while we must hold people responsible for their actions, a leader who blames does not take responsibility for her world or domain.

Blaming and persevering cannot comfortably coexist in one mind. Perseverance means choosing to keep applying yourself when circumstances appear unfavorable and your enthusiasm has waned. Blaming, on the contrary, means that you squander your power and externalize responsibility to someone or something beyond you. The leader who blames abdicates her sense of responsibility; she squanders her personal power and with it her ability to press through difficulty or doubt. When you find yourself caught in a conversation of blame, pause and ask yourself, "What is my part in the situation? What is my responsibility here as a leader?" Yes, the urge to blame is instinctive, but the habit of blaming is not acceptable for leaders on the hero's journey.

20

PARTNERING FOR PERSEVERANCE

We've all heard that misery loves company. Well, misery is not the only extroverted emotion dancing on the stage of our minds; perseverance loves company, too. While on the hero's journey, you will meet multiple foes and challenges, but you're not alone—heroes almost always have companions: Luke Skywalker has R2-D2, Han Solo, Princess Leia, and Yoda; Dorothy travels through Oz with Toto, Tin Man, Cowardly Lion, and Scarecrow; King Arthur has his Knights of the Round Table; even Jack Bauer on the television drama *24* has his allies, helpers, and supporters.

I've seen this play out during a monthly CEO roundtable that I have been facilitating for years. Each one of the leaders in the group is on his or her own hero's journey, and each person is ultimately responsible for the successes and results of his or her organization. While part of a team, each leader has to face challenges on their own. The paradox of the hero's journey is that the leader is both *part of* and *apart from* his or her team. The notion that the hero's journey is performed by some solitary champion who can single-handedly free the town from the dragon is misguided and dangerous—leaders require support and help to maintain their perseverance. In fact, the energy to persevere during difficult periods often comes from their commitment to the team, because the relationship with supporters flows both ways: they provide the leader with resources and encouragement, and the leader provides them with dedication and direction.

Here's an illustration of this principle. Don, the GM of a technology company, took a significant gamble on his division and made a major investment in new equipment and people. Having analyzed market reports and competitive analysis, he believed that it was the right time for the capital expenditure. By all accounts, Don's vision and decision were well placed. His logic and passion convinced his CEO and the board to go along with the plan, but none of them predicted the precipitous decline of the US economy just a year after Don invested the money. A dark six months ensued. Don and his team had to persevere through dangerously anemic market conditions. The money was already spent and committed and everyone was on board, but after two months of intense personal deliberation, Don realized that he could no longer pretend to successfully persevere through this period of time in solitary stoicism. He needed and wanted support.

Don unwrapped his mind from the clingy cellophane of self-centered thinking and looked around for partners and allies. First he engaged his CEO (after avoiding him for two months) in a frank conversation that outlined and described his vision, the current challenges, and his ideas for overcoming them. With his CEO's commitment, they made a plan for a pitch to the board—their investors. Finally, armed with support and buy-in for a revised plan, he reconvened his team and together they devised a plan to curb costs and adjust their go-to-market approach, show breakeven within three months, and profitability within eight months. They persevered together and met their plan. As a result of enlisting support from his team, board, and CEO, Don was able to both grow as a leader and produce remarkable results.

Don overcame the compelling but false delusion of the self-made man. The term *self-made* is misleading. Yes, you have to make continuous choices that move you toward your vision and goals. No, you don't have to exhaust yourself through isolation. The most persevering people have set up an environment that feeds their grit, as grit is more than just clenching your teeth and pushing on—that kind of intensity works well only in short intervals. Gritty leaders are sustained by systems, processes, and relationships that promote and nurture their grit. They orchestrate settings that promote and sustain perseverance and consistency. They surround themselves with allies and guides that provide ideas, insights, emotional support, tools, and introductions to key people.

To illustrate the power of partnerships for building grit, let's look beyond the challenge of leadership to two other widespread and familiar challenges: losing weight and overcoming addiction. For those struggling with alcoholism or fighting to achieve a healthy body mass, perseverance and self-discipline are paramount. The individual's commitment to sobriety and/or to diet and fitness is the hallmark of achieving these goals. If individual commitment were enough though,

It is not weakness to lean on an ally; it is wisdom. Effective leadership blossoms when you acknowledge that engaging allies and guides is a necessity, not a privilege.

then every alcoholic and every dieter would become successful by sheer force of will, but this isn't the case. You attain success by combining your willpower with daily practice and relationships that support you.

You are influenced by your relationships. By applying a mathematical model to data from the Framingham Heart Study, Harvard researchers found that the more obese friends you have, the more likely you are to become obese yourself. This confirms previous research that gaining weight may be "socially contagious"—the people we surround ourselves with directly influence our choices and outcomes; they feed our grit or starve it.

The chances of overcoming the seductive grip of addiction decrease when approached alone. The power of Alcoholics Anonymous mostly lies in the fellowship and environment of mutual support that it fosters. Similarly, Jenny Craig, Weight Watchers, and other weight-loss programs succeed largely as a result of the power of their coaches and peer support rather than their low-calorie meals. Your leadership demands grit in order to continuously press into and through uncertainty and change. However, there is a limit to the amount of grit that is self-generated; it has to be refreshed in relationships that provide encouragement and support.

Inevitably your conviction and confidence will falter, your focus will fade, and your imagination will stutter. During these depleted times, your allies energize, encourage, and remind you of your mission and ability. It is not weakness to lean on an ally; it is wisdom. Effective leadership blossoms when you acknowledge that engaging allies and guides is a necessity, not a privilege.

Types of Allies

As we discussed previously, the myth of the isolated hero renders leaders ineffective if they elect to believe it. Too often, we take on leadership challenges by ourselves, carrying the weight of success and failure on our shoulders, and buying into the myth of the singular hero makes that weight even heavier. The urge to "go it alone" could be driven by selfishness or silliness, but either way it serves ego needs more than team needs.

Even fictional superheroes rely on allies. Robin and Alfred routinely help Batman out of tight jams. Lois Lane emotionally nurtures Superman and serves as a confidant and motivator. And I-Ching mentors Wonder Woman to find her power and direction. Historical heroes who changed the world also leaned on their relationships: Dr. Martin Luther King Jr., for example, led the fight for civil rights flanked by Rev. Ralph Abernathy, Jesse Jackson, and Hosea Williams, among other allies.

The greatest heroes and leaders surround themselves with four types of allies on the hero's journey: mentors, coaches, peers, and loved ones.

Types of Allies

	Mentor	Coach	Peer	Loved One
Qualification	Time and experience	Training in inquiry	Common goals	Emotional commitment
Motivation	Love of teaching	Passion for discovery	Team success	Care and appreciation
Objective	Career evolution	Personal growth	Achievement	Happiness
Contribution	Ideas and connections	Questions and perspective	Encouragement and application	Emotional renewal
Tools	Memory	Inquiry	Collaboration	Connection

Mentors are guides who have themselves already traveled the path ahead of you; they know the territory from experience. Mentors are people you want to emulate; people you want to be like. The word *mentor* comes from *The Odyssey*, Homer's classic telling of Odysseus's heroic journey. When King Odysseus left home to fight in the Trojan War, he entrusted his loyal adviser, a man named Mentor, to care for and educate his son, Telemachus. Mentors serve as resources when you don't know what to do because you lack knowledge and experience, or when your perseverance hits a wall. You can scale these walls more quickly when a trusted mentor boosts you up; your mentor can provide you tools, wise words, or a critical introduction.

I've had mentors throughout my life. Initially, I searched for a single mentor who could provide answers and insights for every facet of my life. However, because my talents, skills, dreams, fears, experiences, and relationships are unique, no one person could match my journey. My mentors are somewhat specialized; I engage with different guides for my business, relationship, and spiritual needs. Even my business mentors are split between those who guide my professional growth as a coach, author, and consultant, and those who guide me as a leader, entrepreneur, and team builder.

A mentor provides support and feeds your perseverance by doing the following:

- Encouraging and motivating you
- Sharing knowledge and experience
- Asking challenging questions with care and kindness
- Contributing to your growth and success
- Investing regular time in your relationship
- Illuminating topics that are scary or overwhelming
- Connecting you with other people and resources

Coaches differ from mentors in perspective. A mentor, having glimpsed your potential future from the perch of his or her own experience, hovers above you and shares direction and instruction. Coaches travel shoulder-to-shoulder with you and help you make great decisions and commitments. Coaches accelerate your results and learning through trust, curiosity, and collaboration.

While your grit is energized by a mentor's answers, it is also fueled by a coach's questions. Archimedes, a Greek engineer and inventor who lived about 250 BCE, famously said, "Give me a lever long enough and a fulcrum on which to place it, and I shall move the world." The curiosity and questioning of an experienced coach is a lever with which you shift your mind. With a coach's help, shifting your mind changes your world.

I spend 35 percent of my work time providing executive coaching. As a coach, I support executives to make better decisions, engage their teams, become more productive, and achieve better results. My clients are accomplished leaders who lead impressive teams; they produce important results and touch many lives. As part of my coaching, I share my experiences in management and leadership and draw on my experience to educate and inform them, but my greatest contribution as a coach goes beyond answering questions; it lies in questioning answers. In the collaborative process of inquiry, we uncover root causes, challenge assumptions, and bring forth new possibilities. Consider what questions can do:

- They initiate a variety of solutions. Questions pierce mental myopia and prompt creative problem solving.

- They inspire thinking, because it's practically impossible to ask a question of a thinking person and *not* have them start looking for an answer.

- They advance your quest (the root of *quest*ion). Curiosity and questions serve as tools of seeking and searching—the gear with which you produce results.

- They unfold your perspective. Curiosity breeds wonder and by extension reveals more details about work, people, and life.

- They open a gate for leaving the comfort zone.
  Questions can lead your mind to places you haven't
  ventured or visited. These unexplored domains contain
  potential, possibility, and the raw material of growth
  and innovation.

- They induce deep thought; they exercise the neocortex,
  our human gift. Questions stretch, grow, and expand
  our mind.

- They momentarily change your pace. Questions can slow
  down your frenzied overwhelm and, in the pause, allow
  the quieter whispers of insight and clarity to arise and
  enter the conversation.

- They cut through to the heart of the issue. Like a warm
  sun rising over a foggy beach, some questions burn away
  the haze and confusion of obsessive thinking and point
  the mind forward and upward.

Peers share your aspiration and your pain. Peers differ from mentors and coaches as they experience your triumphs and challenges in real time, and this shared journey provides context for understanding and partnership, collaboration, and a real potential for competition, too. A peer isn't an automatic ally, and some of my greatest competitors and detractors were my coworkers. I experienced the dark side of peer relationships as a fast-rising manager in a multibillion-dollar corporation. Our GM recognized my abilities and potential and decided to mentor me and accelerate my career. He liked me, in part, because our styles were similar, and he identified with my intensity and drive. I reminded him of his younger self; I was ambitious and goal directed and primarily concerned with accomplishment rather than with relationships.

Following a quick series of professional wins for myself and my team, he promoted me to senior manager; it was not received well by my fellow managers and new peers that had been with the company longer, were older than me, and were networked with one another. My style was brash, aggressive, and arrogant, and I was neither respectful nor considerate of them, their teams, or their needs. Honestly, in reflection, I was a myopic blockhead who had potential and ability but lacked emotional intelligence and political acumen.

Because of my attitude and newcomer status, the constant doting by our GM maddened my peers as they received less attention, opportunity, and praise than I did. When our GM built a new office suite upstairs, he vacated the large downstairs office and invited me to move into this cavernous space, which I, foolishly, accepted. Wouldn't you? That was the final nail in the coffin of my peer relations and united them in mutually resenting me. Even though I had a mentor in the GM, the competition with my peers diminished my abilities and achievements; they were slow to share resources, left me out of critical information, occasionally neglected to invite me to meetings, and didn't encourage their teams to support mine. In fact, the positive effect of having a mentor was overwhelmed by the damaging effect of negative peer relations. I felt frustrated and humbled in that job as I learned about leadership maturity and relationship intelligence. As I grew, I changed my relationships with my peers and eventually bonded with some of them as allies who emboldened my grit and helped me achieve goals I didn't think I could accomplish.

Mentors offer directions and wisdom from their perch at the end of your path. Coaches probe and question in order to sharpen your decisions and competence. Peers offer perspective and accountability. Peer pressure is the influence exerted by our peer group that encourages us to change in order to conform to group norms—the power of peer pressure can influence us to smoke or cheat, for example. The power of our peers can also influence us to excel or rise above our selfishness.

Peers shape our attitudes and choices. I remember my mother insisting on approving or vetoing my friends in school, and I recall how bothered I was by her opinions. "Dan is impolite and selfish and not a good influence on you," she'd say. "I don't want you to spend any time with him. Why don't you play with Gidi? He's considerate, studies, and gets good grades." I recently realized that I have become my mother in conversations with my daughters as I, too, try to orchestrate my children's peer groups. While my wife and I shape our children's values and teach them good judgment, their peers and friends provide potent modeling regarding grades, behavior, and attitudes. Peer influence is especially strong in the teen years, when children want to separate from their parents, but it continues to shape us throughout our lives. By being selective and purposeful about your peers, you shape your sources of influence, so leverage the peer pressure principle by carefully selecting the makeup of your peers. When your grittiness wavers, you don't have to single-handedly energize it; allow yourself to receive the encouragement and support of your peers.

Peer pressure is positively correlated with grit. The supportive force of our peers gives us the energy and courage to try things we otherwise wouldn't, and their encouragement emboldens us to keep pressing forward when our mind and body want to quit. Yes, leadership is a hero's journey, but a hero isn't a solitary figure.

A peer supports your journey by doing the following:

- Encouraging you in real-time, in the midst of action, not before or after

- Actually shouldering a portion of the burden or challenge

- Empathizing with your feelings and experience

- Collaborating with you in problem solving, especially on shared projects

- Providing the camaraderie that lifts the spirit

Loved ones are allies who care about you. They are emotionally vested in your well-being. When the journey of leadership bruises and scrapes your ego, mind, and heart, the healing salve of love, applied by those who care for you, keeps you whole. My wife's loving hug has the power to melt the icicles of tension in my shoulders. On days when fatigue and frustration have had their way with me, my daughters' doting inspires and restores me. Spouses, parents, children, lovers, and friends can offer us unconditional support; they don't expect that we produce a return for their love. They are able to share of themselves for our well-being.

Given that our loved ones are so important to us, do you wonder why you treat your family in ways that you would never behave with colleagues? Why is it okay to argue intensely with your spouse while you must be considerate and rational with your coworkers? We allow ourselves these intense family interactions because we are secure in the connection; we expect that power struggles with loved ones will get resolved, that mutual care will trump the emotional ebbs and flows of our lives. That sense of security and strength of connections are the reasons why loved ones are critical allies on our journey.

When you turn to a loved one for support or affection, their care for you helps them respond appropriately, to set their own concerns aside in order to address yours. Loved ones help you for several reasons. The first reason is the satisfaction they feel glowing within as they give aid and support to a loved one. The second reason is gratitude, a "goodwill credit" that naturally builds up. We humans have a tendency to reciprocate kindness with kindness.

Each time we act on behalf of the people we care about, we ensure that help and support will come back to us—by being there for our loved ones, we strengthen and energize a network of support. At varying times in your leadership journey, you will find yourself on different sides of the network: sometimes you will be in a position to support the people most important to you, and other times you will receive their help. Each time you consciously choose to consider the needs and feelings of your loved ones, you inspire them to do the same, and the cycle of support that begins with you spreads outward to create a mood of mutual encouragement. In helping others today, you begin building a complex system of support that will serve you when you need help tomorrow.

Learn to receive support and care from your loved ones. Although you provide for your loved ones, they can also provide for you. Willingly receiving nurturance from them increases the trust and bond between you, and willingly receiving energy and wisdom from your loved ones strengthens your grit when you get too depleted to renew it yourself.

21

HOW DO YOU TALK TO YOURSELF?

An unpleasant legal situation at work offered me a clear look at the power of my attitude and its effect on my grit. When a difference of opinion and perceptions became irreconcilable, hurt feelings ensued, and the other party really wanted to win, in part by trying to hurt us financially and legally. It was my first brush with the legal process in my professional capacity; I have been fortunate to have resolved conflicts in person rather than in court. The real source of stress in this process, beyond the obvious, came from my feeling of disempowerment—I was not in control and couldn't unilaterally bend the situation to my will. Two influences dominated my attitude: First, I felt the trembling fingers of my inner victim clawing at my thinking. Second, I was grasping for certainty and trying to force a tight grip on my thoughts. However, in the legal process, I was just one part in a big machine. My attitude faltered. My inner dialogue, the narrative I wove about the situation, gradually turned darker and more desperate.

Our attorney's attitude, by contrast, was positive and hopeful. Her experience and expertise drew very different conclusions from mine about the situation we faced. Yes, the uncertainty of the legal process was as real to her as it was to us, but she thought about it in a different way than I did. Our attitudes differed radically because they reflected different experiences and different internal conversations. Remember that a thought is a thing; you are what you think and you become what you think about most. My attorney's thoughts and story focused on strategy and process, and she felt competitive and energized, whereas my story and mental chatter pivoted around my lack of power and control, and I felt anxious and agitated. As my attitude worsened, I became less available and more distant from my team.

I couldn't force the legal process to satisfy my wishes; the situation had to run its course. Yet if my attitude continued to darken, I would lose my ability to think clearly and remain engaged. I did, though, have the capacity to change my experience of the conflict by addressing the quality and substance of my thoughts, because I have learned that an attitude is malleable and can be reshaped by selecting what I recite in my mind. To bolster my grit, I had to change my attitude, and as I became more selective about the thoughts I dwelled on, my attitude improved and, by direct influence, my team's attitude got better, too.

Leaders' attitudes have a direct impact on the attitude of their organization. When your attitude sinks, when your self-talk and inner story turn hopeless and helpless, perseverance seems difficult and unlikely. Healthy leaders have a choice about what they would like to recite to themselves. The heroic attitude means you choose how you frame and interpret a difficult situation. Data are objective, knowledge is subjective, and we make meaning of the world around us by interpreting data—an interpretive process shaped by what we purposefully attend to.

Leaders who choose to embrace the hero's journey don't magically erase the urge to feel victimized. Feeling overwhelmed by circumstances and environment is not a choice; it is a mental and emotional reaction. When you choose to embrace the hero's stance, you are not removed from the ordinary experience of mind and heart. It is precisely because of overwhelm and our emotional reaction to it that we can practice the heroic mind-set. You will at some point feel hopeless, helpless, overcome, and outgunned, but your interpretation, decision making, and attitude will give you the wherewithal to persevere in the face of difficulty.

Successful leaders have the courage to face those disempowering conversations running through their minds.

I'm not suggesting you overcome your inner struggles simply by applying a thin veneer of positive self-talk on your thoughts; I'm proposing that successful leaders have the courage to face those disempowering conversations running through their minds. You don't have to destroy these conversations; you have to diminish their power over you. You accomplish that with courageous and persistent observation, not by whitewashing with happy thoughts.

The Rolling Stones remind us of this in their popular song "You Can't Always Get What You Want." Circumstances can stimulate, challenge, or threaten us, and our attitude and self-talk color our reaction to circumstances. Our attitudes come from our beliefs (thoughts) and our reactions (feelings) to events. Human beings, regardless of our leadership role, are prone to self-doubt and negative self-talk. For example, if you were turned down for a promotion at work, you could take the rejection personally and interpret it to mean that you are not worthy or unappreciated. In this case, the object of a heroic mindset—of being selective about your inner dialogue—would be to help you realize that, although not getting the promotion was disappointing, it was not an entirely terrible experience. It was not a proclamation of your worthlessness, and it did not necessarily predict a bleak future.

Let's classify beliefs in two general categories: rational and irrational. A person or situation that triggers you and causes you to react emotionally generates both kinds of beliefs in your mind. For example, if a man asks a woman out for a date and she turns him down, he may have a rational thought or belief such as, "Too bad she said no. It's no fun to put myself on the line and be turned down." The upsetting beliefs, however, are the irrational ones, and these upsetting beliefs might include, "She's a bitch for turning me down," "I'm so stupid for asking her out," "I'll never be able to get anyone to go out with me," and "She's totally rejecting me." The type of self-talk that we engage in, and the type of language that we use in doing it, help to maintain the belief systems that we have set up.

I don't know how to stop negative thoughts and feelings from arising. It's normal to react and get triggered by situations or people that upset us. Reactions become irrational only when they generalize, when they reinforce overall feelings of self-doubt or inadequacy, or when they make sweeping statements about another person's character. Irrational thinking is characterized by language I call *absolute and grandiose*. Words such as *should, must, always, never, everyone, no one, totally, absolutely, perfectly*, and *everything* represent careless thinking. Rational reality happens specifically, while irrational thinking happens in general. If you notice absolute and grandiose references in your thoughts and words, pause and examine them; rather than allowing your stream of thoughts to disempower you, identify the specific hurt or complaint and address particulars rather that reinforce the generalities of your irrational story.

Reality deals with actual probabilities. Your attitude begins to sink when irrational beliefs wrap themselves around facts. Irrational conclusions can produce nonconstructive thinking, at best, and destructive thinking at worst. Irrational thoughts are highly exaggerated; they form a negative attitude and pull the wind out of the sails of grit. In the previous example, the man tells himself that because one woman turned down his invitation for a date, all women will reject him. There is no rational basis for this exaggerated, pessimistic conclusion.

Along your leadership journey, countless people and situations will trigger you, but only you make yourself upset. Marcus Aurelius, the Roman emperor from 161 to 180, wrote, "If you are distressed by anything external, the pain is not due to the thing itself but to your own estimate of it; and this you have the power to revoke at any moment." Nobody has the power to make another person angry (or sad, or guilty, and so on)—you upset yourself by responding in an irrational manner to someone else's actions. Actions are not of themselves good, bad, anger provoking, or stupid. Our attitude and beliefs, both irrational and rational, interpret those actions and thereby cause us to feel the way we do. I recently attended a conference with two colleagues, and as we listened to the opening keynote speaker's position on politics I became energized, one of my colleague's became angry, while the second colleague seemed bored. We all heard the same words at the same moment, but each of us reacted based on our beliefs. Our beliefs and thoughts become our attitudes, which derive our conclusions, which influence our behavior.

Your attitude can slip into negative territory when your irrational beliefs contain a sense of indignation at the ways things have turned out—as if things should be happening another way. Leaders on the hero's journey have to acknowledge that things are the way they are, that there are no "shoulds" or "musts." When you learn to embrace and accept this, you can diminish the weight of inadequacy. In short, leaders on a hero's journey aspire to a realistic approach to life. It is rational to desire to promote and pursue your goals; it is not rational to demand that the world conform to your desires. From this distinction, we venture into the final part of the hero's journey: faith.

PART IV

FAITH
What Am I Yielding?

Faith is stepping forward confidently in the absence of certainty; it is dedication not based on proof. Faith resonates in what French author André Gide wrote in his 1925 novel *The Counterfeiters*: "You can never cross the ocean until you have the courage to lose sight of the shore." In part IV, we explore how we need leaps of faith to balance planning, projections, and calculations. Good leaders know how to generate ideas, teamwork, and, ultimately, results. Great leaders know all this, and are willing to let go of what is outdated and "lose sight of the shore."

Faith operates as the keystone for leaders on a hero's journey. A keystone is the central stone at the summit of an arch, locking the whole arch together and enabling it to stand. Focus, courage, and grit are elevated and integrated by faith, the willingness to yield and let go. In this part, we look at the power that surrender brings to your leadership. In particular, we study how mindfulness meditation emboldens your ability to yield and surrender, which, paradoxically, improves your decisions, reduces your stress, and significantly enhances your relationships and your team's engagement.

Letting go—having faith—is the trait that beckons freedom of choice and evolution. The hero's journey is not formed from focus, courage, and grit alone—a leader who is focused, courageous, and gritty can be highly driven yet ineffective. Focus, courage, and grit can also slide into bullying, browbeating, and micromanaging styles of leadership. Faith—"What am I yielding?"—is the trait that binds your leadership presence into a heroic journey. In the absence of faith, a leader can become an autocrat.

22

WHAT AM I YIELDING?

Imagine that you are on a quest to find the Pearl of Great Wisdom. It is the most exquisite jewel said to be located in an exotic, far-away land. This pearl has an inner luminosity that makes it glow in the dark, and possessing it gives you the power to make flawless decisions. You have traveled for months, crossed cold streams, climbed jagged hills, hacked your way through forests, and traversed burning desert paths. Finally, guided by whispers and rumors, you have arrived at a North African bazaar. You find yourself in a dark distant stall on the narrow end of an ancient row of merchants, a space never connected to electricity or the Internet. There, you notice something softly glowing in the dim space. You step closer. Your heartbeat accelerates. Your eyelids open wider to drink in as much of the scene as you can.

> *You must open your grip and release some of what you have accumulated in order to grasp and receive the next wave of great value.*

Your focused direction, your brave adventures, and your persistent exploration have brought you right to the Pearl of Great Wisdom. Barely able to contain your hope and excitement, you reach out your hand to grasp the prize, but as you try to lift your arms to reach toward the pearl, you realize that your hands are full, heavy, and weighed down. You cast an alarmed look at your hands and realize that you are clutching and carrying mementos and artifacts that you've gathered on your journey. Every one of these items seemed important and necessary when you picked it up—the pots, jewels, clothes, and knick-knacks you collected fill your grasp. Your arms are laden, and you cannot take hold of anything new. But now you reach for the great prize, you must make a choice: hold on to what you've gathered, or release it all to take the pearl.

And so is your experience as a leader on the hero's journey. You must open your grip and release some of what you have accumulated in order to grasp and receive the next wave of great value. What are the pots, pans, knickknacks, and objects that we have picked up along the way? They are the beliefs, ideas, skills, and attitudes we have acquired in order to relate to our world. We develop patterns—coping strategies—for dealing with the environmental pressures. We determine ways to deal first with our parents, then with our conflicting desires, an array of emotions, the events we experience, and the incessant competition for resources. We develop a coherent set of beliefs and assumptions; we develop an ego.

Steve works as a successful process-redesign consultant. At forty-four years old, he is facing his ego limitations. Steve's engineering degree and more than sixteen years of leadership experience in operations management have yielded a masterful ability to improve operational efficiency. Steve is focused: he is a strategic thinker who knows what he's creating in his business and with his clients. Steve is courageous: he regularly challenges the status quo and has developed a reputation for wrangling with uncertainty and change. He is gritty, disciplined, and determined as a person and as a professional. He dedicates himself to long-term goals. Steve is a successful consultant, a fierce competitor, popular in his social crowd, and worldly.

In spite of Steve's multiple successes, he continues to feel frustrated in two meaningful arenas: he desperately desires to get married and have children (all of his serious relationships end before marriage), and he passionately wishes to build his business (which, even with the stellar reputation he enjoys, is slow to grow). Steve doesn't require more focus, more courage, or more grit. His strategy is clear, his risk taking is calculated, and his consistency of execution is impressive. What he needs is a leap of faith. He needs to yield. Marriage is a dynamic exchange of power and control that requires vulnerability and trust. Scaling a business is an act of empowering and vesting others with authority and responsibility. Both marriage and growing a business require a sharing of power, responsibility, and rewards, and Steve's real challenge is learning how to yield—how to let go of control and certainty and take a leap of faith.

Steve has already been exposed to new ideas that will enable him to accomplish his outcomes, yet in spite of his education and experience he hasn't accomplished the jump to the next level—he is both educated and stuck. The next level is not a step, but a leap of faith. It isn't enough to be knowledgeable; you must become willing to yield some certainty in order to grow. Growth requires that we release rigid thinking that blocks awareness of fresh perspectives. Too much certainty, it turns out, shuts off nuances of new possibilities, connections, and solutions.

Leap of Faith vs. Step of Trust

The journey to gaining the Pearl of Great Wisdom requires simplifying and releasing our limited ego boundaries. This is the leap of faith that accelerates personal and professional evolution and results. Your hero's mind-set is completed by the virtue of faith—the choice to wholeheartedly embrace something for which you have no proof. Faith is a relationship with uncertainty; it rearranges your relationship with familiarity. It is a distinct virtue that differs from having trust.

Along your leadership journey, trust isn't enough. Trust is a confident expectation of something, but there are times when the path forward is

Trust vs. Faith

Trust: Confident expectation of something	Faith: Belief that is not based on proof
Certainty	Known
Experienced	History
Past	Belief
Unknown	New
Vision	Future

unclear and the data are inconclusive; there are times when you must act with conviction even in the absence of certainty. Trust and faith are distinct and entail different mental and behavioral levers that we can apply, depending on the situation. When we recognize the difference between them, we can skillfully apply the right one at the right time.

Leaders who usher in positive change have certainty about them, but they are also willing to be uncertain about their conclusions, ideas, and processes. Leaders unwilling to face uncertainty barricade themselves against creativity. Overly certain minds don't adapt. I've seen leaders become ineffective because they were certain when they should have been uncertain, and uncertain when they needed to be certain.

Trust is rooted in logic—it is grounded in strong expectation based on past experience and available data. I trust my leaders when I have evidence that they have my best interests at heart, and I trust my peers to keep consistent with the behaviors they have demonstrated in the past. If they consistently follow through on promises, for example, then I trust their integrity.

Faith, on the other hand, means accepting something sight unseen. When you wholeheartedly step into the abyss without any proof of safety, you apply faith. Surrender is an act of faith. Surrendering certainty and stepping forward without proof isn't trust, for there isn't any confident expectation of something. It is an act of letting go, of yielding.

Faith requires us to soften our hold on certainty and give up some safety; it challenges our plans and questions our ideas. More demandingly, faith tests our identity. Focus, courage, and grit prepare you for this virtue. Faith calls you to sacrifice, to forgo what you do, what you know, and what you are, but this sacrifice does not mean yielding your power or abandoning your principles; rather, it is a clearing that makes space for growth and renewal.

Leadership as a hero's journey is characterized by pursuing a significant and difficult prize. Leaders on this journey make sacrifices and face considerable jeopardy and risk, and leaders on the hero's journey always give back; they share the prize with their community. These leaders know that this pursuit is sustainable and effective when yielding counterbalances certainty.

Leaders who understand that everything in life expires become adept at knowing when to let go. Software and hardware become obsolete. Processes and best practices turn into bureaucratic traps. Ideas run their course. New scientific findings routinely replace old scientific certainty. Relationships lose their bond and timing. Even personal values evolve. Holding on to what has expired is an act of nostalgia at best and an unexamined resistance to progress at worst. Leadership is a creative endeavor, and there are moments when creativity is best served by clearing the slate and surrendering to make room for the new.

23

LETTING GO

When my friend Jackie returned from a trip to Costa Rica in the late 1980s, she told me about the howler monkeys in the forest. Howler monkeys are among the loudest animals on earth, but they are also gentle and lethargic, congregating in small groups along the middle branches of trees. Zoos favor them because of their mellow nature but boisterous entertainment. Consequently, they are also favorites for trappers. Jackie relayed a story that her Costa Rican guide told her about how trappers catch these monkeys for sale to zoos.

At first, trappers snuck up on small groups of howler monkeys and threw a large net on the group, attempting to capture the monkeys in bulk. The monkeys, however, panicked and perceived their fellow monkeys in the net as dangerous—they fought and struggled among themselves, biting and scratching and disfiguring one another. Since the trappers needed to deliver live, healthy monkeys, they had to find another way to trap them. What did they do? They recognized that monkeys reacted only to imminent situations and didn't think about consequences or the future, so they devised a simple and safe trap that didn't arouse the monkeys' suspicion.

The trappers built small boxes, about half the size of a shoe box—large enough to hold a banana. The box had a small opening for a monkey to reach in its open, flat hand to grasp the banana. The trappers firmly attached a box to a tree and placed a banana inside, and the monkey, lured by easy access to a banana, would reach its open hand into the box and grasp the banana. The opening, however, was too small for the banana-clutching fisted hand to slip out. As long as the monkey held on to the banana, it remained trapped in the box by its hand. To become free and escape, all the monkey had to do was let go of the banana and slide its open hand right out, but the insistent monkey would not let go of the treasure. The more tightly it gripped the banana, the more securely it remained trapped.

Unlike howler monkeys that get stuck in the moment and don't consider consequences, humans can see the bigger picture. We can let go of the limiting attachments, opinions, and assumptions we're clutching. But do we? The nature of clinging is to remain stuck. Clinging and clutching the banana keeps the monkey trapped. What do you cling to, grip, and clutch that keeps you immobilized? The specifics of what you hang on to will vary, but they fall into one of three broad categories: ideas, things, and people.

Psychosclerosis

I refer to the mental state of rigid, encrusted habits as *psychosclerosis*. It is not a clinically diagnosable condition, but it is prevalent. Psychosclerosis is a stiff and hardened mind that does not welcome change and rejects growth. Compare it with *arteriosclerosis*, the hardening of the arteries that prevents healthy blood flow to the heart and organs. Psychosclerosis hardens thinking and worldview, preventing the healthy flow of ideas and, subsequently, diminishing growth.

Psychosclerosis was clearly affecting a man in his mid-fifties that sat next to me on a flight from San Diego to Minneapolis. After buckling my seat belt, I introduced myself to my flight neighbor. When I asked him how he spent his time, he shared that he was a mid-level manager at a plastics engineering and manufacturing firm. He then asked me what I did for a living. I told him that I coach and consult executives to think more creatively, decide more effectively, and relate more deeply. He wasn't sure what that meant and asked for more detail. I shared with him that I enable executives and leadership teams to make better decisions and produce better results. I explained that our work progresses in four stages: increasing awareness of self, others, and environment; identifying areas of flow or areas of interference; crafting a plan for professional and team development; and providing coaching and facilitation to develop individual leaders and teams. Ultimately, our efforts strive to improve perspective, drive better judgment calls, change behavior, and accelerate results. In other words, by helping leaders grow in awareness and craft new, better decisions, we break outdated patterns and enable growth. We actively exercise against psychosclerosis.

The gentleman turned his face and sank a little deeper into his seat; he paused for a moment and seemed reflective. Then he turned to face me and said, "My company has tried that several times over the years, but they have not been successful in changing me. I'm proud to tell you that I'm exactly the same person that I was twenty years ago!" That's psychosclerosis: a disease of attitude that stems from a hardening of the mind.

> *The hero's journey is an evolutionary process at the end of which the person staring back at you in the mirror is not the same person who began the process.*

Unfortunately, the hero's journey is not available to those who wish to remain unchanged; the hero's journey is an evolutionary process at the end of which the person staring back at you in the mirror is not the same person who began the process. Leadership as a hero's journey is marked by a series of unpredictable and uncertain challenges, movements, and surprises. You cannot lead when you are held back by psychosclerosis; rather, you have to drive for novel results, grow and meet goals, and take leaps of faith.

The Comfort Zone, Revisited

As discussed first in chapter 16, the comfort zone is a two-faced companion that can either soothe our tired spirits or hold our spirit in captivity; it's the routine we've rehearsed to the point of effortlessness. We know what we're doing, we know what we're thinking, we know what to expect, and above all we feel safe. The comfort zone is a base of operation in which we can recover our energy and reduce our intensity, a state within which we can recharge and relax, but leaders who make this their default setting lose their ability to lead. They become project-managing bureaucrats, not growth initiators. Of course, project management is critical to success, but it's not the same as leadership.

Stepping beyond the comfort zone requires a leap of faith. *Faith* refers to your ability to wholeheartedly commit to a person or situation in the absence of proof or certainty; a leap of faith includes calculating risk, making a rational computation of danger. But there is another element, an impulse that beckons you to transcend. This aspect requires that you surrender your certainty and dedicate yourself to the vision for which you don't have complete evidence or data.

The pervasive uncertainty of the leader's journey systematically beckons anxiety. Having spent decades coaching and consulting leaders and executives in all types of industries and markets, I've been fortunate to participate in candid and revealing conversations with countless leaders. I have yet to meet a leader exempt from the foreboding clutches of anxiety and fear. Even the most daring adventurers mix excitement with anxiousness as they stretch into the unknown in order to produce growth.

Potential lies beyond the border of the comfort zone. Potentiality and new possibilities of thought and action require that we leave the familiar mapped-out and well-traveled territory within the comfort zone; it is a land that has been strip-mined for years and is no longer fertile. It's messy, and it's chaotic. The comfort zone, for leaders, cannot and must not be a long-term residence. Neale Donald Walsch, author of *Conversations with God*, wrote that life begins at the end of your comfort zone; leadership, too, begins at the edge of your comfort zone. Growth requires that you stretch into what is unrealized. It is an expansion in size, number, value, or strength, and it requires spreading out past the rehearsed and routine and into the improvised and envisioned.

The Three Zones

Comfort Zone	Growth Zone	Panic Zone
Known	Unknown	Unknowable
Comfort	Growth	Stress
Rehearsed	Effortful	Repulsive
Mastery	Beginning	Inconceivable
Soothing	Exciting	Scary

Finding Strength in Softness

We refer to leaders as "change agents" because leaving the comfort zone and venturing into the growth zone means to deliberately court change. Invoking change and knowingly making yourself, your team, and your enterprise vulnerable is an act of faith. Without this faith, our work and life stagnate, and our experience becomes defined by routine and repetition. While leaders face forward with intention, find courage to tangle with change, and press on with perseverance, they do their work in a vast and formless field of doubt. Uncertainty pervades the hero's journey, and faith provides you with the willingness to yield the known and to leap forward. Faith complements the certainty of your vision with the ability to surrender to the unknown.

Surrender, though, is mostly regarded as undesirable and weak. I, for one, grew up in a military environment and was instructed to never surrender. I vividly recall an incident when I was ten years old and my father saw me kneeling and begging an older neighbor boy to return my basketball. My dad came running out of the house yelling at me to stand up and never bend before another man. My dad's a big man. He was a soldier who fought in three wars and was injured in two of them. He was an entrepreneur who honed his strength of mind and body as a steelworker. When this force of nature came barreling into my young face and commanded me never to surrender, the message was deeply etched in my psyche. For decades, I grappled with a limited understanding of surrender. I struggled to ask for help. I rarely accepted authority, and I would part ways from a group before I yielded my will to theirs.

As an adult, I discovered that surrender has more subtle and nuanced dimensions. There is the feeble aspect we equate with being overpowered—this aspect of surrender entails weakness and loss, capitulation and meekness. Certainly, in war, surrender is a primary concern. Growing up as the son of a soldier, I knew that our primary aim was to survive, and that surrender meant personal and national destruction. As an adult, I believe that we shouldn't surrender to forces that bend upon our destruction, and I believe that some things are worth fighting, dying, and even killing for. But for most of us living in civilized nations, this type of struggle is far from our daily reality. The surrender we grapple with—the surrender that leaders on the heroic journey must learn—is the surrendering of our past, certainty, and ego-based limits.

A leap of faith is an exercise in surrender. Leaders must learn to yield their power and allow the larger power of teams to influence them. Leaders influence others, but they are also influenced by the greater power of the collective, the environment, the market, and creativity. A leader who will not yield and allow himself to be influenced by these powers becomes insulated and, in effect, detached and powerless. Faith for leaders means willingly placing your well-being in the hands of other forces.

Perhaps the most critical aspect of faith is that, without it, there is an absence of reciprocal faith and trust from your followers. We are willing to follow our leaders when we have faith in them, when we trust their judgment. Leaders who don't evoke trust, who don't have faith in us, seldom receive trust and faith in return.

Reilly, the COO of a software company in San Francisco, didn't trust Stan, the director of operations he inherited when he took the COO job. He didn't have faith in Stan's ability, didn't trust Stan's intent, and actively micromanaged him. In the absence of trust and faith, the relationship vacuum is quickly replaced with mutual defensiveness. Reilly second-guessed and overexamined every decision that Stan made, and Stan was suspicious and bothered by Reilly's constant hovering. Reilly scheduled two meetings per week to review Stan's progress and decision making, and Stan showed up to every meeting cagey and withholding. The process became a cycle of suspicion spiraling into deeper control behavior, increased mistrust, and growing detachment and distance. What Reilly and Stan needed to collaborate was not just competence and independence, but interdependence. They needed faith in each other and some measure of letting go, of surrendering their personal safety.

As I mentioned earlier, trust is grounded in evidence and faith is grounded in possibility. Think about the difference this way: facts are the raw material for trust and fiction is the raw material of faith. Stan and Reilly had accumulated evidence proving their beliefs about each other; they were locked in a cycle of evidence-based distrust. To repair and change their working affiliation, they had to craft a new story for their relationship, and in order to collaborate they had to articulate a compelling shared vision of their future, take charge of their own behavior, focus on what was working and do more of it. For this to work, they had to stop blaming and yield their individual need to be right.

Leaps of Faith

Søren Kierkegaard, one of the fathers of existential philosophy, popularized the term *leap of faith*. Much of his work explored the emotions and feelings of individuals when they faced difficult life choices. In his 1846 book, *Concluding Unscientific Postscript to the Philosophical Fragments*, he wrote, "When someone is to leap he must certainly do it alone and also be alone in properly understanding it is an impossibility. The leap is the decision."

Sometimes leadership moves forward in measured steps, and sometimes it moves forward in leaps of faith. For example, starting my own consulting firm was a big leap of faith for me, but it was a giant leap of faith for my wife. Getting married was a significant leap of faith for both of us. Here are a few other examples.

Mary was a thirty-five-year-old senior director who recognized an opportunity right under her nose. Her division was being spun out, and she made an offer to her corporation to buy out the division. She took a leap of faith to grow the division into a full-fledged independent company. Her master's degree in biology, though, hardly prepared her to be a CEO.

Jeff was promoted to senior director, and his confidence received a tremendous boost. He had spent the previous year formulating ideas to improve his department's efficiency. Now, with his increased confidence and new role, he decided it was time to take a risk; he took a leap of faith and made a proposal to his GM to do something that had never been done before.

When Michael saw the nature of the Internet changing, he recognized how it would impact his business and his clients; after eight years of guiding the firm in a clear strategic direction, he committed to a leap of faith to invest in new technology and bet his company on his vision of the future.

Jane spent twenty years growing her business to a $90 million company. She felt extremely proud of exceeding her wildest dreams for the business that she had started in her garage, but she also recognized that she didn't have the skill or energy to grow it to the next level. Her leap of faith felt almost unbearable as she began the search for a president to replace her.

Leaps of faith do not guarantee success; in fact, we call them "leaps" of faith because they entail considerable chance of failure. Masters in every domain develop themselves through learning and practice combined with leaps of faith. Just as achieving mastery calls for leaps of faith, maintaining mastery requires them as well. Those who achieve mastery exude a sense of confidence and ease in their craft, an ease that comes from effort, focus, and leaps of faith.

I recently attended a guitar concert; as I sat in the front row I was transported on waves of sound and awed by the beauty of the music, as well as humbled by the profound competence of the guitarists. Andy McKee, the concert headliner, transformed an ordinary guitar into a one-man band—strings, percussion, melody, and background. As a master of his craft, he was in his comfort zone on stage, yet he shared with us that he was consistently experimenting and exploring new ways to express himself through the medium of music. I found it telling that his path to mastery directly related to his willingness to grow—an urgency to explore, experiment, and expand with leaps of faith.

The leap is the decision to leave the certainty of the known, the tried, the quantifiably certain. To leap is an act of faith because you respond to being pulled forward by a belief in something unproven, something for which there is little or no evidence. A leadership leap of faith manifests as you articulate your vision and guide people toward it. A vision is unproven and uncertain. It compels you to yield the familiar and journey forward. As such, it requires courage to navigate the inevitable anxiety birthed in the womb of uncertainty; it also requires grit to sustain the journey of creation. Finally, it requires faith—a leap forward without proof.

24

FAITH IS SURRENDER

Those of us who grew up in democratic cultures have been instilled with the values of independence and control. Western ideals promote self-reliance—our culture perpetuates the folklore that we are our own masters. We overemphasize a belief that we don't need much help from others, and that we succeed because we control our own destinies, but look more closely at these ideals and you will notice that they are glued together with myths. Examine them in your personal experience, and you'll see that they are merely aspirations. Once we pierce this egotistic veil and look closely at the nature of achievement, we see that lasting success comes with elements of surrender—the opposite of control. Rarely, if ever, do we accomplish great feats on our own without help. The idea that we can do so is an illusion that causes most of us a significant deal of suffering.

Once we pierce this egotistic veil and look closely at the nature of achievement, we see that lasting success comes with elements of surrender—the opposite of control.

Surrender comes when we see that illusion and we let go of trying to attain the impossible. Surrender is, in fact, an act of great strength rather than weakness.

Consider the possibility that surrender is not a position of weakness. In military terms, this black-and-white thinking is associated with humiliation, loss, and even death. It is a simplistic and one-dimensional interpretation, most often the reflection of our unexamined cultural biases regarding surrender. In our discussion of leadership, we must understand that the essence of faith—surrender—is critical to the hero's journey, and that there is actually an upside to surrender.

Surrender literally means to let go and form a new lease, a new commitment. It takes mental and emotional strength to surrender, but as a leader you don't surrender your power; you surrender your limited worldview. You give up your narrow identification with ineffective habits and limiting ideas; you release your sense of identity and the well-rehearsed voice of your ego.

The ego is your intact sense of "me" shaped by life experiences. The ego (Latin for *I*) is a sense of a defined and separate self that is a conglomerate of memories, ideas, beliefs, assumptions, and expectations. Your ego shapes your ongoing experience of life, and proceeds forward with behavioral strategies you developed in your lifelong drive for physical, emotional, intellectual, and social survival.

Physical survival is the first concern for our ego. Second, the ego focuses on emotional survival: the survival of your pride—what we call "saving face." It is what we do to prevent a loss of dignity or self-esteem. Our ego survival also manifests in terms of recognition and accolades—because the ego is our identity, its task is to make itself known. Being ignored or rejected can feel like a small death to the ego structure.

The ego is not a negative structure. As a mental and emotional constellation of memories and desires, it represents our drive to maximize joy and minimize hurt. As such, our ego always strives to serve us. Commonly, though, the servant becomes the master, and while most of our behaviors have a positive intent (e.g., accomplishment, recognition, safety, love, or creativity), the basic state of the ego is fear. To evolve our ego and release our fear-based patterns, we must establish new, productive behaviors that fulfill our need for safety and survival.

Consider the case of Stan, a thirty-six-year-old IT director of a nationally growing staffing company. Stan's boss, a man in his mid-fifties, relied on Stan's strategic approach to IT. He had a lot of respect for Stan's people and project management but felt increasingly frustrated about Stan's dress and punctuality. In fact, Stan's infractions of timeliness and appearance had become such an issue that his boss placed him on disciplinary notice, and Stan risked losing his dream job because he often arrived late and dressed too casually.

My first reaction to Stan as he described the situation was bemused disbelief. "Really," I thought to myself. "You're an adult professional who's about to lose your job because your outfits are too casual and you roll in late to the office?" But Stan's concerned look moved me. I asked him to explain his rationale for his behavior. He shared that he's a night owl who has a hard time sleeping and often gets quality work done in the middle of the night, and he also claimed that what he wore was immaterial as he didn't interact with clients. Even though his answer was rational, his job was still at risk and he had to change his behaviors if he wanted to keep it.

Stan's perception was one-dimensional; he was right for the obvious reasons and his boss was out of touch with current trends and culture. Stan insisted that this was a generational issue; his boss was old-school. I realized that we had to approach our conversation from a new direction and asked him to set aside all generational excuses and tell me how he benefited from arriving late and dressing unacceptably. Stan tilted his head and looked at me for a long quiet moment. Finally he said, "This is my rebellion. This is my power and control over my own choices." We both sat quietly as we took in the importance of what he had said; I was impressed by his keen self-reflection and honesty. As soon as he heard himself identify this ego-driven need, he began to see the path to change.

Stan's professional development quest was guided by a new question, "How can I achieve a sense of control and power, but not sabotage my job or my relationship with my boss?" From that day on, Stan changed his workday outfits to meet company expectations. Getting to the office on time proved more difficult as he was legitimately a night owl, but Stan began a dialogue with his boss that addressed his autonomy and decision rights. He matured in his professional journey.

Our ego is a socially developed construct ingrained within us by social forces and the naïve decisions of early childhood. We don't hold children completely responsible for their choices because they are not conscious enough. Becoming an adult means that we have developed enough discernment so that others now consider us responsible for our actions. When Stan was a child, he competed with his sister and brother for their parents' attention and his young ego decided that being passive-aggressive was the most effective way to cope with the situation. His sister's primary pattern was competitiveness and one-upping her siblings, while Stan's brother took on the role of the loner who minimized contact, withheld thoughts and feelings, and became immersed in books and movies.

We each have our own coping strategy. We develop a primary ego structure that becomes so well honed and familiar that it eventually feels natural. As leaders on the hero's journey, however, we are called to recognize our worn-out old patterns. When a snake's body outgrows its skin, the snake sheds its outer layer in order to continue to grow. Similarly, we need to drop our protective layer of beliefs and behaviors in the service of growth; this is our leap of faith—jumping from the familiar to the unfamiliar. Sometimes the only way to travel is by leaps of faith, by surrendering the certainty of the known.

Leadership as a hero's journey begins when we leave the familiar. Leaving the known is often interpreted "geographically"—leaving home, moving to a new city or country, or starting at a new company. But the deeper experience of leaving the familiar is the journey away from our beliefs and identity. This is the great work of surrender—to release outdated aspects of our self-concept, and to embrace the awkward uncertainty of discovering new dimensions of our self.

25

HOW TO SURRENDER

Carl Jung wrote that "the greatest burden a child must bear is the unlived life of the parents." The people who care for us and raise us deeply impress our infant minds. Watching family patterns and behaviors, it seems as though psychological behavior is hereditary. In fact, the question of nature versus nurture is a false dichotomy: the issue is not *versus*—it's not a black-and-white abstraction of either/or. The issue is how they operate together.

An unlived life of a parent haunts the parent like a shadow. Most parents are not conscious of the presence and pressure of their unlived lives—their disappointments, desires, deep-seated fears, and hurts elude daily attention. The parents therefore do not consciously choose their subtle influences, and because they are not actively aware of their unlived lives, they can't control them, and so their shadows press them along a scripted path. But there is more to the shaping of our ego than parental shadows and influences; there are visible patterns and preferences that manifest in newborns. Our pattern—our ego structure—forms from predispositions combined with early life conditioning.

I, for example, have been insisting that our daughters learn to play a musical instrument. I have several good reasons to support my position: Research demonstrates that music develops the brain and helps with mastering math and language. Music provides a social venue for connecting with friends, and offers an outlet for creative expression important for the mind and heart. In addition, the persevering practice required in order to master the flute or guitar will help our daughters flex their discipline, their grit.

These are the rational and logical arguments. But when I get angry because they won't practice, and my determination becomes stubbornness, I have to look below the surface of the rational to find the source of my reaction. Indeed, upon close examination, I found my own disappointment and frustration, my unlived life and failed musicality. I regret that I abandoned music lessons and didn't learn to play an instrument, and, by all means, I don't want my daughters to have that regret. There, lurking below the surface of articulated awareness, my unlived life, my unfulfilled dream casts itself upon my children.

These influencing factors shape us as people and as leaders. The assumption and values you bring to your leadership role and function are often deeply seated and unexamined as your ego structure is mostly invisible. My parents, for example, instilled in me punctuality. Arriving on time is as deep-seated a value of mine as it is for them. Is it right? Is it critical? It's not a universal truth; it's a preference. However, punctuality shapes my life, both in how I behave and how I judge others. My wife was almost not my wife as she arrived twenty minutes late to our first date, and I interpreted her delay as not caring, and I felt annoyed at her lack of responsibility. All this, by the way, before I even knew her.

We are held prisoners to the "mechanicalness" of our patterns. We are moved to react like puppets on the ends of strings, the filaments of ego identity.

That's the power of an ego structure, the force of assumptions and strongly held (and unexamined) beliefs. My mother-in-law is an impressive and accomplished lady whose sense of time is fluid and unstressed, and my wife learned from her mom and their culture that arriving on time is less critical than being in the moment. My future wife was late because her childhood values differed from mine, not because she lacked responsibility or respect.

We are held prisoners to the "mechanicalness" of our patterns. We are moved to react like puppets on the ends of strings, the filaments of ego identity. This is true even for leaders who are charged with infusing positive change into their organizations. Every organization tends toward inertia, toward simple perpetuation rather than growth and evolution. You have your work ahead of you as you protect those elements that are effective and efficient, and challenge and change those aspects that need to be culled and updated.

The very same principle of being updated and current applies to you, the leader, at a personal level. Growth and change demand that we let things go, that we surrender. Although I'm still driven by punctuality, I have learned to challenge my assumption that punctuality outshines its alternatives.

Remember that three elements define leadership as a hero's journey: departing from the familiar, making sacrifices, and serving and contributing. Leaders influence and inspire their team and organizations into growth and change in the pursuit of meaningful results, but there are no guarantees. The process is exciting even as it yields uncertainty. Letting go, yielding, and surrendering to the uncertainty of the unknown is a vulnerable state that evokes discomfort, but fighting for maintaining the safety of the known is not leadership. Surrendering and releasing require a leap of faith. Making a decision to evolve, explore, and grow is an act of service and surrender that develops with these four elements: confidence, humility, discipline, and honesty.

Confidence

We earn confidence from practicing courage. *Courage* refers to your ability to step toward what you'd rather step away from, specifically discomfort and fear. Confidence grows as we face and engage challenges. The physical aspect of a challenge, like climbing a mountain, is just one part of cultivating confidence—the emotional and mental challenges are the greater part.

Visualize a log as long as a school bus resting on the ground. Walking along this log challenges your balance, but it's not particularly scary. Now imagine that this log is suspended between two balconies on the fourth floor of a building. As the relative condition changes, so do your thoughts about it. Anticipation and worst-case-scenario mental projections awaken your anxiety-producing visions of damage and hurt. Context—the circumstances that form the environment within which something takes place—influences our mental states.

You don't have to venture away from your daily activity to develop confidence; you don't have to seek special situations to practice surrender. You can change the context of your experience by simply committing to remain vulnerable. There is always opportunity for something to descend on us that will threaten our sense of ego, our sense of safety: delegating authority, learning to say no to peers, making a game-changing decision, entering into a new and untested strategic alliance, or applying for a big promotion. If we commit to remaining vulnerable rather than reacting defensively, we choose to remain open and engaged with the person, situation, or idea. The opportunity to practice this choice lies in our daily lives. We have it when communicating with direct reports, while driving, or in forming new relationships.

Confidence grows with deliberate practice. Seek out the opportunities, and they will become obvious in your day.

Humility

The ability to yield and let go of ideas, beliefs, people, and situations is also bolstered by humility. It's all too familiar to meet leaders whose success and growth in power have also inflated their ego and self-importance. Rather than loosening the hold of the ego, it becomes more prominent. We commonly observe leaders who have become controlling; rather than move toward surrendering—toward releasing their identification with their sense of self—they develop an increasingly tightened bond to it. Courage, vulnerability, strength, and confidence have to be constantly contained by humility. Pride is nearly synonymous with ego. As ego power grows, so does pride.

Humility is widely associated with acts of service. Service turns attention and care to others, not the self. Pride is fed by absorbing and demanding attention and recognition, and service turns the stream of attention in the opposite direction. To be humble is to subordinate yourself. In some religious practices, people achieve humility by subordinating to God, and in leadership, you practice humility by subordinating yourself in service to your people and mission. Leaders on the hero's journey, like the mythical Knights of the Round Table, serve others and make sacrifices. These knights were considered heroic and humble, and their fame and honor stemmed from their feats of bravery in service: they served the king and queen and the people of the kingdom, and they sallied forth to fight dragons and enemies and to find treasures. Not only did they risk survival but they gave the glory and the benefit to others.

Ultimately, surrender means releasing your limited sense of self. Releasing your well-rehearsed patterns of defense and protection provides access to greater awareness, choices, and power. Surrender is a collaborative relationship with fear, not a cowering one; it is an ability to release your limited boundaries and merge with possibilities. Surrender reduces the separation that emanates from fear and survival and expresses a soft power energized by the humility of service. Power without humility is self-centered and, at times, abusive. Power without humility seeks conquest, not development.

I propose that we achieve surrender—the release of our rigid boundaries of self—through a journey of personal power. When our power infuses our confidence we can legitimately think, "I feel strong." The confident self can finally relax its fear-based vigilance, and that relaxed self can think, "I'm available to engage and to express!" Some martial arts teach this gentle power; masters teach how to use an ounce to deflect a ton. An individual's raw strength doesn't deflect the ton; it's the strength that comes from erasing the barrier between attacker and defender. The warrior accesses this strength when his humility allows his power to blend with and become energized by the power of the other.

When you approach the world with humility, you become more prepared to notice, connect, and engage. When confrontation arises, rather than closing off to the power and energy flowing your way, you have the capacity to absorb and engage the attacker. In so doing, their energy becomes yours to direct. It's through remaining open and willing to surrender our all-important self that we can absorb this power and redirect it.

Discipline

Discipline, more than a cornerstone of perseverance, is also a core element of surrender. *Discipline* refers to a committed series of choices you make that align your behavior with your focus. Discipline balances two inner forces: commitment to your vision and resistance to temptation. For leaders on the hero's journey, surrender is not a defeat at the hands of an overwhelming force; surrender is a capacity to let things go and let them be, a capacity that emanates from tremendous confidence. Confidence in yourself and certainty in your abilities arise from disciplined effort and repetitive practice. Disciplined efforts promote personal confidence that, in turn, fosters self-trust. The blend of confidence and self-trust promote the presence of mind that enables surrender.

Surrender differs from giving in. We give in when we're exhausted; we give in when an outside force overwhelms us. The surrender I'm discussing happens when you stop denying reality. It's an embrace of the moment that happens when you trust yourself and aren't afraid you'll get overwhelmed. Self-trust is a means to surrender. Consistency of choice promotes self-discipline, which in turn fosters self-trust, which provides the strength to yield outmoded beliefs and behaviors. One of the payoffs of self-discipline is the ability to trust yourself, an ability which emboldens you to accept reality as it is.

Discipline is a string of choices to stay on track, choices you make from moment to moment to bring your focus back to your commitment. Leadership development must include dedicated effort at self-discipline. What, then, interferes with discipline? The disruptors of discipline generally fall into two large buckets: the outside environment and our internal impulses. The environment includes people, projects, and problems—the constant stream of activity that clamors for attention and energy. Our impulses include fears, dreams, and multiple appetites—the ever-shifting grasping of our mind and heart that yearns for fulfillment. In truth, these are not interferences to our discipline; they are the landscape of experience within which we practice and develop discipline. Were it not for the outside environment and internal impulses pushing and pulling at your attention, we would not require choice and focus; we would not require discipline.

Self-discipline and humility are disciplines, and so is service. Serving means tending to the needs of others. Serving is a practice of surrender because we have to release our personal comfort in order to provide for others. When we are in service, we put forth our energies toward the well-being of somebody else. The act of serving is a nonsurvival behavior, but service is also an attitude, and the attitude of service is a powerful discipline and a context of leadership. It engenders a strong response of followership. In the discipline of service you might, for example, express an unpopular opinion in a meeting with peers because it is important, even though it is inconvenient. You may choose to surrender your immediate ego need for safety when you make a disciplined choice to serve the greater good.

Honesty

Honesty is the fourth exercise on the path of surrender. Consider why people lie: to gain something or to avoid losing something. We lie to defend our rehearsed story of who we are; we lie to protect ourselves, to protect our immediate well-being, our sense of self. Either way, lying is a survival response. Earlier in my life, I felt insufficient and out of touch with my power, and I believed there was not enough in the world—not enough money, time, attention, or space. So I lied to gain power and resources. My lies were never egregious or illegal; they were small and manipulative, intended to prevent competitors from gaining or winning. They were fear-based acts of survival.

My detour through lies reflected my struggle for self-esteem. As my self-worth strengthened, my urge to deceive diminished. At this point in my life, I'm able to clearly hear and attend to my internal dialogue; I can tell when my desire to exaggerate, eliminate, or distort information increases, and I know that my self-doubt is active. My heroic leadership practices pay off exactly when I feel the urge to protect my ego with a lie, and, instead, I practice honesty in order to surrender and release the fear that haunts me.

Honesty and integrity are two sides of a coin: integrity is being truthful to yourself and honesty is being truthful to others. Honesty and integrity are training areas on the path of faith, on the path of surrender. When we practice honesty, we release the fear of loss or rejection. By releasing attachment to the ego and being honest we become available and undefended in the present moment.

Why do I trust somebody? Because I know that they will follow through with what they promise. Why don't I trust someone? Because they say one thing and then do something else. The same is true for trusting ourselves. I trust myself because I know that when I say that I am going to do something, I do it. As the trust in self grows, so grows self-confidence. As self-trust and confidence increase, I become more secure in my own competence and safety. Trusting others enables me to relax in their presence, to surrender my mind's pervasive vigilance. Similarly, when I trust myself, I relax my vigilance about myself. I gain the ability to be at ease in my skin and honest with my community.

These practices—confidence, humility, discipline, and honesty—are the stepping-stones that we take toward growing in surrender. We mature as we develop with practice, feedback, and support. Yet there is another important set of practices designed to strengthen the psychic muscles required to surrender: self-awareness and mindfulness. Self-awareness and mindfulness quicken the evolution of self-trust. Mindful awareness gives us the capacity to understand our internal reality; as we grasp the mechanics of our inner world, we discover how our outer world reflects our beliefs and expectations. As we grow in self-awareness, we develop self-empowerment and self-trust. Self-awareness shines a clear light on our limitations and our strengths; in that awareness, we grow as people and as leaders. Since mindful attention works as a catalyst to leadership as a hero's journey, we now turn our attention to mindfulness and mindful practice.

Educating the *Heartmind*

Prayer is a common and familiar practice of surrender. Prayer accesses higher wisdom and guidance as we turn our attention away from our ego as the primary object of importance. In praying, we release the pattern of self-limited boundaries and shift from our habituated ideas and knowledge to become open to greater guidance and wisdom. Consider Reinhold Niebuhr's Serenity Prayer:

> God grant me the serenity
> to accept the things I cannot change;
> courage to change the things I can;
> and wisdom to know the difference.
> Living one day at a time;
> Enjoying one moment at a time;
> Accepting hardships as the pathway to peace;
> Taking, as He did, this sinful world
> as it is, not as I would have it;
> Trusting that He will make all things right
> if I surrender to His Will;
> That I may be reasonably happy in this life
> and supremely happy with Him
> Forever in the next.

While some people pray in order to transcend their self-centered limits, others meditate to achieve the same goal. Deciding whether to pray or meditate (or both) reflects your culture and personal style—both call forth wisdom that transcends our day-to-day reasoning. Prayer and meditation guide us to surrender to a vast field of perspective, to a wisdom we can access but not necessarily conceive. Prayer and meditation help us to sidestep habitual mental patterns and arrive at a place beyond our repetitive story line with its assumptions and expectations. By setting aside my limited ego identity, I create space for greater wisdom to come forth.

You probably know the old adage mentioned earlier, "If you always do what you have always done, you will always have what you always had." Surrendering and yielding during prayer and meditation humbles us as we encounter and admit our limitations. We gravitate toward certainty; we are also intimately familiar with the limits of certainty and with the vast, endless aspects of our limitations. When we honestly acknowledge our limits, we can begin to open ourselves to the vastness of the unknown in which lies the potential for new ideas and behaviors. There is much wisdom that we don't carry in our head, but that we can access through prayer and meditation, and that wisdom flows to us when we stop clutching at the well-rehearsed thought patterns already within us.

Mindfulness meditation is a practice for setting aside the overidentification with our thoughts, beliefs, and internal dialogue. It is a method for developing receptivity toward greater wisdom. Mindfulness teaching repeatedly calls for cultivating a "beginner's mind"—the mind of a beginner is malleable and flexible, not yet hardened by assumptions and conclusions. A beginner's mind remains receptive and supple.

Leaders on the hero's journey are most effective when their minds are supple, as a supple mind moves freely, creating and innovating. The opposite of the supple mind is a calcified mind—a mind affected by psychosclerosis. Surrender learned from mindfulness enables flexibility of thought, action, and relationship that defies the calcification of a habit-driven mind. The investment of yielding the familiar returns an ability to adapt, adjust, and lead through multiple possibilities.

WHAT IS MINDFULNESS?

Mindfulness meditation is not a religious practice, but psycho-emotional training. It unfolds from the seeds of concentration. In fact, mindfulness meditation is a name for a level of concentration. As a way to focus and direct your attention, mindfulness provides a practical acceleration to leaps of faith and the process of surrendering. Mindfulness practice develops an ability to deliberately manage the grasping and clutching nature of our mind—an ability to open the fist of our thinking and yield our habitual attachment to beliefs and behaviors.

Mindfulness is the English word we use for a Pali (old Indian) word *sati*. Originally, it meant to take mental note, witness, observe, or pay close attention. It describes an activity of mind. Jon Kabat-Zinn is a mindfulness teacher and the founder of the Mindfulness-Based Stress Reduction program at the University of Massachusetts Medical Center. His definition of mindfulness is succinct and modern: "Mindfulness means paying attention in a particular way—on purpose, in the present moment, and nonjudgmentally."

> *Mindfulness practice develops an ability to deliberately manage the grasping and clutching nature of our mind—an ability to open the fist of our thinking and yield our habitual attachment to beliefs and behaviors.*

Paying attention "on purpose" means to consciously direct our awareness, deliberately choosing where we place our attention. Paying attention differs from passive awareness—being aware that you're eating, for example, differs from eating mindfully. Eating mindfully means purposefully attending to the sensations of taste, texture, temperature, and pressure, for example. It means noticing when your attention wanders, and then bringing it back to the process of eating.

In unmindful eating, our mind and attention wander and flit from thought to thought, to the TV, talking, reading, or all of the above. While a portion of our awareness attunes to the process of eating, it's happening on autopilot; we are not purposefully immersing our attention in the experience of our physical sensations, thoughts, and emotions. Thoughts and feelings wander without restriction. In the absence of deliberate effort to pay attention to our eating, there is no purposefulness. Purposefulness is a core aspect of mindfulness. Purposefully engaging our experience—breathing, emotional reactions, conversations—means that we are actively directing our minds.

Paying attention "in the present moment" is the second aspect of Kabat-Zinn's definition. One of the wonderful powers of the mind is its ability to travel through time—we can visit the recent and distant past or we can project into the near and far future. The mind constantly engages in this form of time travel and gravitates toward pleasant thoughts, memories, or fantasies, while working to reject unpleasant thoughts. Our thoughts turn to planning and worrying (future focus) and analyzing and reflecting (past focus). And with these thoughts we give rise to a range of emotions, including anger, envy, depression, revenge, self-pity, and so on. As we indulge in these thoughts of the past and future, we reinforce those emotions and perpetuate our suffering and struggle. Actual reality, the experience of life as it *is*, happens now, in this present moment—a moment we miss or avoid if we are not being mindful. Mindfulness is the practice of attending and noticing the experience unfolding right now. Of course we can plan for the future and reflect on the past, but we can do so mindfully—remaining aware that in this moment we're thinking about the past or future.

During specific meditation practice, however, we dedicate our attention to experiencing what arises in the present moment. When our mind wanders to thoughts about the past or future, we notice that the mind has wandered and return to experiencing this moment. Holding our attention to the present experience diminishes the habitual pull of past and future-based thoughts. In particular, it begins to reduce anxiety and stress, as these are always anticipatory thoughts and concerns.

Kabat-Zinn's third requisite of mindfulness, paying attention "non-judgmentally," has proved the hardest for me to master. It is also a significant contribution to leadership, as it brings about a centered grace. We instinctively judge some experiences as pleasant and desirable and others as unpleasant and aversive and, therefore, naturally want to shrink away from the unpleasant and move toward the pleasant. Applying nonjudgment means to simply notice whatever the experience is and let it be—to simply notice the upset or the excitement, the fear or the passion, and accept it. We observe mindfully and say yes to the experience. We notice most of all the transient and temporal nature of the experience—it arises, passes through us, and ceases to exist.

During meditation, whatever experience arises—pleasant or painful—we treat it the same way. We refer to this quality as "equanimity"—stillness and balance of mind. With practice, equanimity transcends the formal meditation practice and shapes our daily presence.

The Nature of Mind

We can study and examine the brain with technology, but the mind proves difficult to quantify. To make the most of our mind, however, it helps to understand how it works. Metaphors allow us to compare the mind to familiar phenomena and shed light on the nature of mind, so I'd like to offer air as a useful metaphor for explaining the nature of the mind and its function in meditation.

Of all the resources we require to exist (food, water, and air), air has the most immediate impact on our survival. We can abstain from food for long periods of time without endangering our survival. I once fasted for fourteen days, and, sure, I was weak and ravenously hungry, but I survived just fine. There are documented cases of people surviving for as long as a month without eating, living on water alone. We can't survive as long without water—maybe a week tops—but being deprived of air will kill most people in five minutes or less.

Air functions in a number of ways. As wind, it pushes the oceans and forms waves and currents, moving ships from port to port. Air holds aloft airplanes. Birds fly in the wind. Some flowers spread their seeds in the wind. Wind-borne sand has the power to carve solid rock, and raging tornados can rip tops off mountains and buildings. Sound travels through air. Our speech, the expression of our thought, is possible because of air. Yet air is neutral; it makes no distinction in what it carries, whether sounds or birds or clouds, or even the pollution and smog we manufacture. We hear melodies as well as mayhem through air. Life-flight helicopters and Scud missiles use air with equal measure and effectiveness.

Air is the medium, the context, within which objects are suspended and through which these objects move. Our mind, much like air, is filled with a variety of objects and sounds; it is a medium within which objects are suspended, move, arise, fall, and flow. Within the mind, these objects are forms of thought. Just as there exist a variety and quantity of objects in the air, a rich variety and quantity of thoughts inhabit the mind.

We have learned to categorize, manage, and protect the air we live, work, and play in. The United States, for example, has several agencies related to air. The EPA protects air quality, the FAA determines flight travel routes to prevent midair collisions, and NASA has found ways to extend past the farthest reaches of air and enter outer space. Few people, though, make similar efforts to manage, direct, and protect their mental environments. The practice of meditation bears resemblance to the efforts of the EPA, FAA, and NASA. Meditation is a path to understanding and managing the rich resource of our mind and all it contains.

When you look at the air, you can clearly see a jet plane or a dove, and even bees and mosquitoes. Dust particles are visible to the naked eye. Yet there is also an unseen aspect of airborne elements: tiny particles of dust floating in the air with germs and tiny viruses. And completely invisible to the eye even with magnifying equipment are sound waves, which, nevertheless, are in the air. The mind is like this, too. The longer you study the mind through observation, the more you notice what was unnoticeable before. You might discover during a meeting that an obvious thought ("Brian is aggressive") follows a subtle thought ("I really need to make everyone happy"). As we have studied and observed air, we have unlocked its secrets, enabling flight, communication, and power generation. If you want to enable the powers of your mind, therefore, you must also understand and direct it. The meditation practice that enables this mastery begins with stilling the mind.

27

STILLING THE MIND

I magine a crystal glass filled with water. The water in the glass contains silt and soil. Now imagine stirring this water and watching as the beige silt spins and twists. By its nature, the glass is clear, just like the water, but when stirred the water becomes murky and lightless. Now consider what might happen if you stopped stirring the water: no longer pushed to move, the water will stop spinning and twisting, and the silt, no longer excited and mixed, will settle to the bottom of the glass. As you visualize the settled crystal glass, what do you

> *The constant stirring of the mind with planning, worrying, analyzing, preparing, and categorizing, however, turns it murky and dim.*

see? You see the glass and clean water sparkle in their natural properties, and you see clear water and a layer of silt lining the bottom of the glass. Neither the glass, the water, nor the silt have changed their physical features. What changed was their state—from active to still.

Similarly, the mind is naturally clear and brilliant. The constant stirring of the mind with planning, worrying, analyzing, preparing, and categorizing, however, turns it murky and dim. Making time for the mind to become still allows the silt and sand of our hopes, fears, and worries to settle, and the natural property of mental clarity to return. Stilling the mind is an act of surrender. You can't still the mind by force, but by yielding and letting go of habitual attention. Here are a few documented benefits of a mind clarified with stillness:

- Innovative problem solving
- Effective decision making

- Accurate analysis and synthesis
- Engaged dialogue and conversation
- Comprehensive planning and preparation
- Creative perspectives and ideas

Meditation practice allows you to stop stirring your mental content and thereby bring forth the natural state of mental clarity. Studies show that meditation practice restructures your brain and can train it to concentrate, feel more compassion, and better cope with stress. But that doesn't make the practice easy.

"I tried to meditate once," Kelly, a thirty-eight-year-old VP of finance shared with me, "but my mind just wouldn't stop squirming and jumping from thought to thought. I couldn't get comfortable or stay still. I can't get my mind blank. It's just not for me." If you've tried to sit quietly and meditate, you probably found it challenging, especially if you've tried to stop thinking. Attempting to stop the stream of mental material from flowing and racing can increase your awareness of how much goes on in your mind: worries, self-criticism, old memories, fantasies, and pervasive to-do lists. Meditating requires patience and time. So is it worth the struggle? In a word, yes. I've found my experiences of twenty-five years of meditation reflected in the scientific articles proliferating over the past two decades. Learning to sharpen your mind and hear your heart definitely cultivates focused attention, better decision making, compassion, enhanced emotional intelligence, and contentment. These are not just the promises of Patanjali and Buddha, the ancient teachers from India. These results have been scientifically supported.

Our first step in discussing meditation is to debunk a perennial myth: meditation practice is not about making the mind blank. Trying to stop thinking would be like trying to stop digesting or pumping blood—the stomach processes food, the heart circulates blood, and the mind thinks. That's what it does. The brain is a processing instrument: it weighs and measures, compares and contrasts, labels and anticipates. If your brain is normal, then it constantly generates thoughts. Your brain works constantly in the background of your experience, just as your digestion works without effort and your heart pumps blood without your attention.

At this moment, your physical and mental processes operate automatically in the background, while your attention focuses on reading. A blank mind is correlated with death, not meditation. The objective of mindfulness meditation is to direct your attention on purpose and without judgment. During mindfulness you might, for example, hold your attention on the various steps and aspects of inhaling and exhaling. Thoughts about past and future don't cease to exist, and awareness of your environment registers automatically in the background, just as your heart continues to pump and your digestive system turns food into energy. The goal of achieving a blank mind is a fantasy from Kung Fu movies and tales of the East, not a realistic expectation.

Our science, though two thousand years more "advanced" than the science of ancient Indian teachers, now firmly supports the value of meditation practice. Neuroscientists have demonstrated that meditation, even in small daily doses, can influence your experience of the world by remodeling the physical structure of your brain. A generation ago, doctors and scientists believed that the brain developed in childhood, peaked in adulthood, and remained static until it degraded in late adulthood. However, by using the penetrating real-time photography of fMRI, researchers can now examine the living brain and its functions, and as a result the brain, once thought static, is now known for its incredible elasticity. The term for lifelong brain development is *neuroplasticity*. You can strengthen and condition your brain as much as you can your biceps or heart with exercise and practice. Everything we do, and every experience we have, actually changes the brain.

Meditation modifies the brain in some specific ways. In 2009, Eileen Luders and her colleagues in the Department of Neurology at the UCLA School of Medicine published their study comparing the brains of twenty-two meditators and twenty-two similarly aged nonmeditators. Several differences between the two groups were identified. Specifically, the meditators had more gray matter in regions of the brain important for attention, emotion regulation, and mental flexibility.

The functions of your brain and the effectiveness of your leadership are proven to improve with mindfulness meditation. To lead is to direct attention, regulate your own and others' emotions, and adapt and innovate through mental flexibility. These leadership skills and abilities are the drivers of effectiveness that catalyze your leadership results. Increased gray matter in an area of the brain causes that area to process information more efficiently and powerfully; consequently, this increases your effectiveness at controlling your attention, managing your emotions, and making mindful (deliberate, clear, and intentional) choices as a leader. Since the brain you have today is a product of the demands you have placed on it, it's a matter of training to develop these abilities.

Learning to meditate is no different from learning other mental skills like reading financial reports, problem solving, strategic planning, or playing music. Like anything else that requires practice, meditation is a training program for the brain. I discovered Rollerblading in college. I was determined to master the flowing, easy motion that I saw experienced Rollerbladers demonstrate as they glided along the boardwalk under the bright San Diego sun. I was new to Rollerblading and had to invest concentrated learning and practice to become skilled, but I could practically feel how my efforts and practice formed new neural connections in my brain. I didn't react to my many falls as setbacks, but accepted them as part of the learning process. I bought knee and elbow pads to reduce the damage, and continued to practice until my movements became familiar and fluid.

Meditation skills, like Rollerblading, develop with repetition and consistency. Meditation teachers have insisted for millennia that students practice and repeat in order to learn. Now fMRI technology shows that repeated effort and practice lead to visible changes in the structure of the brain. So, as I mastered the Rollerblades, my physical brain got better at the task. Dedicated practice helps musicians' brains get better at analyzing and creating music, mathematicians' brains get better at solving problems, and executives' brains get better at thinking strategically.

Recall part I, Focus: What Am I Creating? Focus does more than direct your attention; it actually changes your brain. If you take up juggling, your brain develops the area that anticipates moving objects.

For my physician brother-in-law, the intense learning in medical school changed his hippocampus—the area of the brain connected with memory. The brains of mathematicians have more gray matter in the regions connected with arithmetic and spatial reasoning. The premise that a thought is a thing and that you become what you think about most can be physically confirmed with neuroimaging studies. We can choose which thoughts to emphasize and which thoughts to ignore; that's the human gift of being able to direct our attention.

Leading is stressful and demanding. Being an engaged and engaging executive demands exceptional energy and concentration. Focused energy and concentrated attention are the hallmarks of meditation. What, then, do meditators' brains get better at doing? Studies show that they improve processing ability in at least three areas:

- Concentration: remaining attentive to important facts and relationships in the face of distraction

- Stress management: containing and redirecting the brain away from worry and anxiety and toward real-time problem solving

- Emotional regulation: developing a capacity for compassion, which, in turn improves employee engagement and team productivity

Concentration

My meditation teachers were adamant that I learn to "hold a point"—an active process of directing your attention in two distinct ways: narrow focus and open awareness. Narrow focus, similar to looking through a microscope, reduces your scope of attention and reveals fine detail. Narrow focusing improves your capacity to attend to something specific while blocking out distractions as it narrows the aperture of your mind, filters out extraneous data, and magnifies the object/idea/person/situation you're investigating. Open awareness, on the other hand, expands and increases your attention. Open awareness resembles looking through a telescope; it reveals a wider field of data all around you. Open awareness places a fish-eye lens on your mind and enables you to take in a tremendous volume of data as you notice what is happening around you. It gives you a fuller perspective of the present moment.

Mike, the marketing executive we met in our discussion of courage, had to flex his concentration muscle when he sat down to restructure a critical contract with his largest client. He had to focus exclusively on thinking through the benefits and implications of the new contract. Like many leaders, Mike subscribed to an open-door policy, which, while it added value to teamwork and engagement, diminished his ability to concentrate. I strongly urge you to practice closed-door concentration sessions along with maintaining a policy of an open door. Closing your door for a period of time doesn't make you detached and unavailable; it makes you productive and efficient. For most of us, the start of the day is when our brain is fresh and our mind is sharp—this makes the morning an optimal time for concentration sessions. Mike experimented on a Wednesday morning when he came into the office and set up a temporary "fortress of solitude" in order to nurture space for his concentration; he closed his office door and instructed his assistant to deflect incoming calls and requests.

Important leadership decisions sometimes require undistracted time for concentrated reflection and thought. I recommend you reserve thirty minutes to an hour at the beginning of each day to be focused and uninterrupted in order to contemplate the four questions we have explored in depth to this point:

- What am I creating? What are my missions and priorities, and what shall I/we accomplish today to advance that mission?

- What am I avoiding? Are there any projects or people that I'm avoiding because they cause me to feel anxious, angry, or confused?

- What am I sustaining? Where do I/we need more discipline and perseverance in order to advance our mission and priorities or diminish breakdown or errors?

- What am I yielding? What leap of faith can I take today? Which project, task, or plan can I let go of or empower someone else to drive?

By answering these four questions at the very beginning of your workday, you bring focus and priority into your activity and into the work and efforts of your teams.

Tom, a VP of engineering in an equipment manufacturing plant, was a smart and ambitious leader who directed a department of four hundred people. His open door became a revolving door. Dozens of complex machines, thousands of manufactured parts, hundreds of thousands of components, and thousands of work hours can make for a rich cocktail of problems and mishaps. Even though Tom developed competent managers on his team, his skills and expertise were in continuous high demand. Tom also had three elementary-school-aged daughters, and his wife urged him to spend more time at home. When I asked him to experiment with closing his door for an hour in the morning and half an hour in the afternoon, Tom chortled nervously. I assured him that concentrated time would improve his productivity.

"My people need me to solve problems and answer questions in real time," Tom explained, "and I need them to stay on task. There's no way I can cut myself off from them." Tom was convinced that his open-door "best practice" ensured constant communication with his team, but he was mistaking quantity of time for quality of communication; he believed that more time produced better exchanges.

Tom needed concentrated time to plan, analyze, and prioritize. He reluctantly agreed to an experiment: for two weeks he closed his door for one hour early in the morning and thirty minutes toward the end of his day. To his surprise, he found that this uninterrupted time provided him mental focus and an accelerated ability to solve complex problems, plan, review, and prepare for meetings. His concentrated time improved both his decision making and productivity. Equally as important, as his efficiency improved, Tom was able to calmly leave work with more time for his wife and three daughters.

Scheduling time to perform concentrated work is proven to enhance work output. And learning how to optimally harness the mind during those focused times multiplies efficiency. Cultivating your attention through meditation practices will also enable you to wield concentration with even greater precision. Researchers at the Waisman Laboratory for Brain Imaging and Behavior at the University of Wisconsin at Madison have shown that concentrated meditation activates regions of the brain critical for controlling our attention. Fortunately, this outcome occurs even after brief training in meditation, and more experienced practitioners show even stronger activation in these regions.

The work of leading is concentration-intensive. Your leadership attention gets directed to multiple fronts: people and relationships, projects, markets and competitors, processes and operations, and customers. You have to pay attention in order to make good decisions about strategy, processes, and culture. If you can't concentrate, you are bound to miss critical details and compromise your decisions. Even hyperactive entrepreneurial leaders I've worked with have developed an ability to concentrate intensely, if in short bursts.

Meditation enables you to look beyond the obvious and below the surface. To be a change agent, you must challenge yourself to seek the truth and see things as they are, not as they should be or how they used to be. Mindfulness meditation shares that objective in that its practice develops insight—the ability to see things as they really are. That can't happen when the mind is distracted and unfocused. Recall a conversation with one of your colleagues, for example, when you were so caught up in your own thoughts that you missed what she said. Or perhaps while driving you narrowly missed an accident as the car in front of you suddenly stopped and you snapped to attention just in time to avoid the collision.

Psychologists refer to our gaps in noticing as "attentional blink." This unfocused mental state is common, but it's also a barrier to effective leading. We visited Dr. Baumeister's research on decision fatigue and limited attention resource earlier. Fortunately, Dr. Antoine Lutz of the Waisman Laboratory discovered that you can do more with that limited mental energy than was previously believed—by learning to harness attention through meditation, you can reduce your attentional blink and achieve a more accurate and complete perception of reality, since you will notice more and miss less. To put it simply, meditation develops an ability to spend less energy paying attention, which frees up your capacity to take in larger aspects of reality.

Managing Stress

Your leadership includes the daily balance of two forces: uncertainty and accountability. Mary, for instance, has strategic objectives that she must accomplish; her job depends on it, and she's a savvy leader who has gathered a talented and committed team. But despite her planning, she has no guarantee that they will successfully accomplish their objectives. She is, after all, pressing into new territory of services and clients; she is seeking to accomplish what has not yet been done. The inherent uncertainty of traversing the unknown is ever present on the path of leadership. It is also the material upon which anxiety feeds and from which stress arises.

Stressful tension grows in the gap between current reality and desired reality; you develop stress when you set out to accomplish something difficult and desirable. More simply, when you care about a goal you open yourself to stress—people who don't care don't have stress. When your imagination dwells on your limited control and all the things that could cause you to falter or miss your goal, anxiety becomes activated and stress builds. In our discussion of courage, we studied anxiety in depth. In addition to courage, meditation provides another tool to mitigate anxiety and manage stress.

All people experience mental turbulence such as worry, self-doubt, anxiety, and even panic. People with anxiety disorders, however, get caught in repetitive mental loops of these clusters of thoughts. Their lives are dominated by them. Research shows that mindfulness meditation offers release for people with anxiety, as part of its effectiveness lies in changing the way the brain responds to negative thoughts. Participants in an eight-week mindfulness-based course in stress reduction reported greater control of their mental experience as well as reduced anxiety compared with their experience before the mindfulness practice.

Using fMRI technology, researchers compared brain scans from participants before and after the course. The findings of what happened after just two months of daily mindfulness practice were surprising: these novice meditators' brains registered greater activity in a neural network associated with processing information when they reflected on negative self-statements. In other words, they paid more attention to the negative statements than they had before the intervention. This counterintuitive result happened because the increased attentiveness to negative self-talk simultaneously decreased activation of the amygdala—a region associated with stress and anxiety. In other words, the participants became more aware of their internal negative dialogue but learned to mentally distance themselves from their thoughts; they learned to question the accuracy of their thoughts and, therefore, suffered less. They reported less anxiety and worrying. They put themselves down less, and their self-esteem improved. If we can mitigate clinical anxiety disorders through mindfulness meditation, imagine the benefits for leaders affected by leadership stress. Leadership, with its focus on growth, change, uncertainty, and results can expose you to continuous stress and anxiety.

Remember, mindfulness meditation doesn't attempt to ignore or deny the negativity of thinking. Rather, it teaches you how to handle distressing thoughts and emotions without being overpowered by them. In part II on courage, we discussed how leaders on the hero's journey turn toward their fear and anxiety. Mindfulness practice is a tangible and extremely valuable tool for engaging and facing your negative thoughts rather than rejecting them. It provides a "how-to" practice to cultivate courage in the face of fear.

Leaders I work with typically fall into two categories when facing fear: repressing or obsessing. Neither of these methods works too well and both enhance anxiety. Quite frankly, after almost three decades of meditation practice, I haven't discovered how to stop my mind from generating worrisome thoughts. Fortunately, the aim of meditation is not to get rid of these thoughts and emotions. The intent is threefold: to become aware of the stream of thoughts, to choose where to place attention, and to move through the thoughts without getting stuck. Mindfulness meditation practice teaches you how to become a curious observer and thereby learn to experience negativity from a distance rather than being an engaged participant in the thought pattern. Ultimately, the aim of meditation practice is to embrace reality as it is.

A study by Massachusetts General Hospital and Harvard University has confirmed that mindfulness meditation can lead to lasting positive changes in the brain. Participants who reported stress reduction after an eight-week mindfulness-based stress reduction course also registered physical brain changes in brain scans. Specifically, their brains showed decreases in gray matter density in the amygdala. Previous research has revealed that trauma and chronic stress can enlarge the amygdala—more gray matter in the amygdala (increased processing power in that region) makes it more reactive and leads to more habitual stress and anxiety. Now we know that change occurs in the opposite direction, too. We can actually train the brain to become less reactive and more resilient.

The implication of brain changes for leaders is significant. Leadership, in general, and executive leadership, in particular, involve constant consideration of the future, which is the same mental orientation of anxiety—a state arising from negatively reflecting on the uncertainty of the future. The very role of executive leadership provokes anxiety. This dynamic creates a leadership bind: your creative thinking is a significant component of your leadership, but this thinking also activates anxiety and stress. Learning the skills of mindfulness meditation and applying them to your work can positively affect your brain and enhance your hard-won leadership skills.

A friend recently shared an "applied mindfulness" story: A psychology professor walked around the classroom while teaching a stress-management workshop. As she raised a glass of water, everyone expected her to ask if the glass was half-empty or half-full. To their surprise, and with a mischievous smile, she asked, "How heavy is this glass of water?" Participants called out answers ranging from eight to twenty ounces. She replied, "The absolute weight doesn't matter. What matters is how long I hold it. If I hold it for a minute, it's not a problem. If I hold it for an hour, I'll have an ache in my arm. If I hold it for a day, my arm will feel numb. In each case, the weight of the glass doesn't change, but the longer I hold it, the heavier it becomes." She continued, "The stresses and worries in life are like that glass of water. Think about them for a while and nothing happens. Think about them a bit longer and they begin to hurt. And if you think about them all day long, you will feel paralyzed—incapable of doing anything."

It's important to your organization, your family, and yourself to manage your stress. Meditation supports your leadership by changing your experience of stress in two ways: First, you learn to mitigate your stress in real time by releasing—surrendering—your tightly gripped thoughts. Second, you discover how to prevent the buildup of stress in the first place by becoming selective about which thoughts you nurture and which to let be. You can still have water in the glass, but you learn how to put the glass down.

Emotional Regulation

More than just concentrating on problem solving and planning, leadership is a relational competency. Leadership works in the context of followership: people's willingness to emotionally commit and engage with you, your vision, and the rest of the team. Can meditation practice impact engagement and your ability to achieve better results through others? The answer is yes. Let's explore why.

First, some basic concepts about engagement. Engagement is a level of emotional commitment, and there's a demonstrably direct relationship between employee engagement, employee productivity, and company profitability. While we can emotionally commit to ideas (freedom, fairness, or creativity) and to institutions (my country, basketball team, or children's school), we most frequently commit to people. Engagement at work associates strongly with relationships to peers and leaders.

Fortunately, there are as many ways to be emotionally engaged as there are styles of personality. Tom's style is rational and "arm's-length." Mary is caring and nurturing. Mike is jovial, energetic, and fun. These three leaders are stylistically distinct, yet they are each successful because their people are engaged. Engagement emerges from a quality of connection and relationship, not from any particular style, and it can be cultivated. Our emotional range is not fixed at birth. You can cultivate compassion, for example, by increasing your attention to it and to practices related to it. Feeling connected to others can be learned like other skills, and meditation practice can cultivate compassion as evidenced both in behavior and brain function.

Compassion is a two-part experience: feeling sympathetic for someone who is suffering and experiencing a strong desire to alleviate that suffering. While compassion isn't commonly discussed in companies, we expect leaders to have empathy and relate to others' feelings, thoughts, or attitudes. Compassion is often relegated to social and spiritual work, and I've even heard people say that it has no place in environments that require accountability and disciplinary action. I would argue that intensity of drive and compassion are not mutually exclusive. There is no question that leaders must press for change, results, and productivity, but increased compassion does not diminish that leadership drive.

On her heroic journey, Mary had to balance her compassion with her drive. Kim, Mary's senior researcher, was a highly skilled scientist but interpersonally clueless. Kim's staff members reported frustration at what they described as Kim's gruff and self-centered behavior. Mary, driven by her compassion, provided Kim everything from benefit of the doubt to leadership seminars and executive coaching, but Kim remained unmoved. Eventually, Mary had to fire her. It took her four years to do so, however, as her compassionate nature dominated her decision making.

Mary had to balance her compassion and accountability. After her experience with Kim, she fired Chris in just two years, she let Brian go in four months, and she fired Nicole within forty-eight hours. Yet Mary is no less compassionate today than she was seven years ago. In fact, her awareness of others' suffering and her urge to help has sharpened; she has also grown in her ability to balance these feelings with her leadership responsibility to all stakeholders. Mary's determination to remain compassionate has increased the intensity of her team's loyalty and engagement. This increased loyalty is not limited to her team but also affects her clients, investors, and even her bankers.

Compassion is the invisible glue in the delicate construction of trust. The answer to "Do I trust you?" depends on a mental qualification we make by asking, "Do I believe you have my best interests at heart?" Mary's compassion and her desire to help earn her an unambiguous yes to that question. Her people feel confident that Mary has their best interests at heart. These are critical variables in her decision making. Mary's employees trust her, and that trust in Mary reduces their anxiety about the business uncertainty. Therefore, they commit themselves fully to her and to her vision and stay deeply engaged.

Mary is naturally compassionate. My native strength, however, lies in logic. My heart-based connection has grown from decades of practice, but it remains secondary to my rational powers. I have found one significant aspect of mindfulness training quite instructive in nurturing my compassionate presence—*lovingkindness*. In lovingkindness meditation, practitioners direct their attention to generating a state of care and compassion. The practice begins by thinking about someone you care about and experiencing the loving feelings that generates. You then extend these feelings of care to yourself, to other people, and, finally, attempt to extend it to the world. With the use of fMRI, researchers have measured what compassionate practice physically does to the brain. Meditators showed a larger brain response in areas important for processing physical sensations and for emotional responding, particularly to sounds of distress. The researchers also observed an increase in heart rate that corresponded to the brain changes. The brains of meditators who engage in lovingkindness are more attuned to care and compassion. These are powerful building blocks of relationship, and evoke a response of trust and connection.

These findings suggest that lovingkindness meditators experienced a genuine empathic response along with greater compassion. In other words, compassion meditation appears to make the brain more naturally open to a connection with others. A study by psychologist Barbara Fredrickson and her colleagues at the University of North Carolina, Chapel Hill, found that a seven-week lovingkindness meditation course increased participants' daily experiences of joy, gratitude, and hope. The more participants meditated, the better they felt. Participants also reported an increased sense of self-acceptance, social support, sense of purpose, and life satisfaction, while experiencing fewer symptoms of depression. This study provides strong evidence that practicing a path of compassion, and chipping away at the illusion of separation, can open us up to a far more meaningful connection to life.

Practicing Mindfulness

As I stated earlier, the practice of mindfulness meditation promotes self-awareness and the ability to direct your attention; you can then apply the mindful attention you develop in meditation to life and leadership. The practice begins with concentration and observation. To observe is to notice and examine dispassionately—without judgment or interpretation. Observation demands a form of objectivity often associated with scientific research. Scientists studying aerodynamic phenomena, for example, engage with their object of study without regard to subjective emotions and moods; they approach their study with consistency and make detailed notes about the data they collect. The key to effective observation is detachment—a dispassionate objectivity that unlinks what is observed from meaning. Similarly, mindfulness practice requires that you become an observer of your own self. In order to develop your observer self, you learn to split your attention.

Mentally recall a meeting in which one of your colleagues was passionately promoting his point of view. Picture him leaning forward, his voice pitched in excitement, his skin flushed as he's adamantly pressing on about his idea. Remember how you deciphered the signs of his intense commitment: voice, posture, pace, facial expression, and word choice. You observed these details and made some conclusions about his commitment, intent, and anxiety.

Great leaders are great observers. Yes, you have to articulate vision and mission and you have to effectively express goals and shape processes. But if you don't learn to observe, you won't fully activate all your leadership responsibilities. Strong observation skills lie at the heart of leadership abilities such as effective communication, engaging interpersonal skills, influencing people, managing change, managing group dynamics, and selling (getting buy-in) ideas, plans, and strategy. Modern leadership depends on relationships; it works in the context of rapport, bonding, and association. Meaningful relationships emerge when you know and understand the other. Observing others and consequently understanding them is key to your leadership effectiveness.

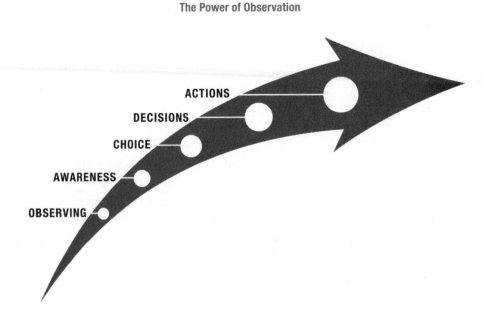

The Power of Observation

ACTIONS

DECISIONS

CHOICE

AWARENESS

OBSERVING

Observing and understanding others is key to relationship building. Observing and understanding yourself is equally key to making better decisions and your own professional evolution. Remember: if you always do what you've always done, you'll always have what you've always had. Observation yields awareness, awareness yields choice, choice yields expanded decisions, expanded decisions yield new possibilities for actions, and these different actions yield different results. Observing and understanding others enables you to lead them effectively toward your desirable shared vision. Observing and understanding yourself enables you to lead yourself toward your own desirable vision.

Mitch is a respected SVP at his architecture firm. Now journeying into his mid-fifties, he is known for his deep expertise, keen problem-solving skills, and passion for the business. Oddly enough, his passion keeps him from advancing to COO. He is a visionary with a huge appetite for problem solving and drive for results, but Mitch didn't pay attention to subtle cues in personal relationships; he infuriated his team and managers in spite of being respected for his organizational abilities.

Mitch agreed to engage in executive coaching for his leadership evolution. We first looked at Mitch's 360-degree feedback assessment results and, as expected, there was a clear gap in perception of his communication and listening skills. On a scale of 1–5, Mitch graded himself a 4 on his listening abilities; no one else gave him a higher rate than 3 (he averaged 2.35). Mitch couldn't explain the gap in perceptions, but he sincerely wanted to improve and become an effective leader. To his credit, he recognized that he had to change his behavior, and the feedback he received clarified the discontent of his people. But he didn't know which behavior to change or how to change it. Without data about the particulars of his actions, without awareness, he was powerless to make positive changes. Mitch needed to increase his awareness to improve his leadership. In addition to feedback from others, he had to glean firsthand knowledge of his patterns; he had to observe himself.

Developing the observer-self isn't complicated; it starts with your choice to pay attention in a focused and dispassionate way. The easiest way to conceptualize this is by imagining a micro version of you sitting on your shoulder: It has a single task—observe and report. It pays attention to what you say, how you move, how you feel, and the effect you're having on others. Your observer-self gathers information in real time, and as you become aware of what you are doing, you create an inventory of reality. From this inventory you can choose and select the behaviors you want to demonstrate; you may choose to conduct yourself as you have all along, but at least you'll be doing so more consciously.

The observer-self is an objective witness that notices, perceives, and takes in data and information; it cannot make interpretations, judgments, or changes. It is never the critic. This exercise is *not* intended to add self-criticism and internal disapproval. Observing and witnessing are acts of discovery, not judgment.

At first Mitch felt silly placing an imaginary, note-taking micro self on his shoulder. Fortunately, the observer-self is invisible, weightless, and doesn't require batteries; all it requires is a portion of attention—attending to what you're doing at the same time as you are attending to your environment. If you've learned to play a sport or a game, then you've learned how to think about what you're doing and what others are doing, too. You learned to quickly calculate what might happen and how to prepare to respond to it. This is a skill of splitting your attention. Observing the self is directing this mental skill in a particular way.

Mitch's observer witnessed how he communicated and interacted with people and became aware of his loud, gravelly, and driving voice. He observed his coworkers' reactions to him—their posture, faces, and speech—and he was genuinely surprised as he made the connection between his actions and his coworkers' reactions. Mitch observed the drive and intensity that he wielded regardless of the circumstance. He saw that he exaggerated when he spoke in absolutes—using words like *everyone, all the time, everything, nothing, always,* and *never.*

The first leg of the journey of growth is not change; it's awareness. Through his observer self, Mitch became aware of his actions and of other people's reactions. In fact, I specifically asked him *not* to change a thing about his behavior in the first week of observation. He failed. Awareness, you see, changes us. As Mitch grew in awareness, without even trying to change, his behavior began to shift. As he gained first-hand understanding of his actions and how they impacted the people around him, he made real-time choices about his behavior. His relationships at work improved in direct proportion to the effectiveness of his observer-self.

Mitch discovered that his observer-self gave him an ability to witness and experience his surroundings with objectivity. Imagine the benefit of engaging in an emotionally charged debate at work and, while remaining intellectually engaged, also accessing an emotionally neutral part. How valuable would it be to analyze a mistake, for example, as you feel your passion to win, but not succumb to the frustration of losing? How might you benefit from traversing a lawsuit without letting your fear, indignation, and anger dominate?

A developed observer-self heightens emotional and leadership maturity. An observer-self is not a path to becoming robotic or emotionally flat; it's a path to wisdom that breeds better decisions and better leadership results. It's also a partner to the concentrative ability to fix your mind on a single point. Observation allows attention to remain open and unfettered, not caught up and lost in stimuli, and a mind prepared with observation can turn the strength of its attention to an object of concentration. During concentration—as a myriad of objects and ideas try to grab center stage—observation allows them to wait their turn.

Learning to Hold a Point

Concentration is a process of harnessing and holding your attention to one predetermined object or idea. Returning to the metaphor of air, an observation would include notes of all the birds, their songs, and their flight patterns. In concentration, you purposefully attend to the red-breasted sparrow flying overhead and concentrate on its song and flight pattern.

Meditation is a process of organic growth. To grow a beautiful and bright sunflower, you plant the seed and provide it with water, sunlight, and fertilizer. As it unfolds from its striped shell, you tend to the shoot, remove weeds, and keep the birds and rabbits away. When the shoot grows three inches above the soil, you can't tug on it to accelerate its growth; you have to nurture it, protect it, and stay patient. Similarly, while developing your concentration muscle, you can't grit your teeth, squint your eyes, tense your shoulders, and scream at your mind to keep quiet. Doing so will bring you no closer to the mindfulness you are trying to attain.

Try this simple observation exercise: Sit in a comfortable position and close your eyes. Direct your attention to your body and notice any physical sensations: pressure, heat, movement, tension, and so on. In your observation, make simple labels of your experience: "feet pressing on floor" or "the room is warm." You don't have to interpret or reject any of the observed items; simply notice them and form a thorough inventory. Take note of the inevitable thoughts, ideas, and feelings running through your mind, and treat your thoughts like clouds in the sky—notice and observe. Allow them to float by and out of sight.

For concentration, sit in the same comfortable position and close your eyes. However, only focus on your breathing process and experience. Gently and persistently return your attention to noticing your breath. Every time your attention wanders to one of the other "birds in the air," gently draw it back to the simplicity of breathing.

When you meditate, you will notice how much variety fills the air of your mind. Inevitably, your attention will want to flit from attraction to attraction like a child in a toy store. Try as you might, you can't force your mind to be motionless; in fact, fighting and forcing your mind to stop thinking only creates tension and struggle. This forced strain and constant vigil against a natural process assures that you won't be able to relax and let go.

I offer you another metaphor to consider as you prepare for mindfulness practice: the boiling pot. Imagine your mind is a large pot of water. Thinking and living have turned up the heat, boiling the water in the pot. Each thought is a bubble that forms on the bottom of the pot—it grows, detaches from the bottom, travels to the surface, disturbs the surface with a boil, and then changes into steam and vanishes. Instead of fighting to suppress thoughts, allow them to rise and disappear into the air. Since the stream of thoughts never ends, you don't need to control or suppress them; it's easier to learn to simply notice the thoughts moving through the water, arising and disappearing like bubbles.

Practice for a Change

As evidence of the benefits of meditation grows, one of the most important questions is "How much practice is enough?" Or, from the perspective of beginning meditators, "How little is enough to see positive change?" Experience among practitioners indicates that several benefits happen early on; noticeable change occurs in a matter of weeks among novices. Experience matters, however. More practice leads to greater changes, both in the brain and in a meditator's mental states. So while a minimal investment in meditation can pay off for your well-being and mental clarity, developing a practice habit is the best way to experience the full benefits.

Learning a new language, software, or accounting method require focused effort, consistent application, and repetition. Grit, as we've discussed, is a key trait of successful leaders; it transforms learning into ingrained behavior, into habit. Adopting meditation as a lever for making better decisions, developing people, and improving personal productivity requires us to practice the habit. Begin your practice with ten minutes a day and experience firsthand the life-changing benefits. Even with advances in brain technology, there are changes both subtle and profound transmitted only through direct experience. Fortunately, all you need to get started is the willingness to sit and be with your own body, breath, and mind.

Simple Mindfulness Meditation

"Pay no attention to the man behind the curtain" says the Wizard in the 1939 movie *The Wizard of Oz*, as Dorothy, the Tin Man, the Scarecrow, and the Cowardly Lion cower before the Great and Powerful Oz, a mystical figure shrouded in a curtain of fire and smoke.

They don't realize that the force behind the Wizard is a lost little man from Omaha, Nebraska. In this critical scene, Toto, Dorothy's dog, pulls the curtain back and reveals the operator behind the veil. The form of the Great and Powerful Oz is revealed as a distorted reflection of the man—removing the curtain of appearance reveals his essence. Mindfulness, like Toto, works to remove the shroud of our own thinking and reveal the essence of our reality. The purpose of mindfulness is to engage reality as it is.

Through mindfulness we learn to direct awareness to whatever is present in that moment rather than getting caught up in a single object or idea. Here is a simple practice: Take a comfortable seat and bring your attention to the experience of your belly rising and falling with your breath; this will start your awareness of breathing. As you observe and notice your breath related movements, you will find yourself naturally attuning to other sensations and physical data. You can have a meditation practice no more complex than spending ten-minute sessions simply observing and noticing your belly rising and falling with your breath.

Once you feel settled, widen your awareness to include all the sensations of breathing. Notice your chest and shoulders rise and fall. Notice the stream of air as it passes through your nostrils. Notice cool air flowing over the skin of your upper lip and through your nostrils as you inhale, and how the breath changes to warm moist air flowing out your nostrils as you exhale. Move your attention like a flashlight beam that brings details into focus. Direct your attention to your throat and sense the air flowing back and forth, in and out—dry, cool air flowing in, and warm, moist air flowing out. Simply attending to the process and sensations of breathing concentrates the mind and settles the body. Without a doubt, your attention will wander to other thoughts or evaporate into forgetfulness; when this happens, gently—without guilt or self-criticism—return your attention to the breathing experience.

After some practice, your body will settle with attention to your breath. When you're ready, add this simple visualization (made popular by Jon Kabat-Zin) to further settle and relax your mind: Imagine yourself as a mountain—its base rooted in the earth and its top touching the sky. The air of the sky is your thoughts. Some thoughts are stormy, with thunder, lightning, and strong winds. Some thoughts are like fog or dark clouds. Some thoughts are bright and alluring. But rather than getting caught in the thoughts, focus on the mountain. As you inhale, think to yourself, "Mountain." As you exhale, think quietly, "Stable." Use your breath to focus on the present moment; cultivate the ability to weather the storm. If you find yourself swept up in a thought or emotion, observe it and simply return to the breath. The key is to simply notice, to observe the ever-changing process of thinking. You don't have to get caught in the contents of your thoughts; as you begin to see that they are indeed just thoughts, they begin to lose their power. You will no longer believe everything you think! Continue to watch and become mindful of your thoughts, feelings, and sensations for five to twenty minutes.

HOW DO YOU RENEW AND GROW?

Leadership becomes a hero's journey at the intersection of ambition, sacrifice, and service. Effective leaders spend their energy ensuring their organization's well-being. They form a personal shield they feel safe behind; they form an organizational shield of strength within which they function safely. Effective leaders also extend effort challenging themselves and their people. And effective leaders champion and stimulate growth, valuing it not for its own sake, but as a contribution to the market and to the community.

Growth is not objectively sacred; you necessarily commit to growth in order to avoid decline and irrelevance. As people and organizations, we either evolve or decay, but we cannot maintain a status quo. When the shield of protection becomes a cage of stability, it must be broken. Entropy, the second law of thermodynamics, claims that all closed systems move toward average performance and eventual decline. Leadership responsibility includes infusing and importing fresh energy into the system to avoid decay and to sustain growth. Leaders are the primary promoters of organizational renewal; it's their responsibility to yield the shield, personally and organizationally.

Growth and renewal represent the ability to exceed current limits and expand. One way to grow is by acquisition; another way is by elimination. You make room for new projects, products, and processes when you shed old ones and release outmoded approaches; this lightens your load and speeds you up. Leading involves a perpetual calibration of what to maintain and what to terminate. Releasing a familiar process, idea, or team member can bring anxiety, but it is a necessity for the future and for organizational well-being. Yielding the shield of protection energizes movement from the comfort zone to the growth zone.

Sometimes we learn lessons in the most unlikely places, and we can learn a lot about growth through yielding by examining the life of crabs. Crabs have an exoskeleton (external skeleton), while mammals have an endoskeleton (internal skeleton), and, because of their hard outer shell, crabs don't grow like mammals. To grow, they must shed their shell in a process called molting that begins by absorbing large amounts of seawater and swelling like a balloon. This swelling expands until it forces the shell apart, eventually tearing along a seam that runs around the body. The crab pops open like a lid. Having cracked its shell, the crab extracts itself from its constricted old suit. As it leaves behind the old casing that held it safe and constricted, it immediately begins to secrete a new shell. Anytime you've walked past what looks like a dead empty crab, it's likely a cast-off exoskeleton. After molting, the crab lives in a spongy plump state that you know as a soft-shell crab. Over time, the soft, stretched-out shell hardens and the water in the crab is replaced with muscle. The shell becomes rock hard after a month.

Scientists have researched the remarkable phenomenon of crab molting for decades. A king crab may molt six times in its first year, four in its second, two or three times in its third, and after that, perhaps only once a year. I promise that this *National Geographic* detour has direct and crucial implications for your leadership.

When a crab outgrows its armored container, it must abandon it, and this growth activity means becoming vulnerable. Regardless of how effective and useful the shell once was, it is now a constriction, and when protection overwhelms development, it is no protection at all. The crab that wants to grow and evolve has to surrender its armor and risk a soft new shell that makes it vulnerable to its surroundings. Similarly, you must molt your protectiveness if you want to evolve and renew your enterprises. Albert Einstein is credited with saying that a problem cannot be solved at the same level of thinking that created it. As your organization grows, its problems grow, and the solutions must grow, too.

I don't like being vulnerable and susceptible to hurt, so I have made a life for myself that is physically safe. My neighborhood is safe, my friends are not violent, and my professional peers don't resort to physical fighting. But I live in danger nevertheless. My ability to accomplish goals; to be recognized in the community; and to tend to my personal and professional reputation, power and authority at work, relative ranking among my peers, and social acceptance and popularity are under constant threat. I am socially, emotionally, and professionally vulnerable as a leader and as a man. So I maintain a hard-shell casing about me as a conditioned response to this pervasive threat and vulnerability; this shell—this armor—is composed of mental and emotional patterns and habits, not steel or leather.

Like a crab, you have to step out of your armor—your calcified boundaries of thought, action, and relationship—in order to grow and evolve and take on new ideas and perspectives. The tendency to harden our position, ideas, and attitude promotes psychosclerosis, and this condition will prove fatal to leadership. Yes, when we engage in new ideas and learn new skills, we revisit a beginner state, but the beginner state doesn't invalidate the standing, power, and competence we've achieved. Rather, it reminds us of the vulnerability and the power of growth. Most important, this is the path of renewal for leaders and for their organizations.

While crabs don't choose to exit their shells and grow, leaders must volunteer for the process. You might feel the pressure to break out of your familiar boundary of conditioned responses, but you could select to ignore the internal strain and remain unchanged. Change requires you to engage the heroic mind-set—the combination of focus, courage, grit, and faith—to willingly yield the familiar and embrace the uncertainty and discomfort of being updated and upgraded. Yielding to the pressure to grow is more than just personal expansion; it provides the moral high ground for leading organizational expansion and evolution.

A crab is affected by its environment and bears the evidence of its journey on its shell. Molting, besides allowing the crab to grow, provides a process for recalibration, resetting balance and accuracy. Molting helps to get rid of parasites and barnacles that have attached to the shell. Stephen Covey's book *The Seven Habits of Highly Effective People* names Habit Seven as "Sharpen the Saw." Sharpening the saw means to recalibrate—to purposefully attend to one's physical, mental, social, and spiritual renewal. Recalibration is more often a process of casting off than adding on.

What does removing parasites and barnacles mean to you? Mental parasites come in the form of other people who become stuck in your thoughts and affect your clarity or courage. We are influenced by the company we keep and the people we work with. Consider Steve's experience: He was a partner in a manufacturing firm and the driver of its growth. His typical enthusiasm for expanding the business was, however, waning after three years of partnering with Kurt—a worrier who wanted to play things safe and avoid stress and anxiety. Kurt's constant fear and focus on stability burrowed into Steve's mind. Over time that influence, like a parasite, siphoned Steve's growth mind-set and contributed to his doubt and anxiety.

As Steve's attitude turned anxious and pessimistic, his wife began to point out the changes, but it took feedback from his peers to pierce through his denial and busyness. By combining feedback with reflection and meditation, Steve recognized the mental safety-seeking parasites that had attached to his thinking. His meditation practice allowed him to apply the steps that cultivate courage as described in chapter 14: feel, face, and embrace:

- Feel: Rather than just contemplate his anxious and pessimistic attitude, Steve began by turning his attention to feeling the physiological sensations—the conditions of his body experience. He felt the tightness and fatigue when the negative thoughts arose.

- Face: Next, Steve turned his attention to the mental realm of thoughts and beliefs, and labeled and named his fears: "failure," "ruin," "loss," "exhausting," and "too much work."

- Embrace: Finally, Steve embraced the experience. At first he gently turned back to his growth-oriented thinking,

but he eventually turned to navigate what the fear
parasites would have him move away from. Ultimately,
he embraced the knowledge that his partnership with
Kurt had reached an end; he realized that they would
both be better served on separate journeys.

Unlike parasites, mental barnacles are calcified reactions. We can recognize barnacles in the form of assumptions and sweeping conclusions.
Barnacles distort the shape and flow of your thinking; they perpetuate
repetitive, black-and-white thoughts. Here are a few examples:

- "I have to be ruthless to get ahead."

- "I have to make all the critical decisions, because I can't
  find anyone willing to step up and take responsibility."

- "I don't have time for long-range planning; I'm too busy
  fighting fires set by other people."

- "I'm not worried about morale around here. We just need
  to grow our top line and all will be fine."

- "I know what I'm doing; I've done this exact thing before.
  I don't need to change; they do."

Removing mental barnacles accelerates growth of your leadership
effectiveness. You will make better decisions, engage your people more
deeply, and improve your personal productivity. Scraping off calcified
thoughts and feelings produces fluidity, agility, and responsiveness of
your mind and heart.

As I mentioned in chapter 13, in addition to a daily sitting practice,
I attend five-day silent meditation retreats a couple times per year as
part of my personal renewal and recalibration process. There is no
magic in the retreats. There are no miracle workers there, and the
experience is not relaxing (sitting cross-legged from dawn till night is

far from comfortable). Retreats are not an escape; they are an embrace. My intent during long silent periods of meditation is to find and feel the edges of my shell, to press through it, and to slough off the barnacles and parasites that cling to my mind and heart. While I may not feel relaxed during a retreat, I emerge clear and focused.

Last, in addition to removing mental barnacles and parasites and enabling growth, surrendering the shield and becoming vulnerable provides the only time that crabs can mate and reproduce; it is their only chance at perpetuating their species. Their ability to mate, to transfer their DNA, and to form the next generation only happens when their defenses are down and their protection gives way to connection.

The final gift of the virtue of faith ("What am I yielding?") is regeneration. Crabs must be able to access one another to ensure their survival and succession. Leaders, too, have to learn to shed their shields and become accessible and open in order to perpetuate their teams and organizations. Shedding the shield is surrender—a letting go of certainty, a leap of faith. Robert Greenleaf, a visionary of the modern Servant Leadership movement, says that the best test of a leader comes from answering one question: "Do those served grow as persons?" Your leadership becomes a multiplying force when you devote a portion of your attention and energy to fostering the development and growth of leaders around you. More than perpetuating the health of your organization, developing other leaders is an act of service and giving—an integral aspect of leadership as a hero's journey.

Recall that leaders traverse the hero's journey when they meet three qualifications: they take on a significant commitment, they place themselves at risk and make sacrifices, and they share their gains with their community. You share your gains by developing and nurturing the people and leaders that work with you; in the absence of giving back, you have not fully embraced the hero's journey. Those who have learned to give of themselves know the vulnerable feeling of anxiety, the fear of becoming obsolete in the face of a new generation coming into power. It is a leap of faith that permits you to give, that emboldens you to crack open your shell, be vulnerable, and willingly give of yourself to others.

CONCLUSION

Leadership is measured by results, but it's attained through followership. Your followers willingly sacrifice a piece of their individual identity in order to blend with your vision and the rest of the team. To attain leadership results, you build a community that you guide on an unfamiliar expedition toward a desirable shared vision; your people produce the results for which you are accountable, so the ultimate measure of leadership is followership. The people you hire barter their time for money. You pay them for their presence and efforts, but what you really want is their creativity and commitment—more than showing up, you want your people to care and engage. In order for them to give of themselves, they have to feel safe, and safety cannot be guaranteed. Trust is the value traded for safety; trust is what people demand from you in exchange for safety on this expedition of uncertainty.

Trust is the currency people charge in order to willingly take a risk. Your people must have trust in you as their leader for them to sacrifice comfort, move toward the unknown, tangle with uncertainty, and remain engaged. Being trusted and becoming trustworthy is the greatest gift you will receive from approaching leadership as a hero's journey.

This book has been an exploration of focus, courage, grit, and faith. You can skillfully face uncertainty and manage your anxiety by applying these virtues; you can become grounded and centered. Specifically, we have looked at the being-thinking-doing continuum that bestows trust upon leaders, and we have mapped the mental and emotional expedition leaders embark on when they take on responsibility for people and outcomes. You have journeyed through the process required to becoming emotionally mature—the path to becoming an engaging person—who people choose to follow.

Your leadership journey is yours to shape. While I have endeavored to invite, educate, challenge, and inspire you to take on leadership as a hero's journey, only you have the authority and ability to awaken your hero's spirit. Now, as always, the decision is yours.

Orienting Questions

Intense demands of time and attention can easily overwhelm your journey through life and work. How do you stay the course toward your intention, as a seeker and as a leader? How do you fulfill your duties *and* press toward evolution? How do you keep your mind, heart, and feet on the hero's journey? We have successfully traversed this book guided by four virtues. Each virtue answers a critical question. My experience tells me that you will most likely forget the majority of the details you read; it also tells me that you can and will remember a few simple questions.

Going forward, you can embolden your path—your leadership as a hero's journey—by asking yourself a few simple, but profound, questions. Rather than taking my word for it, experiment for a week and determine the veracity of this process for yourself. Questions have the power to guide the mind and set your filters of perception; they focus your curiosity and facilitate innovation and growth. I offer you the questions below to orient your daily efforts. By asking them you will activate the four virtues: focus, courage, grit, and faith.

Start of day:
- Which belief do I commit to nurture today?
- What scary person or situation will I engage?
- Where do I need to be more vigorously disciplined?
- What gap do I see that is calling for a leap of faith?

End of day:
- How well did I challenge my limiting beliefs today?

- What steps did I take toward someone or something I'd rather have avoided?
- Did I make deliberate choices that aligned with my focus?
- Was I able to give up some control?

I implore you to consider that the journey through risk and uncertainty is not really an option; life cannot be guaranteed nor kept free of pain and surprises. Your willingness to encounter fear, challenge, and personal evolution is a prize far greater than any accomplishment at work. Seeking and finding the Pearl of Wisdom bestows far more than flawless choices; the journey to finding the pearl beckons you to unfold your authentic self—to uncover, discover, and display the unique being you are.

Never before in the entire history of mankind have we experienced the exact and precise person that you are. And never again in all of history will we see another exactly like you. So embrace your heroic journey, unfold, evolve, serve, and make this a trip worthy of its unique value.

REFERENCES

Chapter 1

Dawkins, Richard. *The Selfish Gene*. Oxford: Oxford University Press, 1976.

Maltz, Maxwell. *Psycho-Cybernetics*. New York: Pocket Books, 1989.

Chapter 5

Allen, David. *Getting Things Done: The Art of Stress-Free Productivity*. New York: Penguin Books, 2001.

Drucker, Peter F. *The Effective Executive: The Definitive Guide to Getting the Right Things Done*. New York: Harper & Row, 1967.

Frankl, Viktor. *Man's Search for Meaning*. Vienna: Verlag für Jugend und Volk, 1946.

Chapter 6

Lazare, Aaron. "Go Ahead, Say You're Sorry: Apologies Can Restore Relationships—But There's a Right Way and a Wrong Way to Do Them." *Psychology Today*, January 1, 1995.

Viereck, George Sylvester. "What Life Means to Einstein: An Interview by George Sylvester Viereck." *Saturday Evening Post*, October 26, 1929.

Part II

Twain, Mark. *Pudd'nhead Wilson*. New York: Random House, 2005.

Chapter 8

Shaw, George Bernard. *Man and Superman*. Cambridge, MA: The University Press, 1903.

Chapter 9

Pessoa, Luiz, and Ralph Adolphs. "Emotion Processing and the Amygdala: From a 'Low Road' to 'Many Roads' of Evaluating Biological Significance." *Nature Review Neuroscience* 11 (2010): 773–83.

Chapter 10

Gallup, Inc. *Engagement at Work: Its Effect on Performance Continues in Tough Economic Times. Key Findings from Gallup's Q12 Meta-Analysis of 1.4 Million Employees.* Washington DC: Gallup, Inc., 2012.

Tuckman, Bruce. "Developmental Sequence in Small Groups." *Psychological Bulletin* 63, no. 6 (1965): 384–99.

Chapter 12

Williamson, Marianne. *A Return to Love: Reflections on the Principles of a Course in Miracles.* New York: HarperCollins, 1992.

Chapter 13

Pink, Daniel H. *Drive: The Surprising Truth About What Motivates Us.* New York: Riverhead Books, 2009.

Chapter 14

Collins, Jim. *Good to Great: Why Some Companies Make the Leap... and Others Don't.* New York: William Collins, 2001.

Witt, Paul L. "Comparative Patterns of Anxiety and Depression in a Public Speaking Context." *Human Communication. A Publication of the Pacific and Asian Communication Association* 11, no. 1 (2008): 215–26.

Chapter 16

Robinson, W. L. "Conscious Competency—The Mark of a Competent Instructor." *Personnel Journal* 53 (1974): 538–39.

Chapter 17

Baumeister, Roy E., Ellen Bratslavsky, Mark Muraven, and Dianne M. Tice. "Ego Depletion: Is the Active Self a Limited Resource?" *Journal of Personality and Social Psychology* 74, no. 5 (1998): 1252–65.

Duckworth, Angela L., et al. "Grit: Perseverance and Passion for Long-Term Goals." *Journal of Personality and Social Psychology* 92, no. 6 (2007): 1087–1101.

Jung, Carl. *Two Essays on Analytical Psychology.* Princeton, NJ: Princeton University Press, 1966.

Seligman, M. E. P. *Flourish: A Visionary New Understanding of Happiness and Well-Being*. New York: Free Press, 2011.

Seligman, M. E. P. "For Helplessness: Can We Immunize the Weak?" *Psychology Today*, June 1969, 42–45.

Chapter 18

Bayda, Ezra. *Being Zen: Bringing Meditation to Life*. Boston: Shambhala, 2003.

Emerson, Ralph Waldo. *The Later Lectures of Ralph Waldo Emerson, 1843–1871, Vol. 1: 1843–1854*. Athens, GA: University of Georgia Press, 2010.

Gabler, Neal. *Walt Disney: The Triumph of the American Imagination*. New York: Vintage, 2006.

Pausch, Randy, and Jeffrey Zaslow. *The Last Lecture*. New York: Hyperion, 2008.

Weir, Kirsten. "The Power of Self-Control." *Monitor on Psychology* 43, no. 1 (2012): 36.

Chapter 19

Branden, Nathaniel. *The Psychology of Self-Esteem: A Revolutionary Approach to Self-Understanding That Launched a New Era in Modern Psychology*. San Francisco: Jossey-Bass, 2001.

Carroll, Lewis. *Alice's Adventures in Wonderland*. London: Macmillan, 1865.

Cordes, Liane. *The Reflecting Pond: Meditations for Self-Discovery*. Center City, MN: Hazelden, 1981.

James, William. *Principles of Psychology*. New York: Henry Holt and Company, 1890.

Lyubomirsky, Sonja. *The How of Happiness: A Scientific Approach to Getting The Life You Want*. London: Penguin, 2007.

Peterson, Christopher, and Martin Seligman. *Character Strengths and Virtues: A Handbook and Classification*. Oxford: Oxford University Press, 2004.

Chapter 20

Cohen-Cole, Ethan, and Jason M. Fletcher. "Is Obesity Contagious? Social Networks vs. Environmental Factors in the Obesity Epidemic." *Journal of Health Economics* 27 (2008): 1382–87.

Chapter 21

Aurelius, Marcus. *Meditations*. New York: Penguin Classics, 2006.

Chapter 23

Kierkegaard, Søren. *Concluding Unscientific Postscript to the Philosophical Fragments*. Cambridge: Cambridge University Press, 2009.

Walsch, Neale Donald. *Little Book of Life: A User's Manual*. Charlottesville, VA: Hampton Road Publishers, 2010.

Chapter 25

Jung, Carl. *The Collected Works of C. G. Jung: The Development of Personality*. New York: Routledge & Kegan Paul, 1954.

Lutz, Antoine, and Richard J. Davidson. "Buddha's Brain: Neuroplasticity and Meditation." *IEEE Signal Processing Magazine* 25, no. 1 (2008): 174-76.

Niebuhr, Reinhold. *The Essential Reinhold Niebuhr: Selected Essays and Addresses*. Edited by Robert McAfee Brown. New Haven: Yale University Press, 1987.

Raymond, J. E., K. L. Shapiro, and K. M. Arnell. "Temporary Suppression of Visual Processing in an RSVP Task: An Attentional Blink?" *Journal of Experimental Psychology: Human Perception and Performance* 18, no. 3 (1992): 849–60.

Chapter 26

Bergland, Christopher. "Mindfulness Training and the Compassionate Brain: Meditation Cultivates Concentration, Empathy, and Insight at a Neural Level." *Psychology Today*, December 18, 2012.

Finucane, Andy, and Stewart W. Mercer. "An Exploratory Mixed Methods Study of the Acceptability and Effectiveness of Mindfulness-Based Cognitive Therapy for Patients with Active Depression and Anxiety in Primary Care." *Biomed Central, Psychiatry* 6 (2006): 14.

Hölzel, Britta K., et al. "Stress Reduction Correlates with Structural Changes in the Amygdala." *Oxford Journals, Social Cognitive & Affective Neuroscience* 5, no. 1 (2009): 11–17.

Chapter 27

Baumeister, Roy. "Ego Depletion and Self-Control Failure: An Energy Model of the Self's Executive Function." *Self and Identity* 1, no. 2 (2002): 129–36.

Fredrickson, Barbara L., Michael A. Cohn, and Sandra M. Finkel. "Open Hearts Build Lives: Positive Emotions, Induced Through Loving-Kindness Meditation, Build Consequential Personal Resources." *Journal of Personality and Social Psychology* 95, no. 5 (2008): 1045–62.

Luders, Eileen, Arthur W. Toga, Natasha Lepore, and Christian Gaser. "The Underlying Anatomical Correlates of Long-Term Meditation: Larger Hippocampal and Frontal Volumes of Gray Matter." *Neuroimage* 45, no. 3 (2009): 672–78.

Lutz, Antoine, et al. "Mental Training Enhances Attentional Stability: Neural and Behavioral Evidence." *Journal of Neuroscience* 29 (2009): 13418–27.

Chapter 28

Covey, Stephen R. *The Seven Habits of Highly Effective People: Powerful Lessons in Personal Change*. New York: Free Press, 1989.

ABOUT THE AUTHOR

Eric Kaufmann is an executive coach, speaker, and author who draws on two decades of experience in management and leadership. He works with executives and leadership teams of established and growing firms from midmarket to Fortune 1000. Together, they clarify strategy and vision, assess the strengths and weaknesses of the team, and identify and eliminate obstacles to collaboration, trust, and productivity. Ultimately, his contribution leads clients to make better decisions and accelerate results.

Eric is president of Sagatica LLC, a San Diego–based consultancy (sagatica.com). He brings an uncommon mix of skills and perspectives to his roles as leadership consultant, executive coach, and keynote speaker. He is also a scuba diving instructor, licensed hypnotherapist, and lifelong practitioner of Zen meditation. He once spent a year meditating in a cabin he built himself in a remote area of New Mexico. His quest for clarifying his lenses of perception, deepening his insight, and widening his capacity to care shapes his leadership work.

ABOUT SOUNDS TRUE

Sounds True is a multimedia publisher whose mission is to inspire and support personal transformation and spiritual awakening. Founded in 1985 and located in Boulder, Colorado, we work with many of the leading spiritual teachers, thinkers, healers, and visionary artists of our time. We strive with every title to preserve the essential "living wisdom" of the author or artist. It is our goal to create products that not only provide information to a reader or listener, but that also embody the quality of a wisdom transmission.

For those seeking genuine transformation, Sounds True is your trusted partner. At SoundsTrue.com you will find a wealth of free resources to support your journey, including exclusive weekly audio interviews, free downloads, interactive learning tools, and other special savings on all our titles.

To learn more, please visit SoundsTrue.com/freegifts or call us toll-free at 800.333.9185.